D1715848

CONSERVATISM IN ENGLAND

AN ANALYTICAL, HISTORICAL, AND POLITICAL SURVEY

CONSERVATISM IN ENGLAND

AN ANALYTICAL, HISTORICAL, AND
POLITICAL SURVEY

BY

F. J. C. HEARNSHAW

NEW YORK

Howard Fertig

1967

First published in 1933

HOWARD FERTIG, INC. EDITION 1967
Published by arrangement with Macmillan & Co., Ltd., London

Library of Congress Catalog Card Number: 67-24582

PRINTED IN THE UNITED STATES OF AMERICA
BY NOBLE OFFSET PRINTERS, INC.

PREFACE

FORTY years ago it was my privilege to begin my study of history at Cambridge under the luminous guidance of Sir John Seeley. If there was one lesson which, above all others, was impressed upon me by his masterly lectures—lectures solid in substance and flawless in form—it was the maxim that "history, while it should be scientific in its method, should pursue a practical object; that is, it should not merely gratify the reader's curiosity about the past, but should modify his view of the present and his forecast of the future." It was, indeed, Seeley's profound conviction that "history is the school of statesmanship," and that "without at least a little knowledge of history no man can take a rational interest in politics, and no man can form a rational judgment about them without a good deal." History, he consistently maintained, "is an important study to every citizen; it is the one important study to the legislator and ruler." He summed up his teaching as to the intimate relation between history and politics in the admirable aphorism: "History without political science has no fruit; political science without history has no root."

During the long period that has elapsed since I sat at Seeley's feet, my prime concern has been the study and teaching of history. And, inspired by Seeley's spirit, I have always instinctively sought to find in the records of the past guidance for the present, and even some prophetic indication of the course of the future. But one result of my historical approach to politics has been that I have never felt myself able to attach myself to any party. In my early days, under the seductive influence of the Fabian essays, I leaned towards the milder sort of socialism; later I was powerfully attracted by free-trade liberalism. The terrible liberal record of 1906-14, however, disillusioned me, and at present, as the ensuing dissertation will probably disclose, my inclinations are towards conservatism. And towards conservatism, since I have attained the grand climacteric, they are, I think, likely to remain. But I do not belong, and never have belonged, to the conservative or to any other party. I view politics, as a historian, from the outside.

My personal detachment does not, of course, mean that I disparage political parties. As I have occasion to say more than once in the course of this dissertation, I regard them as the indispensable concomitant of effective democratic government. My position, indeed, is precisely what it was fourteen years ago when I wrote the preface to my *Democracy at the Crossways*. Speaking in the third person, I said of the author—that is, of myself: "He believes that the organisation of active politicians into two compact and disciplined parties is an indispensable condition of successful and orderly representative government. But he believes equally strongly that the ordinary elector, like himself, who does not take an active part in the technical business of politics, should avoid party entanglements, and should hold himself free, and indeed by duty bound, to criticise party programmes, accept or reject party leaders, and do his utmost to compel parties to serve the larger ends of patriotism and humanity."

I apologise for dwelling so long upon my insignificant self, my unimportant opinions, and my immaterial detachments; but it has seemed necessary to do so in order to make it clear that this dissertation is wholly unofficial. It represents no one's ideas except my own. The fact that for the past six months I have been writing it at odd leisure moments is, so far as I am aware, totally unknown to any conservative leader. It is, however, based on a course of lectures which I have been allowed to deliver on more than one occasion to the students of the Ashridge College, and it has, I hope, profited by the frank and free discussions that characterise the curriculum of that delightful and wholly admirable educational institution. I need not say to those who know it, but I wish to emphasise for those who do not, that no attempt is made by those who govern the college to censor the utterances of lec-

turers or to restrict any expressions of opinion by
students. It is recognised that only in an atmosphere of
the largest liberty is truth able to flourish or sanity to
prevail. I should like to be permitted, in gratitude and
kindliness, to dedicate this dissertation to Major-General
Sir Reginald Hoskins, the beloved and revered principal
of the college, and to those groups of students who
patiently and sympathetically listened to the lectures on
which the dissertation is based.

F. J. C. HEARNSHAW.

HAMMERWOOD,
OXTED,
SURREY.
October 2, 1932.

CONTENTS

CONTENTS

INTRODUCTION

" Throughout the country men and women, of no fixed political allegiance, are eagerly and almost pathetically inquiring for what conservatism stands, and what message it has to give."—THE RIGHT HON. EDWARD WOOD [LORD IRWIN].

"Conservatives should be articulate about the unassailable principles on which their position is based. When they are not so, they are a source of weakness to their fellows."—A. M. LUDOVICI.

§ 1. THE MENACE OF SOCIALISM

SOME years ago, impelled by an irresistible conviction, I penned a *Survey of Socialism*, wherein I endeavoured to make clear to my fellow-citizens the real nature and the extreme danger of the new political superstition which, within the term of a single generation, had overrun the country, capturing the allegiance of nearly one-third of the electorate.* I based my survey on an exhaustive study of socialistic literature and a careful examination of socialistic experiments. The literature I found to be vast and varied: my bibliography enumerated over three hundred items, and I subsequently learned from my critics and reviewers of a good many other works which I might have included. The experiments, on the contrary, were comparatively few; and they were monotonous in the sameness of their leading features—namely, in the uniformity of their enthusiastic inauguration, their brief continuance, and their explosive end. A survey of socialism, in short, is largely an exploration of a jungle of utopian verbiage, an attempt to attain a bird's-eye view of a confused and tangled mass of fruitless speculation, a critique of pure unreason. History occupies but a small part of the socialistic terrain, and such part as it does occupy is regarded without any sort of pride or satisfaction by the

* *A Survey of Socialism, Analytical, Historical, and Critical*, 1928 (Macmillan and Co.).

socialistic zealot. As I remarked in my book (p. 327):
"The history of socialism in all its protean forms—
Utopian, Marxian, Fabian, Guild—is a long and lamentable record of unrealised theories, addled experiments,
and disillusioned dupes."

It is true that since I wrote my *Survey* the world has
been edified by some new efforts—efforts, indeed, of unprecedented magnitude—to embody the socialistic idea in
institutions. First and foremost, of course, must be placed
the bolshevist attempt, by means of the "five years plan,"
to demonstrate to a sceptical capitalism that communism
really can produce something; and that its successful
activities are not, like those of the bandit and the murderer, wholly confined to the narrow limits of confiscation
and assassination. Its strenuous and protracted effort
cannot be said as yet to have demonstrated anything
except that bolshevism's powers of persecution are un-
diminished: it has appropriated churches and converted
them into atheistic museums; it has seized the savings of
the thrifty and used them as doles for the lazy and incompetent; it has suppressed the enterprising and energetic
in order that an equality of pauperdom may universally
prevail; it has employed all the resources of the scientific
criminal in its endeavour to create a community of soul-
less slaves. Happily, its failure seems to be complete.
Human nature, even in the plastic and submissive Slav,
cannot be crushed or evicted by any sort of inquisition.
Man's innate passion for life, for liberty, and for property,
refuses to be frustrated by all the tyrannies of fanatical
Ogpus, or all the machinations of malignant Chekas.

A second socialistic experiment, less frightful in its circumstances, but equally conclusive in its results, has been
carried through in Australia. In that undeveloped paradise, rich in the natural resources of a continent, predatory
taxation, reckless interference with private enterprise,
suicidal attacks upon capital, foolish panderings to labour,
prodigal extravagance in doles and pensions, rash indulgence in unprofitable state-industries, have resulted in
their natural and proper consequence—namely, state-bank-
ruptcy. Australia is now engaged in the painful but

fortunately not hopeless task of returning to capitalism, conservatism, and common sense.

The third great socialistic or semi-socialistic experiment has been that made in our own country during the two years 1929-31. In the general election of May, 1929, the socialist-labour party secured 287 seats (as against 260 conservative and 59 liberal). Its victory was mainly due to the blatancy of its confident assurances that it, and it alone, could solve the pressing problem of unemployment. At that time the number of the unemployed had reached the distressing and alarming figure of 1,112,000. From May, 1929, to October, 1931, the labour government wrestled with this and other social and economic problems, displaying, together with benevolent intentions, the utmost incompetence, ineptitude, and futility. When finally it was driven by the disillusioned electorate from office, the number of the unemployed had risen to 2,714,000. Meanwhile, the national expenditure had increased from £691,000,000 per annum to £751,000,000; our exports had fallen by the enormous proportion of 45 per cent.; instead of lending money to foreign creditors (who normally borrowed from us some £200,000,000 a year) we ourselves had been compelled to borrow first £50,000,000, then another £80,000,000, in order to finance a dole distributed with reckless prodigality and with an almost criminal lack of investigation. From all quarters came the same story of the once prosperous reduced to indigence by devastating taxation; of great industries ruined by foreign competition, by trade-union restrictions, and by governmental extortion; of paupers prospering in idleness, and of honourable citizens corrupted and degraded by indiscriminate charity. Rarely has a great nation been so deplorably debauched and demoralised as was Great Britain during those disastrous two years of socialist misgovernment. Only when, in the autumn of 1931, it was actually face to face with ruin and disgrace did it rally to the call of duty, shake off the socialist incubus, and set itself to recover its lost integrity.

§ 2. CONSERVATISM AS THE ALTERNATIVE
TO SOCIALISM

The only practical alternative to socialism is conservatism. At one time liberalism might have offered a third possibility. But liberalism has obviously completed its work, lost its soul, sunk into senility, and died. With the attainment of complete religious emancipation, the establishment of unmitigated democracy, the reduction of the Crown to impotence and the House of Lords to insignificance, its programme is worked out; it cannot find or create sufficient new grievances to enable it to maintain itself in existence. If only it had remained faithful to its old cries of individualism, laissez-faire, personal freedom, and national economy, it might have continued to form a party round which could gather those sections of the community who desire to limit the functions of the all-encroaching state. But, under the fatal fascination of Mr. Lloyd George, who recks nothing of the great liberal tradition, it has abandoned its old principles, and has become an ineffective rival of the socialists in the mad race of collectivism and extravagance. The fate of most of its representatives is to be absorbed into the ranks of socialist-labour. The small remnant of genuine liberals who remain true to the principles of Gladstone and Rosebery find their natural affinities in the large and sympathetic conservatism of Mr. Baldwin.

A happy day for Britain and the Empire will it be when the disintegrated and distracted liberal party buries its defunct organisation and frankly transfers its sections, the left wing to the socialists, and the right wing to the conservatives. For, in order that the institutions of representative democracy should work satisfactorily, it is essential that there should be two, and only two, parties. The three-party system, which is really only the initial stage of a multiple-group system, is fatal to majority rule—that is, to true democratic government. It means minority control; a weak executive; an irresponsible, divided, and ineffective opposition; unstable and short ministries; perpetual temptations to log-rolling and corruption. And the hope that these obvious defects can be remedied or removed by such devices as proportional representation, or alternative votes, or second ballots, or any other of the expedients by means of which minorities try to secure the advantages of majorities, is a mere delusion. All that they would do would be to bemuse the electorate, and increase the probability that organised and responsible parties will be supplanted by bunches of ideological and irresponsible coteries, each bent on the realisation of its own little fanaticism. We should have a parliament made up of incoherent handfuls of such sects as communists, anarchists, teetotalers, anti-vivisectionists, feminists, seventh-day adventists, and flat-earthists. Indeed, every band of unbalanced enthusiasts would endeavour by concentration of voting power, and in total disregard of all considerations of national policy, to secure representation in the supreme council of the state. The consequence would be chaos. The only sure safeguard from this descent into political perdition is a return to the two-party system. We have to remember that, however desirable it may be that every important shade of opinion should be represented in parliament, it is incomparably more important that the country should have a strong and stable government, together with a coherent and organised opposition capable of providing a strong and stable alternative government when so the electorate wills.

Conservatism and socialist-labour at the present moment provide the only two practical possibilities of effective and consistent government in Great Britain. Socialist-labour will no doubt, in course of time, under the painful tuition of experience, free itself from the insanity of its socialism, and become an economically sound as well as a constitutionally safe party. But, meantime, under the leadership of obsessed ideologues, and impelled from behind by the goads and jeers of communists and syndicalists, it constitutes an inconceivably grave menace to the honour, the security, the solvency, and the very existence of Great Britain and its Empire.

In these circumstances it is imperative that conservatives, upon whom the salvation of their country and its

dominions ultimately depends, should carefully consider
the principles for which they stand; should make themselves conversant with the problems that they have to
solve; and should prepare themselves for the controversies
and conflicts that lie before them.

§ 3. A Source of Danger to Conservatism

Compared with socialists, conservatives are as a rule
conspicuously unready to state precisely what they believe
and why they believe it.   It is true, of course, that no two
socialists believe quite the same things, and that even in
respect of the mere definition of the term " socialism,"
quot homines, tot sententiæ.   But whatever it may be
that a socialist holds to be the truth, he commonly holds
it consciously and conscientiously; he commonly maintains it with conviction and enthusiasm; and he commonly
expounds it with a certain degree of lucidity and plausi-
bility.   Socialism lives and grows by means of a vigorous
and incessant propaganda.

Conservatism, on the other hand, tends to be silent,
lethargic, confused, incoherent, inarticulate, unimpressive.   Conservatives may not be what John Stuart Mill,
with that inoffensive insolence which is the peculiar
property of politicians, called them—namely, " the stupid
party "; but it may be admitted that they do not always
appear to be so wise as they are.   All too frequently, as
the present writer has had occasion to discover, they are
unable effectively to give reasons for the faith that is in
them.   Mr. A. M. Ludovici puts the case even more
strongly when he says : " The principles of conservatism
have but seldom been properly understood by those who
have all their lives professed to be conservatives."*   The
same truth is brought home with almost monotonous
iteration in Mr. W. H. Mallock's *Memoirs of Life and
Literature.*†   On one occasion, Mr. Mallock tells us, he
stood as a conservative candidate in a radical constituency.
He was depressed to find how inadequately equipped were

* Ludovici, A. M., *A Defence of Conservatism* (1927), p. 25.
† 1920 (Chapman and Hall); *cf.* pp. 20, 157, 158, 159, 194, 200.

even his devoted supporters to meet the foe in the gate. Conservatism to these faithful souls, he laments, "was no more than a vague sentiment, healthy so far as it went, but incapable of aiding them in controversy with any glib radical opponent." He also tells an amusing story, derived from his uncle, Mr. J. A. Froude, the historian. It comes from Devonshire, where during the course of an electoral canvass someone asked the local conservative agent, a Mr. Emmot, if he could tell him the difference between a conservative and a radical. "Well, Mr. Froude," reported the Devonian agent, "I don't rightly know the philosophy of the thing; so I just said this: 'You know me; well, I be a conservative. You know Jack Radford—biggest blackguard in the parish—well, he be a radical. Now you know.'" This *argumentum ad hominem* and *de hominibus* may have been effective at the moment, and within the geographical limits of the parish in question; but with lapse of time, and in regions whither the fame of Mr. Emmot and the reputation of Mr. Radford have not penetrated, it would undoubtedly lose some of its force. In the larger world of our modern electorates it is essential that agents and canvassers and all who take a practical part in politics should know something of "the philosophy of the thing."

If we ask how it is that the average socialist is so much more alive and alert than the average conservative; so much more ready to argue and orate; so much more full of fervour and devotion, I do not think that we need go far for a satisfactory answer. Conservatism is primarily a defensive creed: it aims at preserving and safeguarding the old, the familiar, the beloved, the well-tried. Socialism is offensive: it has the charm of experimental novelty; it essays the comparatively easy task of advancing in order to attack, along lines selected by itself, fixed and well-surveyed positions. Again, conservatism bases its appeal on existing fact or on historic record: it has the prosaic and unexciting duty of displaying the merits of things as they have been and are. Socialism is not thus restricted to fact, or limited to the tracing of the narrow course of actual events: it has the infinite inane to fly in, and the boundless resources of imagination to draw upon. Further, conservatism springs from contentment; it tends to tranquillity and to a desire to be left alone; it is frequently either satisfied with things as they are, or apprehensive that any change will be a change for the worse. Hence it prefers not to argue or to agitate; it assumes the existence, the continuance, and the general adequacy of established institutions; and, taking these for granted, it devotes its attention to what it regards as the proper business of life—namely, work, or recreation, or culture. Socialism, on the other hand, is the creed of the disgruntled and discontented. Its devotees do not desire stability and quietude. They are eager for change, even to the extent of a social revolution, because they believe that by the overturning of the present system they stand to gain and not to lose. Hence they are eager, vociferous, energetic, aggressive, and seductive. The lure of booty draws them on, and the potent spur of self-interest causes them to rack their brains in order to find plausible arguments by means of which robbery can be rationalised, or excuses fabricated for such iniquities as the " socialisation " (*i.e.*, confiscation) of capital and the " nationalisation" (*i.e.*, appropriation) of land.

§ 4. THE LACK OF CONSERVATIVE LITERATURE

The same considerations as explain the comparative inarticulateness of conservatives also explain the comparative scantiness of conservative literature. To describe and to defend existing institutions is a much less interesting task to a literary man than to criticise and attack them. Nothing seems so up-to-date as abuse; nothing so old-fashioned and stale as sober appreciation. Moreover, since things which exist are unique, each of them having its single objective reality, there are limits to the number of works that can profitably (or at any rate saleably) be written about them, from however many different points of view they may be regarded. I suppose that the best textbook of British conservatism is the constitutional history of England; but the works of Stubbs, Hallam, and

May are decidedly stodgy, and not even Maitland, for all
his brilliance, is easy reading. Then again, it rarely seems
necessary to defend existing institutions until they are
attacked by radicals or revolutionaries. In normal times
it is considered sufficient that they work with moderate
efficiency, and provide, as well as may be expected in this
imperfect world, the conditions of the good life. Well
says Mr. Arthur Boutwood: "Modern conservatism has
never developed a distinctive philosophy of politics, or
defined a distinctive ideal. It has been a practical attitude, rather than a reasoned creed or an articulate hope."*
Mr. A. M. Ludovici draws marked attention to the same
fact, contrasting the lack of conservative writings, the inadequate formulation of conservative ideas, and the
absence of a conservative "thinking staff" with the
wealth of pamphlets, the precision of policy, and the
phalanx of philosophers presented by such socialistic
organisations as the Fabian Society. "At the present
day," he observes, " a political party cannot survive that
is not supported by an independent body of students and
thinkers from which it can obtain its ideas, its policies,
and its programmes."†

From the nature of things, conservatism can never
produce, and can never require, such masses of verbiage
as are produced and required by socialism. For socialism
is little else than literature. Destroy its tracts and its
manifestos, and most of it vanishes into thin air. What
remains is merely the lamentable record of its few disastrous experiments. It shuns the appeal to history. Conservatism, on the other hand, although deficient in formal
treatises, is rich in historic monuments. Its very genius,
as a writer in *The Times Literary Supplement* well says,
" is the escape from theory to history." It inherits from
Burke, he adds, " this distrust of the abstract, this reliance upon history, this insistence upon political institutions as things that cannot be made, but must grow."‡
But, although conservatism lacks a copious literature, it

* Boutwood, A., *National Revival* (1913), p. 4.
† Ludovici, A. M., *A Defence of Conservatism* (1927), p. 244.
‡ *The Times Literary Supplement*, June 19, 1924.

has a small select library of great classics which constitute a magnificent heritage of sound principles and inspiring ideas.   In so far as these relate to England I shall comment upon them one by one in due course.   But apart from these, it must be remembered, there is an inexhaustible storehouse of the finest conservatism in much of the best of the general literature of our country. Where, for instance, can the genius of conservatism be found more magnificently embodied than in the historical plays of Shakespeare?   How finely inspired by the conservative spirit are the poems of Dryden, Pope, Wordsworth, and Coleridge!   What wealth of conservative thought is to be found in the prose works of Swift, Johnson, Southey, and Scott !*

During recent years, moreover, something has been done by the younger generation of conservatives to supply the demand for formal statements of the conservative creed. The histories of toryism which have come from the pens of Kebbel, Feiling, and Woods; the expositions of conservative policies and the formulations of conservative ideals that have been produced by Cecil, Butler, Banks, Elliot, and Bryant have materially helped to remove the charge of inarticulateness from the conservative party as a whole.†   Nevertheless, there still remains the task of attempting a survey of conservatism in its entirety—an analysis of its ideas and a history of its development in England; and that is the task which in this essay I venture to take up.

* *Cf. Saturday Review*, July 6, 1929: " The tone of English literature is so incurably aristocratic that the conservatives have no need to worry about propaganda. They have but to encourage the sale of cheap editions of the national classics."

† For the titles of the works alluded to above see the book list at the end of this volume.

PART I
ANALYTICAL

CHAPTER I

CONSERVATISM IN GENERAL

" Ask for the old paths, where is the good way, and walk therein, and ye shall find rest for your souls."—JEREMIAH vi. 16.

" Stare super antiquas vias."—CLARENDON'S MOTTO (*from the Vulgate version of the above*).

Conservatism stands " for the most permanent, and hence the most vital and entirely natural interests of the people as a whole."—KEITH FEILING.

§ 5. THE TWO CONFLICTING IDEALS : ORDER AND PROGRESS

MR. W. S. GILBERT, it will be remembered, when in 1882 he wrote *Iolanthe*, was much impressed by the curious dichotomy of nature :

> " I often think it's comical
>   How nature always does contrive
> That every boy and every gal
>   That's born into this world alive,
> Is either a little liberal,
>   Or else a little conserva-tive."

He wrote when as yet there was no labour party, and even before the rise of that temporarily separate middle group, the liberal unionists. But though by the emergence of the Home Rule crisis, and by the growth of organised labour, the obvious duplicity of British politics was changed during the closing decades of the nineteenth century into apparent multiplicity, what Mr. Gilbert said fifty years ago remained substantially true all the time, and remains substantially true to-day. Fundamentally there are only two political parties, by whatever names they may be known. Just as—however long men may let their hair grow, or however short women may have theirs cut—there are only two sexes ; and just as in the last judgment there will be only sheep and goats, no matter how many mixtures and

13

crosses there may appear to be on earth; so, amid all the
medley of groups, and all the babel of titles and designations, there are only two distinct political parties—namely,
the party of order and the party of progress.

The party of order, although it necessarily moves forward with the process of time, does so cautiously and
circumspectly, lest it should in the unfamiliar present, or
in the unmapped future, make some irremediable mistake
in direction. It constantly turns its eyes to the past in
order that it may learn the lessons of history, and profit
by the rich experience of the human race. It reveres and
cherishes the institutions of religion and politics as they
have been established and developed by the genius of the
generations past. It respects tradition and social custom;
it reverences law and morality; it exalts authority; it
practises obedience; it lays stress on civic duty rather than
on individual right; it distrusts the unknown and the untried; it is suspicious of unverified and abstract theory; it
prefers to follow the guidance of ancestral instinct rather
than the lure of youthful logic.

The party of progress, on the other hand, moves with
less caution and more rapidity. It laughs at the slogan
" Safety first," and is eager for enterprise and adventure.
It looks to the future rather than the past; it tends to
deny that history has any lessons to teach, or that the
experience of the human race is much more than a record
of crime and folly. It is quick to discern the defects of
existing institutions, and prone to believe in the merits of
visionary novelties. It repudiates tradition, delights to
abandon custom and to shock convention. It criticises
law, questions the canons of morality, defies authority,
exalts disobedience to the rank of a virtue. It stresses
individual rights—such as the right to the vote, or the
right to work, or the right to maintenance—to the obscuration of civic duty. It finds a peculiar fascination in
the unknown and untried, the speculative, the new. It is
devoted to abstract theory and has a profound faith in the
processes of abstract logic. It enriches the language of
politics with countless formulæ.

Now both these parties—the party of order and the

party of progress—are necessary for the proper working of a democratic state. The party of order, in the absence of the stimulus of its progressive opponents, might degenerate into a party of mere reaction, stagnation, and immobility. Its cautious movement might slow down into sleep, and even into ultimate death. It might become a mere monument of antiquity, or a pillar of obsolete salt. On the other hand, the party of progress, if unchecked by the prudence and restraint of the party of order, might well, in the rashness of its enthusiasm for novelties and in its revolutionary zeal, repeat on a gigantic scale the tragedy of the Gadarene swine.

The difference between the two parties, indeed, is one of emphasis rather than of essence. There are, of course, in the party of order, extreme reactionaries who would discountenance all change of any kind; and there are, on the other hand, in the party of progress, violent revolutionaries who would make a clean sweep of the whole heritage of the past. But these are a minority in each case. The more moderate members of both parties— happily the immense majority—have a good deal in common. The wiser members of the party of order recognise the need for circumspect progress, and the wiser members of the party of progress recognise the importance of continuity and of a certain amount of conservatism and caution. In times of tranquillity and prosperity, in fact, the differences between the moderate progressives and the moderate conservatives tend to become very slight. In England, for example, between 1855 and 1865 the divergence between the liberalism of Palmerston and the conservatism of Disraeli was almost indiscernible: Disraeli, indeed, was much embarrassed by the necessity of maintaining an organised opposition to a statesman with whom in general he so cordially agreed. Times and circumstances largely determine to which of the two parties a prudent and patriotic citizen shall attach himself. If he feels that things are moving too fast, or are moving in the wrong direction, he will become a conservative. If, on the other hand, he considers that they are not moving fast enough in any direction at all, he may become a progressive. I suppose that most English conservatives if they were domiciled in Thibet would become radical reformers; and I hope that all English radicals, if they had the misfortune to be domiciled in Soviet Russia, would have the grace to become reactionaries.

These, then, are the two essential parties—the party of order and the party of progress. There is no other. For when any political problem is analysed into its constituent elements, when complicated issues are disentangled, and when the ultimate and simplified questions are put one by one, two answers alone are conceivable in each case—either an unqualified Yes or an unqualified No. Similarly, when in any democratic assembly, such as the British parliament, all the various arguments are ended, and the time for voting is come, the multiform debaters, however numerous and finely graduated their opinions, if they vote at all, have to divide into two lobbies—the lobby of the Ayes and the lobby of the Noes. In the last resort, and in the supreme issues, not even neutrality is possible : all who are not with us are against us.*

§ 6. The Psychological Bases of Conservatism

The two parties have their respective foundations deep in the substratum of human nature. Here, again, the differences between the two are rather of emphasis than of essence, of quantity rather than of quality, of degree rather than of kind. For however widely individual human beings differ from one another, the main characteristics of the nature of man are universal and uniform. No sane conservative is wholly devoid of the instincts dominant in the progressive; no sane progressive entirely lacks the instincts dominant in the conservative. It is a matter of relative prominence and of proportion. So much is this so that it is not at all an uncommon phenomenon for a conservative such as the young Gladstone, owing to change in circumstances, insensibly to be transformed into a radical. Still less uncommon is it for a raging revolutionary, under

* *Cf.* a most important and illuminating passage in Dr. Robert Flint's *Philosophy of History* (1893), p. 34.

the influence of experience and responsibility, to be gradually and unconsciously sobered into conservatism.

What are the qualities prominent in the progressive? They are dissatisfaction with things as they are; discontent with existing institutions; discomfort, disillusionment, disgust. The progressive finds himself out of harmony with his environment. He feels that his merits are unrecognised or inadequately rewarded; that his powers lack scope for their exercise; that his possibilities are prevented from becoming realised actualities; that he is cribbed, cabined, and confined by circumstances. And what he feels in respect of himself he probably feels with somewhat diminished force in respect of the class to which he belongs, or with which he has peculiar sympathy. But not only is he dissatisfied with the present; he is hopeful regarding the future. He is apt to think that any change will be for the better. He tends to an optimistic view of human nature in its raw state; he inclines to believe that man is primitively good, and that if he sinks into folly and crime the fault is due to causes extraneous to himself. He, therefore, is disposed to be confident that if only he can " take this sorry scheme of things entire " and destroy it, he will be able to " remould it nearer to the heart's desire." He is energetic, resourceful, youthful (even when not young), full of ideas, enthusiastic, a creature of abstract theory and of vivid imagination. It is well that the world should have its relays of progressives. They keep things moving. They prevent stagnation and putrefaction. As they grow old and learn wisdom they often become the soundest and the sanest of conservatives. They save conservatism from sinking into mere reaction and immobility.

But what are the distinctive qualities of this sound and sane conservatism? We are told by a brilliant and able social psychologist, whose sympathies are rather too patently progressive, that the primary conservative emotion is fear. He distinguishes various kinds of fear, such as fear of the unknown, fear of the unfamiliar, fear of the unconventional, fear of social disapprobation. But he says that " all conservatism, both interested and disinterested, is essentially a safety-first attitude. Its root desire is for security."* Now fear is not usually regarded as one of the heroic virtues, and it is evident that when this eminent progressive psychologist has characterised conservatism as an embodiment of fear he considers that he has sufficiently condemned it. But fear is contemptible and reprehensible only if it leads to flight. If, on the contrary, it results in a steeling of the will, in a suppression of the instinct to run away, in a quickening of the intelligence, and in a courageous facing of a crisis, it is wholly valuable and commendable. For there are certain things that ought to make one afraid, and that do actually cause fear to every sane individual. Persons who in the presence of mortal peril do not feel fear are apt to be destroyed; for fear is an instinct which has played an all-important part in the preservation of the human race. We are told that " the fear of the Lord is the beginning of wisdom," and this assuredly is not a fear of which any man need feel ashamed. Similarly, a fear of rash and ill-considered change is the very first feature of political prudence. For, as the conservative realises, civilisation is a frail flower doubtfully struggling for existence amid a jungle of old luxuriant barbarism; it may also be compared to a thin and fragile crust, barely supporting humanity, over molten oceans of volcanic savagery. The conservative dreads changes which may conceivably destroy the frail flower of culture; changes which may crack the crust of civilisation and let loose upon the world the flaming floods of banditry and bolshevism. He tends, therefore, to see the best in existing institutions; he is anxious so far as it is possible to maintain things as they are, lest they become worse instead of better. One of the wisest of conservative mottoes is : " Unless it is necessary to change, it is necessary not to change." The conservative reverences antiquity; he feels that habits and customs, conventions and traditions, embody the wisdom of the ages, and that they should not lightly be abolished or cast aside. He trusts to what Disraeli describes as " the sublime instincts of an ancient people," and he is suspicious of what calls itself " reason "

* Wolfe, A. B., *Conservatism, Radicalism, and Scientific Method* (1923), pp. 21-60.

when it is opposed to these inherited and immemorial feelings. Above all, he is inspired by a passionate loyalty to the saints and heroes of the past, and to the institutions which embody the genius of all preceding generations.

Again, the conservative does not share the roseate view of primitive human nature which characterises the typical progressive. He does not believe that man, in the absence of corrupting circumstances, is necessarily innocent and good. He recognises the fact that, together with the good elements in human character, there are also bad elements that require suppression or discipline. Man, he knows, is uneliminated ape as well as undeveloped angel, and he is aware that if the development of the angelic element in him demands freedom and opportunity, on the other hand the eradication of the bestial element calls for the exercise of authority and for the stern enforcement of law. The conservative views man and the state of nature rather with the eyes of Hobbes than with those of Rousseau. He sees things as they are rather than as he would like them to be.

§ 7. CONSERVATISM A SPIRIT, NOT A PROGRAMME

Conservatism as embodied in, and represented by, an English political party is, of course, a comparatively modern phenomenon. Most historians are content to trace it back to the constitutional struggles of the seventeenth century, and to place its birthday somewhere in or about the year 1640. Mr. Keith Feiling, however, discerns its beginnings in the religious controversies of the sixteenth century, and assigns the year 1583 as that of its nativity. But conservatism as a general principle is, it need hardly be said, immeasurably older. Not only can it in England be perceived as one of the operative factors in all the political and ecclesiastical conflicts of the early and middle ages, but it can in the world at large be observed as active and effective among every people and in every historic period. It would be interesting, if space allowed, to trace its manifestations in the histories of Israel, Greece, and Rome. But to tell the stories of the prophets who tried to keep the Hebrews true to their faith; of the philosophers who strove to maintain the ideas and institutions of the

Greek city-state; of the patriots, such as Cato and Cicero, who fought for the virtues of old Rome against the encroaching corruptions of demagogy, would occupy too much room. Suffice it to say that conservatism in the sense of a spirit opposed to radicalism—*i.e.*, as a spirit opposed to that of rash innovation—can be traced right back to the Garden of Eden itself. In that visionary abode of bliss Adam was the person who represented the conservative qualities of contentment and stability. Eve was the innovator, eager for novelty, ready for reckless experiment, liable to be led away by any such seductive slogan as " Eat more Fruit," or " Free Fig Leaves for All." As to the devil who, in the form of a serpent, tempted Eve, I suppose that he was the nearest approximation possible, before the Christian era, to the idea of Karl Marx. As to the fact that Adam became involved in the tragic fate of Eve, is it not a warning against the lamentable consequences likely to accrue when the conservative adopts the radical programme ?

Conservatism, it has been well remarked, is not so much a fixed programme as a continuing spirit.* It is sometimes taunted because of its lack of a sharply formulated policy, such as that of the liberal " Newcastle programme " of 1891. Lord Rosebery, for example, speaks of " the somewhat negative doctrines of orthodox toryism."† So, too, Mr. Arthur Boutwood, who writes from the tory point of view, rather pathetically laments this negativeness of the conservative creed and the indefiniteness of its programme. He says of conservatism that " it was, and continues to be, a practical attitude rather than a reasoned creed or an articulate hope, and its chief electoral victories have been revulsions from things disliked, not achievements of a conquering ideal."‡

There is, I think, no need to apologise for either the negativeness of the conservative creed (in so far as it *is* negative) or the indefiniteness of its programme (in so far as it *is* indefinite). For conservatism, as we have seen, is

* Feiling, Keith, *What is Conservatism?* (1930), p. 8.
† Rosebery, Lord, *Lord Randolph Churchill* (1906), p. 112.
‡ Boutwood, A., *National Revival* (1913), p. 11.

primarily defensive. It exists in the first instance to protect from injury and save from destruction "the old perfections of the earth." Hence the nature of its defence depends on the nature of the attack which it has to repel, and the doctrines which it propounds are largely determined by the radical or revolutionary doctrines which it is called upon to refute. For example, when individualism runs rampant (as it did in the middle of the nineteenth century), conservatism in the interests of the nation as a whole has to emphasise the doctrine of the solidarity of the community and the authority of the state. When, on the other hand (as at the present time), collectivism and socialism are in the ascendant, conservatism, with perfect consistency, is compelled to stress the complementary truth of the rights of the individual to freedom and self-realisation. A still better example of the relativity of conservative doctrine is provided by the history of the long conflict between free-trade and protection. The great conservative leaders of the eighteenth and early nineteenth centuries—Bolingbroke, Pitt, Canning, Peel—were all pronounced free-traders; for they had to emancipate commerce and industry from the fetters of an obsolete mercantilism, imposed upon them by a corrupt and obscurantist whig oligarchy. But when laissez-faire was triumphant—that is, from 1840 onward—and when unmitigated freedom began to display itself in the frightful oppression of the labouring masses, and in the ruin of British agriculture, then the conservative leaders of "Young England," Disraeli and his successors, the founders of tory democracy, began to assert once again the duty of the Government to intervene in matters economic in order to save the nation as a whole from intolerable social evils.

It would be possible to instance a whole series of doctrines and policies in which conservatism has appeared to take, with a certain inconsistency, now one side, now another. In England, for example, sometimes it has advocated war, at other times peace; sometimes it has demanded expenditure, at other times economy; sometimes it has been imperialistic, at others insular; sometimes it has urged parliamentary reform, at others opposed it; and so on indefinitely. It will be found, however, on careful examination, that there has been no inconsistency at all. Conservatism is a spirit, an attitude, a temper, and not a set of dogmas. Conservatives always stand on the same ground; they always defend the same position; their principles remain essentially unchanged. But circumstances, and in particular the nature of their assailants and the direction of the hostile attack, determine the way that they face and the sort of defence that they make.

Their principles, I say, remain essentially unchanged. What, then, in brief, are the essential and stable principles of conservatism?

§ 8. The Principles of Conservatism

If I were called upon to enumerate in summary fashion and tabular form the general principles of conservatism, particularly as it exists and displays itself in the world of modern national states, I should be disposed to say that conservatism stands for (1) reverence for the past, (2) the organic conception of society, (3) communal unity, (4) constitutional continuity, (5) opposition to revolution, (6) cautious or evolutionary reform, (7) the religious basis of the state, (8) the divine source of legitimate authority, (9) the priority of duties to rights, (10) the prime importance of individual and communal character, (11) loyalty, (12) common sense, realism, and practicality. A few words concerning each must suffice.

(1) *Reverence for the Past.*

The conservative reveres the past, not for its own sake, but for the sake of the present and the future. He feels instinctively that the accumulated wisdom and experience of the countless generations gone is more likely to be right than the passing fashion of the moment. He believes that, even though each successive generation of his ancestors was in its day no more intellectually sane or morally sound than the silly and sentimental generation to which he himself belongs, nevertheless a long process of trial and rejection has purified their creations from error and made them fit for their appointed work. He realises, moreover, that it is much easier to destroy than to construct; that a cathedral that took a century to build can be burnt down in a night; that an institution that has evolved during a thousand years can be ruined by a single injudicious reform. He recognises as one of the soundest of conservative maxims the rule, already quoted, that "unless it is necessary to change, it is necessary not to change." He tends to faith in the great motto "Securus judicat orbis terrarum." He stands for the universal and permanent things of life; for the ancient traditions of the race; for the fundamental laws of his people; for established customs; for the family; for property; for the church; for the constitution; for the great heritage of Christian civilisation in general.

(2) *The Organic Conception of Society.*

One main reason why he values and strives to conserve the past is that he feels that in a real sense it is one with the present. He has an organic or biological conception of society, as opposed to the inorganic or legal conception prevalent among the philosophical radicals. To him the great community to which he belongs—*e.g.*, the national state—is a living entity, albeit of a psychological rather than a physical type; a spiritual organism to which every individual of the community belongs. He feels with St. Paul that we are all members one of another; all joined together in the large and enduring life of a mystical body, whose abode is a mother-country or a fatherland. Hence he is impressed by the need to preserve the integrity of this communal life, which is larger and more enduring than his own brief individual existence; he strives to safeguard the body politic from injury at the hands both of malignant enemies and injudicious friends; he struggles to maintain the communal identity amid all the changes that time inevitably brings. He studies with loving care the records of the past growth of his people and of their institutions, in order that he may to the extent of his power help to keep the necessary new developments along the old lines of progress.

(3) *Communal Unity.*

An all-important corollary to the conservative conception of society as an organism is the fine and inspiring idea of the essential oneness of the community. Conservatism is utterly opposed to the horrible dogma of the class-war which is one of the most damnable features of Marxian socialism or bolshevism. It denies the existence of any irreconcilable antagonisms in a healthy body politic. It holds, on the contrary, that the efficiency and prosperity of each class—upper, middle, lower, each with its countless internal gradations—is essential for the well-being of the community as a whole. It recognises the distinction between the classes as natural, fundamental, and beneficial; the same sort of distinction as exists between the head, the body, and the limbs of a man or an animal. But it regards the distinction as one of function mainly, and not necessarily one of honour or emolument. And it realises that if any one of the three great classes suffers or is diseased, the whole organism is weakened and incapacitated. " We may say," exclaims Mr. Harold Begbie, " that at the centre of conservative thinking is the idea of unity."* Similarly, Lord Irwin, with his noble and catholic spirit, maintains that " the conservative stands for the unity of the nation, and of all interests, classes, and creeds within it."† In saying this they, and all good conservatives, are but following the fine tradition of Bolingbroke, Burke, and Beaconsfield.

(4) *Constitutional Continuity.*

A second and hardly less important corollary to the conservative conception of society as an organism is the idea and ideal of continuity. Such a breach in the natural and orderly development of the constitution as occurred in seventeenth-century England or eighteenth-century France fills the conservative with repulsion and alarm. He regards

* Begbie, H. (" A Gentleman with a Duster "), *The Conservative Mind* (1924), p. 145.
† *The Times*, March 14, 1924.

it in much the same way as a normal individual would regard the action of a physician or surgeon who, when called in to treat the ailment of a parent beloved, should, by way of experiment in some novel therapy, inflict upon the sufferer an all-but-fatal injury. So prominent in conservatism is this principle of continuity—this conception of the vital connection between past, present, and future; this idea of a communal life ever one and the same, although constantly evolving in order to correspond with a changing environment—that Mr. Walter Elliot regards it as its " major tenet," and says that conservatism is " first of all the creed of continuity."* An anonymous but excellent writer in the *Saturday Review* expresses the same opinion more at large in the words : " Conservatism is not a bundle of political expedients, but the very imperfect expression through political action of certain deep-rooted and far-reaching convictions in regard to both the national and the individual life. These convictions are hard, nay impossible, to define. They amount in sum to a passionate belief in the principle of continuity."†

(5) *Opposition to Revolution.*

The principle of continuity, of course, implies instinctive and emphatic antagonism to revolution. For the essence of revolution is complete severance from the past. The revolutionary, as distinct from the reformer, seeks to destroy existing institutions, not to amend them; to slay and not to cure. In place of communal unity he stirs up civil war. Instead of treating society tenderly as an organism liable to injury and death, he smites and blasts it as though it were a mechanism which can be scrapped and made new again. He is, as a rule, obsessed by some abstract (and viciously erroneous) theory, such as the Jacobinical theory of the rights of man, or the bolshevik theory of the wrong of private property. He is commonly a gloomy fanatic, filled with envy, hatred, malice, and all uncharitableness ; a raging Philistine wholly devoid of both

* Elliot, W., *Toryism and the Twentieth Century* (1927), pp. 18-19.

† *Saturday Review*, July 6, 1929.

sweetness and light. The conservative, however, while unalterably opposed to revolution, recognises that the revolutionary is a natural, if horrible, product of ignorance and wretchedness. Hence while resisting revolutionary violence and denouncing subversive dogma, he seeks to find the causes that produce the would-be destroyer of society, and to remove them in so far as the demand for their removal is real and rational.

(6) *Cautious or Evolutionary Reform.*

Since ignorance and wretchedness are the prime propagators of the revolutionary virus, the conservative policy is one of education and betterment. Nothing could be more contrary to fact than the statement that conservatism is opposed to reform. Reform is of its very essence. Well says Mr. E. J. Payne concerning Burke: "He led the way in reform, while raising his voice against innovation," adding: "The spirit of conservatism and the spirit of reform are the necessary complements of each other: no statesman ever pretends to separate them."* And Burke himself remarked with his usual profound wisdom: "A state without the means of some change is without the means of its conservation."† No persons are less true to the conservative genius than the reactionaries or "diehards" who resist all alteration whatsoever without ever inquiring into the causes that have led to its demand. Nothing could be more alien from the true spirit of conservatism than the famous saying of the Duke of Cumberland (son of George III.): "Any change, at any time, for any purpose, is highly to be deprecated." If the Cumberland spirit should at any time gain possession of the conservative party, the day of triumphant revolution will have dawned. And the Cumberland spirit has had many embodiments among those who call themselves conserva-

---

* Payne, E. J., *Select Works of Burke*, vol. i., Introduction, p. xxvi.

† Burke, E., *Reflections on the French Revolution*, iv., 23. On Burke's attitude generally, see Opzoomer, C. W., *Conservatismus und Reform, eine Abhandlung über Edmund Burke's Politik* (Utrecht, 1852).

tive. Indeed, the very man, Mr. J. W. Croker, who gave
currency to the term " conservative," a hundred years
ago, was one of them. Mr. Keith Feiling has presented us
with an unforgettable picture of the man—able, honest,
energetic, but hopelessly obscurantist and out of touch
with reality. His dread of novelty, and his worship of the
fetish of stability, made him blind to the immense trans-
formations that were going on around him. " Who," says
Mr. Keith Feiling, surveying his well-intentioned but disastrous career—" who can measure the damage inflicted on
sane conservatism by one reactionary of high character and
personal charm ?"* The true conservative attitude is that
of Sir Robert Peel, at one time but not always Croker's
friend. Writing about " conservative principles " in 1834,
he said : " Those principles I for one consider to be perfectly compatible with cautious and well-digested reforms
in every institution which really requires reforms, and with
the redress of approved grievances."† Mr. Ludovici puts
the matter well when he remarks : " Conservatism is not
a brake on progress . . . it is a brake on indiscriminate
change," adding, " It is the lofty mission of conservatism
to prevent national changes from degenerating into a process of general decomposition."‡ But the true key to the
whole problem is found in the organic conception of
society. For if, on the one hand, the principle of life
negatives any breach in the continuity of communal
development, on the other hand the principle of healthy
and vigorous growth (which is the only alternative to the
doom of decadence and death) demands the constant
adaptation of the enduring organism to the ever-changing
environment. Conservatism accepts and applies the
doctrine of organic evolution.

(7) The Religious Basis of the State.

The conservative doctrine of organic evolution implies
the existence of a corporate Being—the Great Society, the

* Feiling, K., *Sketches in Nineteenth-Century Biography*
(1930), p. 55.
† Clark, G. K., *Peel and the Conservative Party* (1929), p. 176.
‡ Ludovici, A. M., *A Defence of Conservatism* (1927), pp. 11-13.

Community-as-a-Whole, the State—a Being possessed of a social conscience, a communal intelligence, a public opinion, and a general will; a Being vaster and more permanent than any of the individuals who at any time constitute its members. Devotion to this Being, which Hobbes termed "Leviathan," and defined as "that Mortal God to which we owe under the Immortal God our peace and defence,"* is itself a religion. Devotion to the state was, indeed, the real religion of both Greeks and Romans. Athena was but Athens personified, and in Rome the worship of the emperor's genius was no more than a symbolic reverence for the dominion of which the emperor was the momentary representative.

To the Christian, however, religion means more than it did to his pagan predecessor. He recognises society as existing by the will of God; he regards it as continually directed and guided by a divine Providence; he considers its end to be akin to that of the church itself—namely, righteousness and peace. Hence, as a rule, he holds it to be right and proper that the state should formally and publicly recognise its sacred character by the legal establishment of religion, and by the association of all the most solemn and important acts of government with the august ceremonial of the service of God. "In a Christian commonwealth," said Burke, "the church and the state are one and the same thing, being different parts of the same whole."† And this great idea, which was akin to that of the *Respublica Christiana* of the Middle Ages, was the very essence of Coleridge's notable contribution to conservative thought in the early nineteenth century.

(8) *The Divine Source of Legitimate Authority.*

The conservative who regards the state as organic in nature, as sacred in character, as founded upon a religious basis, and as akin to a church, naturally tends to accept the ancient Christian view that all legitimate authority is, whether directly or indirectly, divine in its origin. He

---

* Hobbes, T., *Leviathan* (1651), chapter xvii.
† Speech, May 11, 1792.

remembers the cardinal pronouncement of St. Paul : " The powers that be are ordained of God. Whosoever therefore resisteth the power, resisteth the ordinance of God."* He traces the influence of this great utterance through the writings of countless thinkers down all the Christian centuries, and in the acts of innumerable ecclesiastical statesmen. He feels, with Disraeli, that " the divine right of kings may have been a plea for feeble tyrants, but the divine right of government is the keystone of human progress, and without it governments sink into police, and a nation is degraded into a mob." Even conservatives who are not able to accept the Christian view—such as Hobbes, and Bolingbroke, and Hume, and Matthew Arnold—hold that authority springs from a source superior to the individual, " a power not ourselves that makes for righteousness," a spirit universal and eternal. Well says Mr. Keith Feiling in his fine study of Newman : " In the permanent essence of a teaching which is successfully to defend authority, there must be something in the widest sense catholic."†

(9) *The Priority of Duties to Rights.*

There are few things that more sharply distinguish the conservative from the radical or the socialist than his attitude towards rights and duties. The radical concentrates his attention almost wholly on the rights of the individual. He asserts his right to the franchise, even though he use his vote merely to further his own personal interest—*e.g.*, to secure ninepence for fourpence. He maintains his right to freedom of speech, even though his speech be nothing except libel and blasphemy, sedition and nonsense. And so on. Similarly the socialist, with an extreme individualism that accords very ill with the alleged main principle of his creed, proclaims the proletarian's right to work or maintenance (which means the right to compel other people to support him in perennial idleness),

* *Romans* xiii. 1-2; *cf.* also 1 *Timothy* ii. 1-3, *Titus* iii. 1, and 1 *Peter* ii. 13-17.
† Feiling, K., *Sketches in Nineteenth-Century Biography* (1930), pp. 114-115.

or his right to the whole produce of labour (which means
the right to deprive the landlord and the capitalist of their
just dues). And so on.

As against this one-sided and self-centred assertion of
personal rights, the conservative stresses the principle of
civic duties. His ideal is public service rather than private
gain. He regards the franchise not as a possession which
he can claim as his own, but as an obligation which he
must exercise in the interests of the body politic. Similarly, in respect of such matters as freedom of speech and
writing, he thinks rather of how they may be employed
(and if necessary limited) in the interests of the community-as-a-whole than of how he may assert them on his
own behalf in all circumstances. Well says Mr. Harold
Begbie of conservatism : " The great word on its lips is the
word *duty*. It does not stoop to flatter ; it does not wish
to deceive ; it does not seek to infuriate and excite the
passions of the ignorant and the half-educated. It appeals
to what is best in man's nature—to his moral strength, to
his spiritual self-respect, to his human kindness—and it
bids men rise to a level of self-forgetfulness from which
they can see the path of their duty stretching to the land
of their children's glory."*

(10) *The Prime Importance of Character.*

The prime concern of the radical, with his demands for
freedom and franchise, is power. The prime preoccupation
of the socialist, in spite of all his fine phrases, is pelf. The
conservative, if he be true to the genius of his creed, is
concerned neither for power nor for pelf, but for character
—character both individual and national. He repudiates,
in particular, the socialist's gross over-emphasis on the
influence of environment as a determinant of a man's
condition, and stresses the fact that his condition depends
very largely upon what he is himself. Mr. Baldwin put
the point excellently in a great speech delivered on
March 19, 1924, when he said : " The conservative believes

* Begbie, H. ("A Gentleman with a Duster "), *The Conservative Mind* (1924), p. 147.

that the only salvation of the country is to concentrate on the individual, and to continue to cherish in him a spirit of character, marked by the virtues of thrift, hard work, and prudence." In saying this, Mr. Baldwin was but echoing the teaching of his revered master, Disraeli, who in his day proclaimed that "the wealth of England is not merely material wealth . . . we have a more precious treasure, and that is the character of the people." If, then, the conservative resists and denounces the socialist's nostrums of doles and subventions and transitional benefits and all the other euphemisms for poor-relief, he does so not merely or mainly because they are economically ruinous and socially disastrous, but because they are hopelessly demoralising and degrading. They tend to debauch and debase the English people. Rarely, indeed, has a more subtle and deadly enemy to character revealed itself than socialism. Under its malign influence the national integrity is gravely menaced. Rightly says Mr. Arthur Bryant : " Our English character is in danger to-day. We all know it. We can all think of ways in which it is being undermined—its jealous, bold independence by an ever-growing pauperisation of our people ; its frank, just courage—honouring gallant foe as well as friend—by the false sentimentality which is swamping our education and philosophy ; its good nature and humorous tolerance by the alien gospel of class hatred. The overmastering thought of every conservative must be how we can save this precious thing, handed down to us by so many generations of good, honest, clean-living English men and women, from the foes that threaten it."*

(11) *Loyalty.*

Of all the elements of character which the conservative values and cherishes, loyalty stands pre-eminent. He tends to support men rather than measures ; he is devoted to institutions rather than to ideas. In so far as he is true to the high standard of his creed, he is loyal—that is, faithful—to his best self, suppressing all inclinations of his

* *The Ashridge Journal*, No. 5 (February, 1931), p. 33.

baser self towards self-aggrandisement at the expense of
his fellows; he is loyal to his family, to his school, to his
university, to his party, and to whatever professional
group he may be attached. But his larger and supreme
loyalties he reserves for his church, his king, his country,
and his empire. Piety, fidelity, patriotism, imperialism—
these are words that are dear to him, and the noble principles which they connote are among his most treasured
spiritual possessions.

A clever and observant French writer, M. Floris
Delattre, making a survey of post-war England, perceives
loyalty to be one of the outstanding features of its conservative elements. His remarks have been summarised
as follows: "Conservatism lies at the very heart of the
collective psychology of England. Everything runs into it
and converges here—the sense of tradition, the tenacity
with which the people hold to what they have received
from their forebears, the respect for authority, the social
discipline, and even a certain homesickness for the past,
which confers on the democratic middle class of to-day a
sort of aristocratic flavour. No word is dearer to an
Englishman than *loyalty*, which implies a cordial devotion
to his country, his family, his friends, the ideas and even
the prejudices of his group."*

(12) *Common Sense, Realism, Practicality.*

Perhaps in treating of the conservative principle of
loyalty—that is, of fidelity to persons, devotion to institutions, and staunch adherence to causes—we have come
suspiciously near the visionary region wherein abstract
ideas hold sway. We have not, however, as a matter of
fact, crossed the line that divided the real from the fantastic. We are still in the midst of actualities, which are
none the less real for being spiritual. For the conservative
—unlike the jacobite, the non-juror, or other reactionary—
recognises the fact that even loyalty can on occasion be
carried too far. It may be bestowed on persons unworthy,

* Delattre, F., *L'Angleterre d'Après-Guerre* (Paris, 1930), re-
viewed in *The Times Literary Supplement*, September 11, 1930.

on institutions obsolete, or on causes discredited. Mr. Keith Feiling, indeed, says of toryism that it tends "to drag the chain of lost loyalties, superannuated leaders, and indefensible chivalries."* From this excess of an excellent quality conservatism is saved by its balancing common sense, by its instinct for the practical and possible. "The essential strength of the conservative party," it has been well remarked, "lies largely in its claim to be the party of practical compromise and common sense."† It is the party of affairs rather than of theories; the party of strong and efficient administration rather than of incessant and ill-digested legislation; the party which adapts policy to circumstances instead of attempting (like the bolsheviks) to fit circumstances into the Procrustean bed of fixed obsessions. The late Lord Younger, one of the ablest organisers that the conservative party ever produced, summed up the whole matter in the sentence : "Were I asked to define the basic principle of the conservative and unionist party, I would reply in a single word—*common-sense.*"‡

* *The Times Literary Supplement*, September 26, 1929.
† *Ibid.*, June 19, 1924.
‡ *Sunday Times*, June 12, 1927.

CHAPTER II

ENGLISH CONSERVATISM

" Revolution does not occur in this deeply conservative country, only development."—WILHELM DIBELIUS.

" The spirit of toryism, with its sense of an historic past, is the very genius of the national life."—C. B. ROYLANCE KENT.

" Conservatism has it in its power to make an appeal nobler and more potent than that of any other party "; but "it is essential that its disciples should take the trouble to reflect upon the origins and implications of their beliefs, and then be willing to preach their gospel with energy and conviction."—THE RIGHT HON. EDWARD WOOD [LORD IRWIN].

§ 9. THE CONSERVATIVE TRADITION IN ENGLAND

HITHERTO we have considered conservatism in general, and more particularly conservatism as it exists in the modern national state. We have remarked that the word " conservatism " stands as a convenient term to connote the ideals of the party of order, as opposed to those of the complementary, necessary, but (if unrestrained) perilous party of progress. We have observed that conservatism is based upon some of the sanest, deepest, and most enduring instincts of human nature—namely, upon reverence, affection, love of stability and security, suspicion of visionary theory, proper and rational fear of rash and revolutionary change. Finally, we have considered and tabulated the broad and general political principles that naturally display themselves as the results of the operations of the conservative spirit.

It is now time for us to turn more specifically to England, and to ask how the conservative spirit has manifested itself during the long course of our insular history. For, though the conservative spirit is everywhere the same, its manifestations depend very much upon its environment. Such abstract theories as Marxian socialism may try to stamp themselves in stereotyped uniformity

34

upon all the nations, kindreds, peoples, and tongues of a subjugated and terrorised humanity. But conservatism, respecting and cherishing the historic institutions and the traditional loyalties of each distinct unit of the human family, displays its common characteristics with differences in each separate locality. Further, since conservatism is usually called into its most positive activity by attacks upon those things which it holds most dear—upon church, upon constitution, upon crown, upon landed interest, upon family, upon property, upon national prestige, upon independence, upon empire—the nature of its manifestations is inevitably largely determined by the nature of its enemies and by the form of their assaults. And these differ prodigiously from country to country and from age to age.

It will be the task of the second part of this book to trace in some detail the development of conservative principles in England; to describe the organisation of a conservative party during the later centuries of our history; to follow the fluctuations of its fortunes, and the modifications of its policy due to the ever-changing character of the environment in which it has found itself militant. What I wish to do in the present preliminary and analytical chapter is, first, to indicate briefly how and in what order the general principles of conservatism have manifested themselves in England; secondly, to sketch in broadest outline the course of the development of conservative policy in this country; thirdly, to mention the names and works of those great exponents of conservative ideas who may be called the " major prophets " of English conservatism; and, finally, to enumerate among notable English statesmen those who are commonly regarded as the outstanding exemplars of conservatism in practice.

First, as to the general principles of conservatism. The English people more than most have manifested reverence for the past, respect for tradition, regard for custom. Even English radicals have tended to appeal rather to the practices of earlier days than to those abstract ideas that have so much vogue on the Continent. Their demand has constantly been for the concrete ancestral rights of

Englishmen and not for the visionary natural rights of Man. English liberty, as Tennyson remarked, has slowly broadened down " from precedent to precedent." Thus the Act of Settlement (1701) supplements the Bill of Rights (1689); the Bill of Rights confirms and safeguards the Habeas Corpus Act (1679) and the Petition of Right (1628); both these Acts appeal to and define the principles of Magna Carta (1215); the Great Charter itself is based on the Charter of Henry I. (1100), and it professes to make no innovations; the Charter of Henry I. resumes the laws of Edward the Confessor; these again recall the dooms of Alfred, which themselves are but the solemn formulations in writing of the immemorial customs of the Anglo-Saxon peoples. It is not too much to say that all permanent reforms in England have been conservative reforms. Justly does Lord Hugh Cecil observe that so fundamentally conservative are the English people as a whole that " the best way to recommend a novelty to them is to make them believe that it is a revival."*

Few people, moreover, surpass the English people in their sense of solidarity, in their consciousness of national unity, in their passion to preserve the continuity of their rich and splendid heritage. They feel that England is a great and living reality, the mother of them all. They are filled with love for her beauty, with thankfulness for the benefits she confers upon them, with zeal for her honour, with devotion to her service. Of course, unhappily, from time to time some sections of the English people become disgruntled by adversity, or poisoned by the virus of alien dogma. These misguided sections, under the impulse of misery or of madness, turn against their mother-country and try to injure or destroy her. They divide the nation in hopeless schism; they attack their fellows with merciless ferocity; they temporarily break the unity of the people, threaten the continuity of the constitution, and menace the very life of society. Such were the fanatics of the Puritan reformation; such were levellers of the Stuart rebellion; such were equalitarian demagogues of the eighteenth-century period of revolu-

* Cecil, Lord Hugh, *Conservatism* (1912), p. 25.

tion ; such are the Marxian socialists and communists. It has been, and is, the special task of English conservatism to maintain the organic unity of the nation and the living continuity of its institutions, together with the kindly and genial English spirit, as against all the destroyers.

Thus English conservatism has always set its face against revolution, and if it has ever, as in 1689, lent its aid to a violent change of government, it has been—as Burke pointed out—because those whom it opposed and removed were themselves attempting a violent subversion of the constitution. It remained conservative even when it had to ally itself with its usual enemies and adopt their methods. But English conservatism has never in its great periods, or under its outstanding leaders, been merely reactionary. The " stability " of Mr. Croker and the " immobility " of the Duke of Cumberland have not been its watchwords. It has always been associated with reform, but with reform cautious, gradual, experimental, as befits the guardianship of so fine yet perishable an inheritance as the English constitution and the English church.

And especially the English church. For conservatism in England has, from its first conscious and organised beginnings, always been peculiarly associated with religion. Its enduring ideal has been the magnificent mediæval conception of the *Respublica Christiana*—the single great society which is in its spiritual aspect the church, in its secular aspect the state. When in the sixteenth century Christendom divided itself into national churches —Gallican, Spanish, German, Italian, and so on—and particularly when the national churches of the Continent became associated with powers, whether monarchical or papal, hostile to English interests and English independence, then Englishmen as a body rallied round the Anglican church-state, as established by Henry VIII., and the first conservatives proper (although, of course, the name " conservative " was not then invented) were those who rose to defend this Anglican establishment against both the Roman reactionaries who opposed all reform and the Puritan revolutionaries who wished to Calvinise both church and state. Thus English conservatism began by being what it has always continued to be, the creed and policy of the moderate, sensible, pious, and patriotic middle portion of the nation.

These early conservatives were all profoundly convinced of the divine source of authority in both church and state: for a time, indeed, the doctrine of the divine right, and even the hereditary divine right, of kings became an integral part of their profession. The prayers and exhortations of their church inculcated the obligation of uniform and unresisting obedience. They were made continually conscious of duties, and if ever they were impelled to demand and to insist upon rights, it was the rights of the community as a whole, or of the national church as such, rather than the rights of the individual, that they stressed. In respect of both individual and nation they emphasised the prime importance of character, and contended that "the soul of all improvement is improvement of the soul." Above all they stood for loyalty, and if ever conservatism has tended to lapse into reaction—as perhaps it did with the jacobites and non-jurors of the eighteenth century— it has been because the passion of loyalty had associated itself with unworthy persons, obsolete institutions, and lost causes. But next to the church it is the crown which has gathered round itself the most enthusiastic and enduring loyalty of conservatives. And, happily, not of conservatives alone. For just as the church—although its *defence* is the special function of conservatism—is the church of the whole nation, so the king—although the maintenance of his prestige and prerogative is peculiarly the conservative task—is the monarch of the whole nation, standing above all parties, reconciling differences, harmonising discords, symbolising the unity of the state, the continuity of its constitution, and the integrity of its empire.

§ 10. The Development of Conservative Policy in England

We have observed that, although conservatism as a spirit and a principle is as old as the human race itself, conscious and organised conservatism in England—that is to say, something that, under whatever name, can properly be called a conservative party—dates only from the sixteenth century. For, ere political parties of any sort could form themselves, formulate policies, and begin to exercise influence on the course of events, four preliminary conditions had to be fulfilled. First, the sovereign national state had to come into existence; and it was not until the end of the middle ages that the English national state achieved sovereignty—on the one hand, emancipating itself from the control of the Holy Roman Empire and the cosmopolitan Papacy, and, on the other hand, bringing into subjection to its supreme authority all feudal and local powers that had during the mediæval millennium enjoyed a virtual autonomy. Secondly, peace and security had in the main to prevail. So long as order was waging a doubtful battle with anarchy, as it was all through the middle ages, a strong and autocratic kingship presented the only hope of the ultimate establishment of effective and beneficent government. Not until Henry VII. and Henry VIII.—by methods which strike us as brutal, but which were probably inevitable at the time—established the rule of law was any continuous control of the executive by permanent popular parties possible. And, thirdly, not even in the comparatively peaceful England of the Tudors would popular participation in politics have been feasible but for the existence of representative institutions. And the creation of representative institutions in England —in other words, the development of the English parliament—was peculiarly the work of the later middle ages and of early Tudor times. Finally, representative institutions themselves would not have sufficed to secure popular influence by means of coherent parties, in the absence of an articulate public opinion. And until the close of the middle ages public opinion, in so far as it existed at all, was largely inarticulate: on the one hand, it was ordered and restrained by ecclesiastical authority; on the other hand, it lacked organs and instruments of expression. Not until the Inquisition loosened its grip on the throats of men; not until the invention of printing disseminated knowledge; not until men began to congregate freely in cities, did the communal consciousness and the general will find intelligible voice.

The first question on which the voice of the conservative section of the English nation made itself distinctly audible in modern England was, as we have already remarked, the question of religion. And on this first occasion of its utterance it embodied in its pronouncement in a most striking manner the two principles which in the eighteenth century received their perfect expression in the writings of Burke—namely, the principle of careful preservation and the principle of cautious reform. Those who accepted and supported the anglican settlement of Henry VIII. and Elizabeth—and they formed the decisive majority of the politically minded portion of the nation— were bent, on the one hand, to conserve the splendid mediæval ideal of the unity and coincidence of church and state; but they were equally bent, on the other hand, to carry through those reforms in church government, in ecclesiastical discipline, and ultimately in dogma, which the better thought and the rising morality of the age demanded. Thus, as we have seen, they stood midway between the Roman reactionaries who opposed all reform and the Puritan revolutionaries who wished to change everything. They held up the hands of the monarchs and their ministers while, amid the ragings of two opposite groups of enemies, they marked out that unique, but typically English, *via media* between catholicism and protestantism, the anglican establishment.

The second great question concerning which the conservative section of the English nation was called upon to declare itself was the political question of sovereignty, at issue between Charles I. and his parliament. And here again, as we shall observe more at large in the second part of this dissertation, the English conservatives showed at once their determination to preserve the constitution intact, while reforming its working. So long as Charles I. was clearly in the wrong—that is, so long as he himself was violating the constitution (roughly, until December, 1641)—they were against him. Next to the maintenance of the church, the maintenance of the constitution was the conservative task. During the first session of the Long Parliament (November, 1640—September, 1641) Charles I. had no supporters outside the court and official circles : all the great conservative leaders, such as Hyde, Colepeper, and Falkland, joined the progressives in stopping the levies of ship-money and in abolishing the Star Chamber. By the end of the first session the conservative task was accomplished. The accretions to the royal authority made during the Tudor period were swept away; the constitution was restored to the condition in which it had flourished under the Lancastrians in the fifteenth century.

But the puritans and parliamentarians were not content with this conservative reform. They proceeded, first, to attack the anglican settlement of the church, and, secondly, to encroach upon the constitution by demanding, on the one hand, the exclusion of the bishops from the House of Lords, and, on the other hand, the further diminution of the royal power. Hence the conservatives —headed by Hyde, Colepeper, and Falkland—became royalists, and braced themselves for their third great task —namely, the defence of the crown (as head of both church and state) against puritan republicans. The issue came, of course, to the arbitrament of war, and for a time the enemy prevailed. But the Restoration of 1660 saw the counter-triumph of moderate conservatism in the return of the king, the re-establishment of the church, and the revival of the constitution.

Unhappily, the restored Stuarts were unfaithful both to the anglican church and to the English constitution. Hence it became painfully necessary for conservatives (who at that time got the nickname of " tories "), in defence of their prime loyalties, religious and political, to join the progressives (then called " whigs ") in expelling James II. and in setting up the new constitutional monarchy of William and Mary. This so-called " Glorious Revolution " of 1689—the conservative nature of which was always strongly maintained by Bolingbroke, Burke, and Disraeli —immensely increased the importance and power of par-

liament, and therefore of the political parties which in turn
sought and secured control of the parliamentary machine.
All kinds of new questions began to divide the conservatives (*i.e.*, moderate tories) from their opponents (*i.e.*,
the whigs and later the radicals). The tories stood, of
course, like their predecessors, for church, for constitution, for crown, as against dissenters, innovators, and
oligarchs. They also found themselves called upon to
defend the landed interest against aggressive money;
rural England against encroaching industry; a strong navy
against a menacing standing army; non-interference in
European politics against an active and belligerent whig
foreign policy; parliamentary reform against gross whig
corruption; social reform and the improvement of the condition of England against laissez-faire economists; the
unity of the kingdom and the empire against those who
would disrupt them. Details of all these policies we must
defer for the present. Enough for the moment to indicate
the general lines of conservative development in England.

§ 11. The Major Prophets of English Conservatism

Defence of the church, the constitution, and the crown
—such successively in order of time were the main preoccupations of the conservatives of the sixteenth and
seventeenth centuries. And such in order of magnitude
they remained during the centuries that followed. But the
eighteenth century—which brought with it limited monarchy, parliamentary government, and cabinet administration—added many supplementary tasks. To conservatism, in the broad sense of the term, fell the duty of
defending the landed interest; the precious heritage of
rural England; the navy; freedom from continental entanglements; the purity of parliament. In the nineteenth
century still further obligations became incumbent upon
conservatives. The social and economic changes effected
by the industrial revolution brought with them (together
with much material good) evils which menaced the very
existence of the older England. Hence the " condition

of England " problem became prominent in conservative thought. And to this great question of the welfare of the people were soon added the not less insistent questions of the defence of the corn laws, the Irish church, the union of Great Britain and Ireland, and the integrity of the Empire.

Conservatives prefer to defend menaced institutions by actions rather than by words. We have already noted, and endeavoured to explain, the scantiness of avowedly conservative literature, as compared with the fulness of the flood of verbiage which accompanies and largely constitutes socialism.* Nevertheless there are a few great works which can be regarded as the classics of conservatism, and a small band of notable writers who may be termed the major prophets of the cause. It will be convenient to mention these writers now, although detailed discussion of their views will come more appropriately in the historical portion of this work. For most of them wrote not abstract dissertations on political theory, but practical treatises closely concerned with the urgent problems of their own day.

First among them, the one outstanding exponent of sixteenth-century conservatism, must be placed RICHARD HOOKER (1554-1600) with his great work on *The Laws of Ecclesiastical Polity*. He defended with masterly skill and fine catholicity of spirit the Elizabethan settlement of religion, and the anglican conception of the relation of church to state. To him the church was the nation, the whole nation, in its religious aspect. He wished every Englishman to claim his heritage in the national establishment. He strove to show the trivial and secondary nature of those differences of government and ritual, and even of dogma, which caused the puritan sectaries to cut themselves adrift and hold themselves aloof from the anglican communion. His passionate zeal was for the unity of the nation in both faith and allegiance.

The seventeenth century, the supreme seminal period in English political speculation, was, of course, rich in works imbued with the conservative spirit in one form

* See above. § 4.

or other.   Some of these works, however, such as the
writings of King James I. or Filmer's *Patriarcha*, were
too extreme and reactionary to be regarded as representative conservative utterances.   They lacked the essential
moderation of true conservatism; they did not give adequate recognition to the constant need of provision in the
constitution for the abandonment of obsolete beliefs, and
for cautious reform.   James I. stressed most strenuously
the conservative doctrines of the religious basis of the
state and the divine source of all legitimate authority; but
he identified the state with hereditary monarchy, and
centred all legitimate authority in himself.   He emphasised the duty of obedience on the part of subjects to
the point of denying their possession of any rights whatsoever as against himself.   The true conservatives of the
seventeenth century placed both church and constitution
in priority to the crown.   Filmer repeated the errors of
James, although he broadened the basis of political obligation by adding the sanctions of natural law to those of
the divine commandment.   The authentic conservative
note, in all its fulness and balanced harmony, was not
heard in the utterances of these extremists.   It sounded,
however, loud and clear in the works of Clarendon,
Hobbes, and Halifax.

EDWARD HYDE, EARL OF CLARENDON (1609-74), in his
masterly *History of the Rebellion and Civil Wars*, stated
with inimitable power and authority the case first for the
conservative defence of the constitution against the king,
and secondly for its defence of the king against the rebels
and revolutionaries.   Incidentally, he reasserted Hooker's
conservative ideal as to the relations of church and
state.

THOMAS HOBBES (1588-1679), in his memorable *Leviathan*, utterly discarded the obsolete and indefensible doctrine of the divine right of kings, based the duty of
obedience on the ground of an original social contract,
and recognised the validity of other forms of government
than monarchy.   He had the enviable, if temporarily uncomfortable, fate of offending both extreme royalists by
his rationalism, and also extreme republicans by his in-

sistence on the advantages of monarchy and by his firm denial of the right of resistance.

GEORGE SAVILE, MARQUIS OF HALIFAX (1633-95), honourably known as "The Trimmer," instinct with the spirit of sweet reasonableness, helped both by his deeds and by his writings to preserve the continuity of the constitution and the unity of the nation during the great crisis of 1685-95. His writings consisted in half a dozen epochmaking pamphlets which were collected and published under the title of *Miscellanies* in 1700.

In the eighteenth century the literature of conservatism was enriched in the first half by the writings of HENRY ST. JOHN, VISCOUNT BOLINGBROKE (1678-1751), and in the second half by those of EDMUND BURKE (1729-97). Bolingbroke and Burke, together with Beaconsfield in the nineteenth century, are the supreme exponents of conservatism. I shall have to say much of their work and their influence later on. Suffice it here to remark that both of them had the task of defining and defending conservatism as against reaction on the one side and revolution on the other. Bolingbroke marked out for conservatives the middle path between obscurantist jacobitism and oligarchic whiggism; Burke did more than any other man to found and inspire the conservative coalition of 1794, the great war ministry of Pitt which held the moderate middle position between the panic-stricken repressiveness of the "old tories" and the revolutionary recklessness of the "new whigs."

In the nineteenth century BENJAMIN DISRAELI, EARL OF BEACONSFIELD (1804-81) stands unique as the exponent of the new conservatism—the forerunner of the tory democracy of more recent days. Of him much more will have to be said; for he was man of action as well as man of letters. He, too, like his great predecessors, Bolingbroke and Burke, had to guide the party which he led, and ultimately controlled, along a new and untrodden path of compromise and moderation, midway between the reactionary toryism of Eldon and Sidmouth and the subversive liberalism of Russell and Gladstone. His *Life of Lord George Bentinck* is a brilliant defence of the agricultural interest and the charms of rural England; his *Spirit of Whiggism* is a scathing exposure of the " Venetian oligarchy " which had degraded the church, undermined the constitution, and superseded the crown; but, above all, his great trilogy of novels—*Coningsby, Sybil*, and *Tancred*—inexhaustibly rich in ideas, expound with masterly authority and completeness the conservative attitude towards the constitution (including the crown), the people, and the church respectively.

The major prophets of conservatism are unquestionably Bolingbroke, Burke, and Beaconsfield.

Contemporary with the young Disraeli, the " lake poets," Coleridge, Southey, and Wordsworth—all of whom had for a time been lured from the path of sanity by the false lights of the French revolution—maintained the principles of Burke, adding ideas inspired by continental thinkers, and leading the " romantic reaction " in Britain. Scott with his superb novels and Kenelm Digby with his glorification of mediæval chivalry furthered the same great movement. Closely allied to it, moreover, was the Oxford movement in the church—a movement whose leaders, and Newman in particular, proclaimed doctrines essentially conservative when they said that " religion is a spiritual loyalty," and when they argued that " securus judicat orbis terrarum."

In the mid-nineteenth century the ideals of conservatism were set forth admirably by Sir James Fitzjames Stephen and by Sir Henry Maine. And all through the century, the *Quarterly Review* (founded 1809) maintained with an amazing consistency of ability the conservative cause. It was supported, too, by a monthly, weekly, and daily conservative press too vast to specify.

§ 12. The Great Exemplars of English Conservatism

Since conservatism is displayed rather in actions than in words, it is necessary for those who would understand it to study the history of England, and to see the conservative spirit in operation on the field of practical politics.

A systematic, although necessarily superficial, survey of this field will be attempted in the ensuing part of the present dissertation. It will be convenient, however, before we proceed to that survey, to indicate the great men to whose policies and performances special attention will have to be paid. Who were the leading exemplars of conservatism, in the broad sense of the term, during the past four centuries?

Back beyond A.D. 1533 it is not necessary for us to go. Because, as we have already noted, it was not until the time of the Reformation that a conscious, consistent, organised, and effective conservatism began to display itself among the English people at large.* Hence, interesting though it might be, it would be irrelevant to revert to earlier ages and examine such sporadic phenomena as the conservatism of the barons who forced Magna Carta, the safeguard of the ancient liberties of Englishmen, upon the innovating and unscrupulous King John; or the conservatism of the patriots who under Henry III. made, as against the encroaching canonists, the famous and decisive declaration " nolumus leges Angliæ mutari "; or the conservatism of the fifteenth-century Lancastrians who strove to maintain the institutions of feudal England in face of the challenge of the autocratic but bourgeois Yorkists.

The marriage of Henry VIII. to Anne Boleyn was the decisive though discreditable event that brought to a head a quarrel between the English court and the Roman curia that had long been pending. The mediæval church, always and necessarily anti-national, had during the fourteenth and fifteenth centuries become obscurantist, persecuting, extortionate, and corrupt. Long and loud had been the cry from the faithful for reform of the church both in its head (the pope) and in its members (the clergy, monks, and friars). All attempts at conservative reform, however, had lamentably failed. One of the tragedies, indeed, of the later middle ages had been the collapse of the conciliar movement which at one time had seemed to promise reformation of the church from within. The occasion had not evoked the necessary man. It fell, there-

* Cf. Feiling, K., *History of the Tory Party* (1924), p. 13.

fore, to the clerisy and laity of each Christian nation to
effect the reforms which the church as a whole, through
its official chiefs, had shown itself unable or unwilling to
achieve.   In England, the Reformation, although carried
through by a brutal king and accompanied by incidents
of needless violence, was essentially and conspicuously
conservative.   Henry VIII., in fact, might well be ac-
claimed as the first outstanding English conservative of
modern times.   For his ecclesiastical settlement illustrated
the very genius of conservatism : it achieved reform without the sacrifice of continuity; it retained the catholic
doctrines, sacraments, and ceremonies, while abolishing
the inconveniences that had flowed from an alien domination and from an obsolete monasticism.

The moderate anglo-catholic settlement effected by
Henry VIII. was temporarily disturbed by the radical
Edward VI. and the reactionary Mary in turn; but Elizabeth restored it and, with the aid of such ecclesiastical
servants as Parker and Whitgift, and such civil servants
as Burleigh and Walsingham, made it permanent and
secure.

The struggle which Elizabeth and her ministers had to
wage on behalf of anglicanism in the sixteenth century
against Roman catholicism on the one side and Genevan
calvinism on the other, broadened during the seventeenth
century into a conflict in the political sphere.   James I.
was confronted both by papists who tried to blow him up,
and by presbyterians who wished to pull him down.   He
himself, as we have seen, was too extreme in both his
opinions and his policies to be properly called a conservative : he was one of those reactionaries who are the
precipitators of revolution.   And still more so was his
son Charles I., whose ill-instructed conscience compelled
him on principle to refuse the reforms necessary to conserve the constitution.   But though both James and
Charles made the position of their moderate ministers one
of abnormal difficulty, each of them was served by men
inspired by the true genius of conservatism—that is to
say, by a spirit of instinctive preservation combined with
that of conscious adaptation.   Eminent among such ser-

vants were Francis Bacon (Viscount St. Albans) under
James I. and Thomas Wentworth (Earl of Strafford)
under Charles I.   When the troubles broke out, and after
Strafford—hunted by his enemies and betrayed by his
master—was gone, the cause of conservatism was best
represented by Edward Hyde (later Earl of Clarendon),
John (later Baron) Colepeper, and Lucius Cary (Viscount
Falkland).*   Hyde and Colepeper survived to see the
Restoration.   Colepeper's work was done; he died in
1660.   But Hyde—created Earl of Clarendon in 1661—
lived until 1674, and did more than any other man to
make the Restoration settlement a truly conservative
one.   He had to defend its moderation against the
vehement ultra-royalists on the one hand, and its resolute
rehabilitation of old institutions against violent republicans on the other.   Clarendon ranks high among conservative statesmen.   And hardly inferior to him in statesmanship, though less estimable in character, stands Thomas
Osborne, baronet, who became successively Viscount
Latimer, Earl of Danby, Marquis of Carmarthen, and
Duke of Leeds.   After he had served Charles II. as minister (1674-79), he played a great part in carrying through
the eminently conservative revolution of 1688-89.   With
Danby at this critical period was closely associated in the
defence of caution and continuity George Savile, Marquis
of Halifax.   After these two notable men had passed
away, the leadership of the conservative (then called
" tory ") party devolved upon Robert Harley (who became Earl of Oxford) and Henry St. John (who became
Viscount Bolingbroke).   As a practical politician Harley
represented far better than Bolingbroke the essential
moderation of conservatism.   Bolingbroke in the days of
his power was a violent ultra-tory reactionary: only in
exile and adversity did he learn the wisdom that made

* Falkland, a man of inimitable charm, unhappily perished at
the early age of thirty-three in the first battle of Newbury (1643).
Everyone should read Matthew Arnold's sympathetic study of
his fascinating character: it originally appeared in the *Nineteenth
Century* for April, 1877; it was republished in *Mixed Essays*, 1879.

him in later life the prime exponent of conservative principles.

In the eighteenth century conservatism became associated rather with the whigs than with the tories: the whigs were bent on conserving the constitutional settlement of 1689; the tories, on the other hand, became the advocates of changes—e.g., franchise reform, abolition of rotten boroughs, shortening of the duration of parliament, freedom of trade—calculated to terminate the long-drawn ascendancy of the whigs. Perhaps the two Pitts and Edmund Burke may be regarded as the best exemplars of the true conservative tradition at that time. The reign of George III., however, saw the retransference of power and office from the whigs to the tories, and consequently the return of the tories to the conservative tradition, while the whigs became associated with the radicals in demands for drastic constitutional changes. Among the most eminent and representative of the tories who, during the nineteenth century, maintained and exemplified in office the conservative tradition were Canning, Peel, Disraeli, Salisbury, and Balfour, of all of whom more anon.

A Note on Nomenclature

It will be observed by those who follow the course of the narrative set forth in the ensuing chapters that the exponents and exemplars of conservatism have been, during the process of the four centuries under review, called by many names. Some of these names, such as " abhorrers," have had but a momentary vogue: they have served an ephemeral purpose, connoted a passing phase of the eternal controversy between order and progress, and have faded away. Two terms, however, have enjoyed a longer life, and both of them have from time to time been put forward as superior, either in claim or in attraction, to the name " conservative " as the general designation of the party of order. These two terms are the old one " tory " and the comparatively new one " unionist." The claims of neither can, I think, be seriously maintained.

I. *The term* TORY. The word " tory " comes from Ireland. The Ormonde papers (A.D. 1646) speak of " others of the Irish called tories," and four years later Whitelock tells of English officers "murdered by those bloody highway rogues called the tories." These original Irish " tories " were apparently bog-trotters, moss-troopers, or bandits, who, while nominally devoted to the royalist cause, were in reality self-seeking criminals of the lowest type. Mr. Cooke in his *History of Parties* describes them (Vol. I., p. 138), on the authority of Roger North, as " a set of ruffians in the disturbed districts of Ireland . . . the most despicable savages among the wild Irish." The term seems to have been brought to England and applied to English politics by Titus Oates, who, about 1678, denounced as " tories " those who doubted his mendacious fables concerning a popish plot, or who defended the innocent victims of his unscrupulous malignity.* The term was thus to begin with, in the sphere of English politics, an expression of virulent abuse, the worst that could be discovered or devised by frenzied opponents. In the eighteenth century, its original significance having been forgotten, it became a mere party title, accepted as a familiar battle-cry by both friends and foes alike. But the tory programme was by no means always so conservative as that of its opponents, the whigs : in the middle of the eighteenth century, under the influence of Bolingbroke, it was distinctly the more progressive of the two. On the other hand, at the end of the century, under the influence of George III. and amid the alarms generated by radicalism at home and revolution abroad, toryism tended to become not merely conservative, but clearly reactionary and regressive. The term, too, became definitely a misnomer after 1794, when a coalition in defence of order, as against radicalism and revolution, was formed by a fusion of tories and " old whigs." The great ministries of the period of the long war that terminated at Waterloo were not tory ministries, but coalition ministries essentially conservative. No doubt Welling-

* *Cf.* Kent, C. B. R., *Early History of the Tories* (1908), Preface and pp. 263-264.

ton's ministry, 1828-30, can properly be termed " tory " ;
but its achievements were not such as to make any modern
conservative wish to claim .it as his model.   The term
" conservative," indeed, was urgently needed to describe
the party which combined defence of order and continuity
with recognition of the need for cautious evolutionary reform.   Peel's Tamworth Manifesto, 1834, was a true conservative pronouncement ; but the term " conservative "
itself seems to owe its introduction as a party name to
Peel's friend, the famous, or notorious, J. W. Croker, in
1835.*   Its perfect appropriateness caused it speedily to
supersede the obsolete and discredited term " tory," and
it still remains definitely its superior.   The name " tory "
has once again become what originally it was in the days
of Titus Oates—namely, a term of abuse.

II. *The term* UNIONIST.   This term was useful and
indeed necessary during the closing years of the nineteenth century (1885-1900).   It denoted the coalition of
conservatives and anti-Gladstonian liberals who opposed
the liberal leader's novel Home Rule policy for Ireland.
So long as these two coalitionist groups remained separate
and distinct, and so long as the Home Rule question remained the centre of political controversy, the retention
of the name " unionist " was imperative.   But with the
complete fusion of the two groups, and with the rising
into prominence of new and larger issues, the term lost its
significance and its justification.   No doubt it was a good
term, and some who like it contend that, quite apart from
its relation to Ireland, it pleasingly connotes that ideal of
that unity of classes in the nation, and that unity of
dominion in the empire, which is one of the dominant notes
of conservatism.   But unity, as we have seen, is only one
of its dominant notes, and by no means the keynote.
" Conservatism " connotes a much larger and richer harmony of ideas than does " unionism."

* *Cf.* Alington, C., *Twenty Years* (1921), p. 182.

PART II
HISTORICAL

CHAPTER III

THE FORERUNNERS OF MODERN ENGLISH CONSERVATISM

1533–1641

"The first germs of whig and tory in England may be dated from a wedding—the sacrament which united Henry VIII. to Anne Boleyn and signalised our definite disunion from Catholic Europe."—KEITH FEILING.

"Toryism was born with Anglicanism, with the doctrine of church and state implicit in the religious settlement of the Tudors."—*The Times* (June 6, 1924).

§ 13. HENRY VIII.

FOUR hundred years ago religion occupied in men's minds a place incomparably more prominent than that which it occupies to-day. It reigned without a rival. No theatres, concert-halls, picture-palaces, or lecture-rooms drew the multitudes away from the churches. No organised sports distracted their attention; no Sunday newspapers with their fascinating records of the crimes and misfortunes of mankind kept them in bed when they were summoned by the bell to service. And further: when they were in church no doubts assailed them concerning the marvels related, or the miracles performed, by the priest. Heaven with its celestial inhabitants lay within easy reach of earth, and a constant intercourse was maintained between angels and good men. Hell was even nearer: it yawned immediately beneath men's feet. Earthquakes might precipitate mortals immediately into everlasting flames. Volcanoes were the mouths of Hades, and the lava that flowed therefrom conveyed some idea both of the nature and the temperature of the place where the wicked would eternally be tormented. The air swarmed with devils whose crafty devices for snaring immortal souls could barely be frustrated by means of bells and gargoyles, holy water and consecrated wafers, penances and fastings, incantations and prayers.

For a thousand years the spell of the catholic theology had lain upon the minds of the men of the western world. The civilisation that had raised the barbarian invaders of Europe (including England) from their primitive pagan savagery into a condition of crude culture and comparative humanity was a Christian civilisation promulgated by monks and priests. Its finest flower was the life of mediæval sanctity—the life of self-sacrifice, meditation, devotion, and divine communion. But this flower of sanctity was a rare and frail one, for it sprang from a root peculiarly liable to corruption. And in the sixteenth century corruption in Christendom was rife.

The thirteenth-century conflict between the papacy and its creature the empire had witnessed the scandalous prostitution of the spiritual powers of the church to secular ends; the fourteenth-century captivity of the popes at Avignon had degraded their great office, had destroyed their cosmopolitan character, and had hopelessly involved them in national brawls; the fifteenth-century schism, when two and even three popes—each with his college of cardinals, his complete hierarchy, and his inquisition—fulminated and fought, uprooted whatever of respect and reverence remained in the mediæval world. Even when, in 1417, the schism was ended, and a re-united Christendom once more found its centre in Rome, the popes of the renaissance, ignoring the urgent need for religious revival and moral reform, devoted themselves to secular ends, and in particular to the re-establishment of their power over their Italian possessions. The spectacle of such a pope as Alexander VI. (1492-1503)—liar, murderer, adulterer, traitor, and the father of a brood of children even worse than himself—shocked the conscience of Christendom. And even the pope who had to deal with Luther, Leo X. (1513-21), although he was a scholar and a munificent patron of art, nevertheless was a source of scandal by reason of his evil life and his scarcely veiled unbelief. The need of a drastic reformation of the church, in head and members, became every day increasingly evident to all good men. Yet all the efforts of the fifteenth-century reformers failed to effect reform from within. In particular, the disillusionment, defection, and death of Æneas Sylvius (Pope Pius II., 1458-64) made Martin Luther inevitable. Never was a clearer demonstration of the truth that reform is essential to conservation.

England, in common with Germany, had long been restless under the papal yoke. So far back as the eleventh century William I. had laid down rules limiting the power of the Roman curia within his realm; and Henry II. had followed William's example in the still more stringent restrictions of the Constitutions of Clarendon. Not, however, until the reign of John did the barons and people of England begin to regard the papal court as definitely hostile to themselves. They were humiliated by John's enforced surrender of his kingdom to the Roman see, and by its reduction to the status of a papal fief; they were outraged by the pope's denunciation of Magna Carta. It was under Henry III., however, that antagonism for the first time became acute. The enormous exactions of money that gave England the name of " the milch cow of the papacy," coupled with flagrant abuses of papal patronage and gross encroachment on the part of the papal courts, roused general resentment and disgust. When the papacy moved from Rome to Avignon (1305-9) and became the preserve of Frenchmen, the situation was intolerable. Edward III., with the scholastic assistance of Wycliffe, endeavoured to safeguard English interests by means of his Statutes of Provisors (1351) and Præmunire (1353), and by his repudiation of John's surrender, with its consequent annual tribute (1366). Wycliffe, however, warming to his patriotic and anti-papal task, went beyond the fourteenth-century limits of conservative reform : the time was not yet ripe for the foundation of the Rationalist Association. He himself, even with royal protection, barely escaped with his life : his unhappy followers, the Lollards, had to endure the utmost horrors of the stake. The objection of fifteenth-century Englishmen to Rome was rather financial and political than moral and intellectual.

Even in the sixteenth century Henry VIII. was staunchly catholic in his creed. The second son of Henry VII., he was, so long as his elder brother Arthur lived, destined for the church. He was thus trained in theology, and he never lost his ecclesiastical interests. He remained throughout his life resolute in his determination to permit within his realm no deviation from the doctrinal standards of Western Christendom. Early in his reign he entered the lists of controversy against Luther, and won from Pope Leo X. the title of " Fidei Defensor " in respect of his championship of the sacramental system. At the very end of his reign his statute of the Six Articles maintained the same rigid orthodoxy. What he objected to in Rome was not its creed, but its territorial possessions, its financial exactions, its maintenance of benefit of clergy, its claims to jurisdiction and to patronage, its tendency to assert its sovereignty in secular concerns. Almost inevitably a clash would have come during the sixteenth century between the growing royal power and the declining papal authority. The clash was prematurely precipitated by Henry's matrimonial entanglements during the six years 1527-33.

In repudiating the jurisdiction of the papal courts, in stopping the export of money to Rome, and even in dissolving the monasteries, Henry had not the remotest intention of breaking the continuity of the English church, or of founding a new schismatical organisation. He was but completing the work begun by William the Conqueror and continued by Henry II. and Edward III. He was asserting national independence, not starting a protestant sect. The wording of the *Act of Supremacy* (1534) should be carefully observed : " Albeit the King's Majesty justly and rightfully is and ought to be the supreme head of the Church of England, and so is recognised by the clergy of this realm in their convocations, yet nevertheless for corroboration and confirmation thereof and for increase of virtue in Christ's religion within this realm of England, and to repress and extirp all errors, heresies and other enormities and abuses heretofore used in the same; be it enacted by authority of the present parliament that the king, our sovereign lord, his heirs and successors, kings of this realm, shall be taken, accepted, and reputed the only supreme head in earth of the Church of England," and so on. Here is the very genius of conservatism embodied.

There is no innovation : the king already " is and ought to be the supreme head of the Church of England," for the church is merely the nation in its religious aspect. All that he and his parliament do is to reassert an authority that has been obscured by alien encroachments. At the same time the reassertion of these ancient powers prepares the way for needed reform. The church, when free and under its proper head, will be more, and not less, able to " repress and extirp all errors, heresies, and other enormities and abuses " which under the divided authority of king and pope have managed to flourish. The mediæval constitution, the Roman ritual, the sacramental system, even the catholic creed—all are conserved; only the evils due to foreign jurisdiction are removed.

§ 14. ELIZABETH AND HER MINISTERS

The conservatism of the anglican church, as determined by the masterful will of Henry VIII., although it was satisfactory and agreeable to the immense majority of the nation, did not please the extremists on either side. The Roman reactionaries were unable to recognise the royal supremacy; the Genevan reformers could not reconcile themselves either to the Roman ritual or the Catholic creed. Henry VIII. made short work with both groups of dissenters : the Romanists he hanged or beheaded as traitors and rebels; the Reformers he burned as heretics and schismatics. His sanguinary maintenance of the anglican *via media* ceased for a season with his death. Neither his son Edward (controlled by Cranmer) nor his daughter Mary (supported by Pole) was at all disposed to tolerate a church that was neither protestant nor catholic —a church that was Roman in its ritual and dogma, but Lutheran in its repudiation of the papacy and its dependence on the state. Neither Edward nor Mary was conservative : the one was a revolutionary reformer, the other a blind reactionist. Edward's innovations menaced the continuity of the church, Mary's restorations foreboded the cessation of its reform. And, as we have seen, continuity coupled with reform is of the essence of conservatism. Edward would have merged the English church with Continental calvinism; Mary would have subjected it once more to Roman cosmopolitanism : in either event it would have lost its peculiar and intimate association with the English nation; it would have ceased to be distinctively *Ecclesia Anglicana*.

Elizabeth was above all things a patriot and a nationalist. She and her subjects were conscious, as none of their predecessors had been, of " the commonwealth of this realm of England." They were resolved that in things spiritual as well as in things temporal they would be free from any and every foreign yoke : they would not bow the knee either to Geneva or to Rome, any more than they would to Philip of Spain or to the head of the House of Valois. Nevertheless, Elizabeth in the early days of her autonomy had to move with extreme caution : she dared not assert her independence too aggressively; she had to refrain from offending too grossly any of the great interests of the age. For she was surrounded by enemies eager to compass her destruction, and her realm was beset by foes who longed to add it to their conquests. Fortunate, indeed, was it for her that her foreign foes—Hapsburg, Valois, Papal—were divided by animosities so intense as to preclude their combination; otherwise she must have been at once overwhelmed. As it was their mutual wrangling gave her twelve invaluable years (1558-70) in which to establish her strength. With inimitable skill she played them off, each against the others, and so secured immunity from external attack. With respect to her domestic enemies, catholic and calvinist, she tried, with infinite patience and worldly wisdom, to conciliate them and reconcile them to her Anglican establishment. For to the anglican *via media* of her father she returned from the moment of her accession. She could do no other. The daughter of Anne Boleyn could not possibly recognise the authority of Rome (which had declared her illegitimate) and still continue to reign; the daughter of Henry VIII. could not possibly recognise the authority of Geneva (which had denounced the royal supremacy) and remain head of the church.

The Elizabethan settlement of 1559 was a model of conservative statesmanship : it was instinct with conciliation, compromise, and common sense. It was effected by the two great statutes of *Supremacy* and *Uniformity* jointly. The *Act of Supremacy*, of course, emancipated the church from papal control; but it carefully avoided the ascription of ecclesiastical headship to Elizabeth—an ascription which, offensive when applied to Henry VIII., would have been doubly obnoxious if applied to a woman —and merely asserted that the queen was "the only supreme governor of this realm as well in all spiritual or ecclesiastical things or causes as temporal." The *Act of Uniformity* simply required the use of the anglican servicebook by every loyal minister, and regular attendance at the parish church by every loyal subject. Into the personal beliefs of the individual subject no inquiry at all was made. There was no attempt to re-introduce any such inquisitorial test as that instituted by Henry VIII.'s statute of the *Six Articles*. External conformity was enough. The ideal of spiritual unity was lowered to the more practicable ideal of political uniformity. Of course, ultimately the question of creed had to be faced in respect of the clergy and the official classes. The doctrinal standards of the anglican church were finally formulated in the *Thirty-nine Articles*, framed by convocation in 1563 and confirmed by royal authority eight years later. In this admirable settlement—which was incomparably broader, more tolerant, and more comprehensive than any other existent at that date—Elizabeth had the potent and invaluable aid of her statesmanly archbishop, Matthew Parker, a man in whom the historic sense and the passion for continuity were strong. He trod so far as he could in the mediæval ways; that is to say, he conserved all that seemed to him sound in the ancient catholic organisation, ritual, and dogma. As Canon E. W. Watson well says : "The English church was to manifest its continuity by retaining its constitutional position and the immemorial ordination of its ministry, and by a worship and an attire of its clergy that should remind its members of the past; but it was also to be a reformed church, recognising its sister churches abroad and recognised by them. But Elizabeth and Parker had no mind that it should lose its identity and be merged in a new reformed cosmopolitan system."*

One thing, however, must be noted. Elizabeth's *Thirty-nine Articles* were as pronouncedly and unmistakably protestant as Henry VIII.'s *Six Articles* had been catholic. What was the cause of so marked a transition and transformation in a quarter of a century? The answer is twofold. On the one hand, the dreadful persecutions of Mary's reign had turned the English nation definitely towards protestantism and away from catholicism. On the other hand, the decrees of the disastrous Council of Trent (1545-63) had stereotyped catholic dogma, had destroyed the hope of any revision of the mediæval creed, had closed the door to doctrinal reform, and had committed catholicism irrevocably to reaction. The anglican church, then, though it remained catholic in organisation and ritual, became emphatically protestant in its articles of belief.

§ 15. RICHARD HOOKER

The Elizabethan settlement—half Roman and half Genevan, neither wholly catholic nor wholly protestant, but entirely English, illogical, conservative, and practical —happily satisfied the overwhelming majority of the English nation. They went to church and saw the service performed much as it had been from time immemorial. If they were catholic, they imagined that they were still following the missal and assisting at the mass; if they were protestant, they found comfort in the articles and the homilies, feeling that, whatever relics of superstition still remained in the ritual of their worship, the head and the heart of the Elizabethan ministers were soundly calvinistic.

But although the overwhelming majority of the nation accepted the Elizabethan compromise with gratitude and relief, a small minority on either side felt unable to conform to its demands. The catholic recusants suffered severely. For the papal bull of deposition, launched

* Watson, E. W., *The Church of England* (1914), p. 139.

against Elizabeth by Pius V. in 1570, turned them, against their will, into traitors and rebels; involved them in suspicion of conspiracy on behalf of Mary, Queen of Scots, or Philip of Spain; and plunged them into a sea of troubles. When called upon to recognise the queen's titles, and to repudiate the pope's claims to absolve subjects from their oaths of allegiance, many of them felt compelled to refuse, and to seal their refusal with their blood. To some, at any rate, of these sufferers the crown of martyrdom cannot be denied, even though the offences for which they endured death were apparently political and not religious. For it was of the very essence of the Tudor establishment that church and state were one. At the other extreme from the catholic recusants stood the puritan dissenters. They considered that the Reformation in England had gone but half-way, and they were eager to complete the journey (carrying the whole church with them) to Geneva. They objected to the royal supremacy; they denounced episcopacy, and particularly the Elizabethan bishops, who were merely royal officials; they repudiated the relics of the Roman ritual left in the service-book; they demanded a drastic revision of the dogmas of the church. Elizabeth regarded attacks on her bishops as attacks on herself, and attacks on herself as treason. Hence some of the more violent puritans—e.g., Barrow, Penry, and Greenwood in 1593—suffered the death of rebels against royal authority. Thus, towards the close of her reign, Elizabeth took up much the same position as her father. She walked on a razor-edge between catholicism and protestantism, and she struck with nervous ferocity anyone on either side who threatened to upset her equilibrium. In John Whitgift, archbishop of Canterbury (1583-1604), she found a prelate after her own heart, a worthy continuator of the work of Matthew Parker. He was a man of high purpose, clear understanding, and resolute will. A strong disciplinarian and an administrator of the first rank, he was determined to maintain the royal supremacy, the episcopal authority, and the uniformity of practice characteristic of the anglican church. Continuity coupled with reform was the guiding principle of his policy, and, by means of the High

Commission Court, over which he presided, he strove to subdue both puritan separatists who menaced continuity and Roman recusants who repudiated reform. His ideal was the *Respublica Christiana*, the perfect coincidence and co-ordination of church and nation. He was the true Elizabethan conservative.

To the anglican idealist the church and the nation were one and the same; to the Roman catholic the church was more than the nation; to the Puritan separatist it was less. The romanist regarded the church as universal and cosmopolitan, large as humanity itself, and aiming at the conversion and inclusion of all mankind. The puritan, although he too looked forward to the final establishment of Christ's universal kingdom, considered that in the present evil days the church consisted only of the exiguous company of the elect—a mere handful amid the hosts of the reprobate. Whitgift himself, in controversy with the leading puritan apologist, Thomas Cartwright, showed himself to be an able defender of the anglican position.* But he had an incomparably more effective coadjutor in the great debate in his friend and protégé, the judicious Hooker.

Richard Hooker (1553-1600), a man of the finest and most conciliatory spirit, a saint of the lowliest humanity, a thinker of commanding ability and clarity, an unsurpassed master of sonorous and majestic English prose— Richard Hooker is the prime exponent of conservatism as it is embodied in the Anglican settlement of Elizabeth. The great theme of his inimitable *Ecclesiastical Polity* (1594 *et seq.*) is the identity of the anglican church with the English nation; the religious basis of the state; the propriety of the royal supremacy; the validity of episcopacy; the complete harmony of the Elizabethan system with the laws of scripture and the laws of reason rightly interpreted. The argument of the eight books—of which the last three come to us in an imperfect condition—is a miracle of sustained and unanswerable logic : an argument, too, conducted in a tone admirably calculated to conciliate

* See *The Works of John Whitgift*, 3 volumes, edited for the Parker Society by John Ayre (1853).

and convince. After a preface addressed to the separatists, in which the excellencies of Calvin as a theologian and a disciplinarian are generously recognised, he proceeds to his main contention—namely, that the Scriptures, although they are the supreme guide of life, are not, as the separatists maintain, the sole guide; that God has provided man with a second and subordinate guide—namely, reason—to whose directions most minor matters of conduct are referred; that among these minor matters are details of government and administration in both state and church; and that because of these minor matters no rational man ought to sever himself from the church and break the unity of the nation. He speaks of the body politic as an organism, and he has a vivid conception of its unique and indivisible vitality. The weak part of Hooker's—*i.e.*, the anglican—identification of ecclesia and nation is, of course, its necessary obliteration of the distinction between sheep and goats, church and world, God and Mammon. Hooker tries, in his third book, to make out a case for this confusion by expounding the parable of the wheat and the tares, which were to be left to grow up as a single undivided crop until the final harvest. But when he has said all, it has to be admitted that there were among Hooker's contemporaries a considerable number of men whose infernal foliage so conspicuously proclaimed them to be tares that, even if they were not uprooted by excommunication or execution, it seemed difficult by even the widest charity in classification to include them among the celestial cereals.

§ 16. Thomas Wentworth, Earl of Strafford

The persons who found it most difficult to identify the church with the nation, and to regard every Englishman as *ipso facto* a Christian, were the puritans. It was against them that, towards the termination of her reign, Elizabeth, assisted by Whitgift and Hooker, had most strenuously to contend.

After Elizabeth's death their numbers grew, their strength increased, their demands became more insistent, and their antagonism to the Elizabethan constitution spread from the sphere of religion into the sphere of politics. Parliament became dominated by puritan influence, and the parliamentary puritans, not content with demanding the enforcement of the recusancy laws against the romanists, and the grant of concessions to the presbyterians, proceeded to attack the royal prerogative, to object to the presence of bishops in the house of lords, to criticise the king's ministers, to protest against the issue of royal proclamations, to claim a voice in the determination of foreign policy, and to seek to secure the complete control of taxation.

In matters ecclesiastical Elizabeth's successors, James I. and Charles I., signalised themselves by their strong and resolute defence of the anglican establishment. James I.'s attitude may have been opportunist. He had been brought up as a presbyterian in Scotland, and the two indelible lessons that he had learned in his native land were that Calvinism was the creed of rebels, and that the Genevan discipline was incompatible with any effective royalty. In uttering his famous saying, " No bishop, no king," he was obviously thinking of the conservation rather of monarchy than of episcopacy; rather of divine right than of apostolic succession. Charles I., however, supported the anglican settlement with a pure and passionate devotion. So completely, indeed, did the defence of the Church of England dominate the policy of his later years that it is not excessively imaginative to regard his ultimate execution as a religious martyrdom. In maintaining the Elizabethan establishment and defending the Church of England, James and Charles unquestionably had behind them the support of the immense majority of the nation. If they had not gone beyond that, there would have been no trouble. But, unfortunately, they did two things which roused against them the antagonism of large and decisive numbers of moderate and conservative men. On the one hand, they encouraged an " arminian " movement in the church—a movement led by such men as Bancroft, Andrewes, and Laud—which tended definitely to cut off the church from communion with Geneva and bring it nearer to Rome. Under "arminian" influence convocation became formidably aggressive : its canons of 1604 and 1640 were a deliberate challenge to both puritanism and parliament. Countless loyal anglicans who were far from puritan in their sympathies loathed and dreaded the recrudescence of priestcraft. On the other hand, these unhappy Stuart monarchs, who never understood either the English constitution or the English character, began to assert and to act upon an alien and fantastic doctrine concerning the alleged hereditary divine right of kings, a doctrine which menaced not only parliamentary government, but all the hard-won liberties of the nation. They appointed undesirable favourites as ministers and refused to listen to criticisms of their enormities and incompetencies ; they initiated a policy of continental alliances and foreign marriages obnoxious to the bulk of the people ; they levied money, exacted impositions, and granted monopolies in deliberate defiance of parliamentary protest ; they arrested and imprisoned those who opposed their arbitrary will, and kept them in bondage without any form of trial ; they proclaimed martial law in times of peace, and crushed remonstrance with military rigour.

Even in James I.'s reign encroaching puritanism, supported by parliament, nearly came to blows with reactionary absolutism, buttressed by convocation.* Repression faced revolution with none to mediate. The death of James, however, in 1625, for the moment relieved a situation tense with tragedy. But the relief was not of long duration. Charles I., although he possessed many virtues and graces that his father had lacked, had an even higher sense than James of the majesty of the royal prerogative, and an even firmer determination to oppose all constitutional change. He had more conscience than his father ; but even less common sense. Within four years of his accession the issue between king and parliament was fairly joined (1629).

But in this crisis of the national fate appeared the man

* Cf. Canons of Convocation, 1606 : " The king's power is from God, that of parliament from men, gained perhaps by rebellion; but what right can arise from rebellion?"

who, had his advice and guidance but been followed, might have saved both king and parliament from the ruin that overwhelmed them each in turn.   That man was Sir Thomas Wentworth, later Earl of Strafford, the man under whom conservatism in England addressed itself to its second great task—namely, the preservation of the consti- tution.   It is manifestly impossible in a couple of pages to sketch Wentworth's career, portray his notable achieve- ments, or even expound in detail the lines of his masterly policy.   Those who wish to study the life and work of this great man—and none can understand seventeenth-century conservatism without doing so—should turn to Lady Burghclere's fascinating biography.*   Thomas Wentworth, son and heir of Sir William Wentworth, of Wentworth Woodhouse in Yorkshire, was born in 1593.   He entered parliament as member for his native county in the year in which he came of age.   Filled with reverence for the Elizabethan constitution and the anglican church, he found himself compelled to join and ultimately to lead an opposition to the disastrous misgovernment of the Stuarts and their creatures.   The Elizabethan constitution, which remained his ideal throughout his life, had consisted of a patriot queen, a devoted and highly efficient council, and a loyal, respectful, co-operative parliament.   In 1614 he found the country going to wrack and ruin under the mis- guidance of an alien pedant, a band of evil and incom- petent favourites, and an irritated and suspicious parlia- ment.   For fourteen years (1614-28) he stood prominent as an opponent of the Court in general and Buckingham in particular : in Buckingham, indeed, he thought he saw the source of all the trouble.   He actually proposed the famous parliamentary protest of 1621 which roused James to ungovernable fury.   Under Charles he refused to pay his share (£40) of the " forced loan " of 1626, and conse- quently had to endure nearly six months' illegal imprison- ment (July-December, 1627).   Finally, as the climax to this first half of his career, he played the foremost part in formulating and in forcing upon the king the great Petition of Right—the document which stands with Magna Carta,

* Burghclere, Lady, *Strafford*, 2 volumes, Macmillan, 1931.

the Habeas Corpus Act, and the Bill of Rights as one of the four main pillars of English liberties. Hitherto he had fought shoulder to shoulder with Pym and Eliot for reform. But reform to him, though not to them, meant conservative reform : it meant " back to Elizabeth." In 1628 three events occurred which caused him to change, not his ground, but his attitude. First, the king's acceptance of the Petition of Right seemed to ensure a return to constitutional government; secondly, the assassination of the Duke of Buckingham removed the main obstacle to efficient administration; thirdly, the aggressive and revolutionary attitude of Pym and Eliot, who regarded the triumph of the Petition as, not the end, but the beginning of a constitutional conflict, showed him that the main menace to the Elizabethan system now lay with parliament and puritans, and not with king and convocation. Hence with a strength of character based on firm principle, and regardless of apparent inconsistency, he changed front and became the king's ablest and most devoted minister. As president of the Council of the North (1629-32) and as lord deputy of Ireland (1632-40) he provided a model of strong, capable, and incorrupt administration. He, as Lady Burghclere well says (vol. i., p. 217), " had none of the king's distrust of parliaments "; but he was resolved to resist the attempts of his quondam allies, the parliamentary leaders, to encroach upon the proper prerogative of the crown, or to interfere in the rightful province of the executive. Equally, in conjunction with his friend, the well-meaning but less moderate Laud, was he determined to resist the efforts of both recusant Catholics and revolutionary Calvinists to break the religious unity of the nation and wreck the anglican compromise.

During the eight years of Wentworth's absence in Ireland, Charles, governing England without a parliament, contrived by means of ship-money and star chamber to bring his southern kingdom to the verge of rebellion. Meantime the conscientious but extreme and injudicious Laud raised both English puritans and Scottish presbyterians to the temperature of empassioned resistance by his visitations, his canons, his service-books, and his insistence on effective episcopacy. So grave was the situation in 1639 that Wentworth was summoned from Ireland to give advice. By his advice the Short Parliament was summoned (April, 1640); against his advice the king quarrelled with it and dissolved it (May, 1640). Had the advice of Wentworth—created Earl of Strafford in January, 1640—been followed on this occasion and subsequently, almost certainly there would have been no civil war, no martyrdoms, no puritan republic. But in May, 1640, reaction (embodied in Henrietta Maria) prevailed and came to death-grips with revolution. For the time being conservative reform was in abeyance. The triumph of his rivals at court, co-operating in strange accord with the malignity of his overt enemies in parliament, brought the loyal and heroic Strafford to the block in May, 1641. From that moment the civil war and the execution of the king were, we can now see, almost inevitable.

CHAPTER IV

CAVALIERS VERSUS ROUNDHEADS
1641–1660

" For my part I do not like the quarrel, and do heartily wish that the king would yield and consent to do what they desire. My conscience is only concerned in honour and in gratitude to follow my master. I have eaten his bread and served him near thirty years, and I will not do so base a thing as to forsake him; and choose rather to lose my life—which I am sure to do—to preserve and defend those things which are against my conscience to preserve and defend. For I will deal freely with you : I have no reverence for bishops, for whom the quarrel subsists."—SIR EDMUND VERNEY (*two months before his death at Edgehill, 1642, to Edward Hyde*).

" The wide ramifications of the court, poetry and drama, the classic tradition, chivalry, mysticism, reverence for degree and order, all those catholic feelings which make men realise that they are part of an ancient country, or a universal creed, or a great society—such sentiments produced the Cavalier."—KEITH FEILING.

§ 17. CONSERVATIVE REFORM, 1641

At the time when Strafford was brought over from Ireland to advise the king, England had been for eleven years without a parliament. In 1629, indeed, as a culmination to four years of incessant conflict, Charles I. had firmly resolved that, if he could possibly avoid it, he would never call parliament again so long as he should live. The great problem which this resolution had presented to him had been, of course, the problem of how to raise a permanent revenue to take the place of the parliamentary subsidies. The king's ministers—in particular Noy, Finch, Cottington, Windebank, and Portland—had showed themselves ingenious in inventing devices for extorting money from all and sundry, and diligent in exploring ancient records in order to discover precedents. But such expedients as distraint of knighthood and prosecutions for encroach-

ments on the royal forests, though profitable, had been
exhausted in a single use. Not until Noy in 1634 had
introduced the levy of "ship-money" had Charles come
within sight of a regular and calculable income. The levy
of 1634 had been paid by the coast towns, though not
without protest, and its success had caused still more
extensive levies to be demanded in 1635, 6, and 7. The
manifest menace to parliamentary control of taxation had
led John Hampden to make his cardinal refusal : his trial
in 1637 had been an event of outstanding importance.
Meantime, while Charles and his ministers had been subverting parliamentary government, William Laud and his
minions had been, by means of a great metropolitical visi-
tation, attacking puritanism in its strongholds, and enforcing ecclesiastical uniformity with a high hand throughout England. And, not content with reducing England to
conformity, they had essayed to stamp out Scottish presbyterianism by means of new canons of church government
and a new highly-sacerdotal liturgy. England had been
near to rebellion in 1637 ; Scotland actually had risen in
revolt in 1639. This so-called Bishops' War it had been
that had brought Charles's absolute rule to an end, and
had compelled the summoning of a parliament. On the
one hand, the king had had no money with which to wage
a war ; on the other hand, he had had no troops who were
prepared to fight on the bishops' behalf. The Short Parliament (April-May, 1640) had refused to grant supplies
for the war until its grievances—the accumulated grievances of eleven years—had been attended to. The king
had demanded subsidies first, and, when the parliament
had declined to grant them thus unconditionally, he
(following the fatal advice of Henrietta Maria and the
elder Vane) had dissolved the parliament in anger. He
had taken the first irrevocable step on the road to ruin.
Soon afterwards the Scottish rebels, having secured complete control of their own country, had invaded England,
had easily overcome the feeble and half-hearted English
resistance (at Newburn-on-Tyne, August 28, 1640), had
occupied Northumberland and Durham, had advanced
into Yorkshire, and had forced the helpless king to make

a truce with them at Ripon (October 16, 1640). They were to hold the two northern counties; to receive £850 a day towards their expenses; to remain thus settled and subsidised until a new parliament should be summoned, their grievances redressed, and peace concluded. The Scottish rebels had thus become masters of the situation. Such was the frightful and humiliating mess that Charles, under the influence of his pernicious and incompetent court, had made of things. No wonder that Strafford groaned in agony, or that loyal patriots like Sir Edmund Verney sank into deep despair.

The parliament summoned to provide the money demanded by the Scots—the famous Long Parliament—met at Westminster on November 3, 1640. Its first session, which lasted until September of the following year, was unquestionably the most important single parliamentary session recorded in English history. The houses were in no mood for trifling. Their members came together in a condition of extreme exasperation and disgust. They were determined to terminate once for all a system of arbitrary and unconstitutional rule which had resulted in so much oppression, extortion, and disgrace. With the might of the victorious Scottish army behind them and supporting them, they were for the moment omnipotent. They could not be dissolved so long as the money due to the Scots remained to be paid.

During this first session the king and the court had no defenders. Falkland, Hyde, and Colepeper were as firmly resolved as were Pym, Hampden, and Cromwell to abolish both the arbitrary administration of Charles and the inquisitorial tyranny of Laud. Nevertheless, under the influence of Falkland, Hyde, Colepeper, and their like, the reforms effected in 1641 were eminently and essentially conservative reforms. There were no innovations. The watchword of the reformers might well have been "Back to Henry VI." They swept away such accretions to the royal power as had been made by the Yorkists, the Tudors, and the Stuarts. For example, having secured their position by means of a Perpetuation Act and a Triennial Act, they proceeded to abolish Edward IV.'s Council of the

North, Henry VII.'s Star Chamber, Henry VIII.'s Council
of Wales, Elizabeth's High Commission Court, and sundry
other similar tribunals that lay outside the sphere of the
common law. Similarly they declared illegal all those
novel or antique devices, such as "ship-money," by means
of which the king had endeavoured to evade the necessity
of summoning parliament. By September, 1641, the work
of restoring the constitution to the condition of its Lan-
castrian model was accomplished. The conservative reformers—Falkland, Hyde, Colepeper, and their fellows—
were satisfied. They felt that parliament had once again
been established in its proper place in the constitution;
and they believed that Laud's efforts to secure for the
bishops the supreme administrative control of both church
and state had been finally frustrated. Hence they cried a
halt to opposition. Not so, however, their more progressive puritan and parliamentary allies—Pym, Hampden,
Cromwell, and their friends.

§ 18. Conservative Resistance to Revolution, 1642

Even in the first session of the Long Parliament there
were ominous signs that conservative reform would not
satisfy Pym and his coadjutors. Two innovations they had
proposed that clearly indicated that they had in their
minds both a political and an ecclesiastical revolution.
They had brought forward, on the one side, a bill for
annual parliaments which had showed that they adumbrated the ultimate transference of sovereignty in the
state from the monarch to the multitude : with difficulty
had they been persuaded to be content with the Triennial
Act. On the other side, and with more insistence, they
had tried first to get their *bêtes noires*, the bishops, excluded from the House of Lords, and secondly to have
them abolished "root and branch." Their "Root and
Branch Bill" had passed two readings in the House of
Commons, and had only perished in committee (August,
1641). It was clear that nothing short of presbyterianism
would be regarded by them as an adequate safeguard
against the pretensions of the Laudian bishops, who were

asserting that their authority was derived from apostolic succession and not merely from royal nomination. Obviously both the anglican church as established by Elizabeth, and the English constitution as evolved from time immemorial, were menaced by the designs of the puritan revolutionaries. The first session of the Long Parliament, therefore, terminated with unmistakable symptoms of a schism in the hitherto solid ranks of the parliamentary opposition (September, 1641).

During the seven weeks' recess (September 3 to October 20) two things happened which rapidly precipitated a crisis. First, Charles paid a visit to Scotland (the first since his coronation), and there gathered conclusive evidence of the criminal correspondence of Pym and his friends with the leaders of the Scottish rebellion of 1640 : it was clear that, as an expiation to the shade of Strafford, as a sacrifice to his own outraged majesty, and as a vindication of his sovereign authority, he was about to have them arrested, tried, and executed as traitors. In desperate self-defence they prepared a *Grand Remonstrance*—a long catalogue of Charles's arbitrary and unconstitutional acts since his accession, coupled with further demands for safeguards— which *Remonstrance* they presented to him on his return to England. Their object was thoroughly to discredit the king and once more to unite the parliament in opposition to him. This object they failed to attain. The conservative reformers, now thoroughly alarmed by the violence and apparent unreasonableness of their quondam allies, and also deeply disgusted by the revelation of their antipatriotic intrigues with the Scottish invaders of England, rallied to the defence of the king. Hence, after a protracted and embittered debate, the issue of the *Grand Remonstrance* was carried by but the narrow majority of eleven (November 22, 1641). The king had on his side a " royalist " party of nearly 150 members, resolute to prevent any further encroachments on the monarchical authority, any more changes in the constitution, any additional attacks upon the church. If only Charles had behaved with normal prudence and restraint, he would speedily have found himself at the head of a parliamentary

majority. But just when the balance was beginning to
tilt in his favour he threw all his advantages away by his
futile and foolish attempt, through his attorney-general,
to impeach Pym and his four chief colleagues, on January
3, 1642, and by his still more fatuous and futile attempt
next day, at the head of a band of four hundred proto-
fascists, to arrest them in the House of Commons. The
menaced members took refuge in the city, and so threatening was the attitude of the Londoners to the king that
on January 10 he and his court departed from Whitehall,
whither he was destined never to return until he came for
execution seven years later. In January, 1642, civil war
began to come into sight.

The second event which had signalised the fateful recess
of the autumn of 1641 had been the outbreak of a formidable rebellion in Ireland. The strong hand of Strafford
having been removed, the Irish Catholics had risen in
revolt and had commenced a massacre of Ulster Protestants—a massacre frightful enough in reality, but mag-
nified to appalling proportions by popular rumour. Charles,
naturally and properly, demanded from parliament funds
with which to equip and despatch an army for the restoration of order. But the parliament, equally naturally and
justifiably, being profoundly suspicious of the royal
designs, refused (eager though they were to chastise the
Irish rebels) to supply him with the means to raise troops
(which they were sure he would sooner or later wish to use
against themselves) unless he would permit them to
appoint the officers. Here was a demand which, however
consonant with the circumstances, marked an unprecedented encroachment on the royal prerogative. The king
positively declined to surrender the military authority
which he had inherited from his ancestors—an authority
which it was his duty to transmit unimpaired to his successors. Negotiations continued through the summer of
1642, on this and other matters. But meantime the Irish
massacres continued unchecked, and puritan passions in
England were fanned to flaming heat by the stories of
catholic atrocities that came from Ulster. Finally the
parliamentary majority, in a frenzy that threw all restraint

to the winds, presented to Charles, in the so-called *Nineteen Propositions* (June, 1642), an ultimatum which they must have known he could not possibly accept. It was a formal challenge to war. The *Nineteen Propositions* demanded, not only that he should surrender his military sovereignty, but also *inter alia* that he should hand over to parliament the power of determining the appointment of ministers and privy councillors, the control of foreign policy and royal marriages, the custody of forts and castles, the education of the king's children, the creation of peers, and the reformation of the church. This was virtually a demand for abdication, or something worse than abdication—namely, for the continuance by the king in an office all of whose powers and prerogatives had been transferred to his implacable foes. It was a demand for the abandonment of the church to the presbyterians, for the complete abrogation of the constitution, and for the surrender of the sovereignty of the crown to parliament. An issue such as this could obviously not be settled by negotiation. Each side began to collect troops—the parliament by militia ordinances, the king by commissions of array—and on August 22, 1642, the civil war broke out. All the conservative forces in the country were called upon by the king to come to the defence of church, constitution, and crown.

§ 19. CONSERVATISM AT WAR, 1642-49

Rarely have the rights and wrongs in a great quarrel been more evenly balanced than they were in that dispute between Charles and his parliament which came to a head in August, 1642. No one can question the high seriousness, the strict integrity, the profound piety, the sincere nobility of purpose of those dour puritans who felt it their duty, as they euphemistically expressed it, " by battle or other way to rescue the king from his perfidious counsellors and restore him to parliament." They fought for the lofty causes of personal religion, individual liberty, and the sovereignty of the people; and neither the sublimity of their ideals nor the purity of their motives need be doubted, if—perhaps owing to the machinations of the devil, whom they did not sufficiently take into their calculations—what they actually achieved was nauseous hypocrisy, moral anarchy, and military despotism. On the other hand, the cavaliers who fought to maintain the beloved traditions and the revered sanctities of church and constitution and crown were painfully embarrassed by the complications which the conduct of Charles and his creatures had introduced into the controversy. They had no enthusiasm for the Laudian episcopate with its claim to apostolic succession, its aspirations after political power, its inquisitorial tyranny, its merciless severity. They had no desire whatsoever to go back behind the reforms of 1641, so as to restore the star chamber, or ship-money, or any other of the institutions which the Long Parliament had swept away. Above all, they had no love for that favourite but wholly un-English dogma of the Stuarts, the divine right of kings; they felt, too, that Charles had put himself badly in the wrong by his failure to observe the Petition of Right, by his effort to govern without a parliament, by his treatment of the Scots, by his intrigue with the Irish, by his attempt to seize the five members, and by countless other acts which displayed at one and the same time hopeless duplicity, abysmal folly, and extreme incompetence. They clearly realised that if the king had managed his affairs with even normal honesty and prudence he would have had so overwhelming a body of public opinion behind him that there would have been no possibility of war. Nevertheless, now that war had come, and now that such tremendous issues had been raised, they had no hesitation as to their duty. Church, constitution, and crown, all were menaced; and all were far too precious to be allowed to perish, even if their peril was to no small extent due to the actions of aggressive bishops, tyrannical ministers, and an injudicious and untrustworthy monarch. It was for the church rather than for the bishops, for the constitution rather than for the ministers, and for the crown rather than for the king, that the cavaliers in 1642 took up arms.

The armed supporters of the parliamentary cause were,

for the most part, the citizens of London, the burgesses of the greater towns, and the yeomen farmers of the eastern counties; their strength lay in their solid character, their rigid convictions, their command of most of the wealth of the country, and their possession of all the principal ports of the kingdom. To the king's side, on the other hand, flocked most of the nobility, gentry, and peasantry of England. The church, too, was as a whole ardently with the king, and even the catholics preferred him to the puritans. The royalist cause, however, was weakened by chronic and irremediable poverty; but it was strong in the possession of most of the military skill and trained force of the kingdom, and it was fortunate in having a person (however unsatisfactory) on whose behalf to fight, and also a clear objective for its campaign—namely, the capture of London. In the circumstances it was obvious that the best hope of Charles was to strike hard and at once : every week's delay meant the diminution of his own forces and the increase of those of his enemies. If only, in the autumn of 1642, after he had shaken off the parliamentary mosquitoes at Edgehill, he had pressed on vigorously and resolutely to London, he would have been master of the situation. He got as far as Turnham Green, and then the spectacle of 25,000 apprentices behind an extemporised mound caused him to stop. He paused, he hesitated, he turned tail, he was lost. Never again did he come within sight of success. Marston Moor (July, 1644) and Naseby (June, 1645) accomplished and sealed his ruin, and with his ruin the temporary eclipse of church, constitution, and crown. In May, 1646, the beaten and discredited king surrendered to the Scots. For three years futile and exasperating negotiations were carried on with a view to his conditional restoration—negotiations with the Scots at Newcastle, with the parliament at Holmby House, with the army at Hampton Court, with all three at Carisbrooke. Then came the so-called " second civil war " (1648), directly due to Charles's incurable duplicity. This outbreak, suppressed with indignant energy and promptness by the dominant army, was the immediate cause of the determination of the officers " to bring that man of blood to justice." The

outward formalities of a trial were observed: the pre-
ordained verdict was pronounced, and on January 30,
1649, Charles I. was executed.

If we ask how it was that so good and great a cause as
that of church, constitution, and crown—a cause supported
by the loyal affection of at least nine-tenths of the nation—
was overwhelmed in so complete a disaster as that of
January, 1649, the answer is that, on the one hand, the
cause had been irremediably weakened by the military
incompetence and diplomatic dishonesty of the king, by
the intrigues of the queen, by the depredations of the
royalist troopers (whom the king had ceased to be able to
pay), and by the defection of the navy (also starved and
storeless); and that, on the other hand, the puritan army,
organised and directed by the genius of Fairfax and Cromwell, had attained a perfection of discipline and equip-
ment that made it the finest military force existent at that
time anywhere in the world. From the summer of 1647 to
the spring of 1660—superseding both king and parliament
—this " new model " army established a military despotism under which the country groaned and travailed, seeking in vain for relief, and beneath which church, constitution and crown all were crushed out of being.

§ 20. Conservatism in Defeat, 1649-60

The execution of Charles I. was not only an unpardon-
able crime, it was also an act of supreme folly on the part
of the puritan fanatics of the triumphant army. The calm
wisdom of Cromwell had recognised this, and he had
argued against it with all his might: but he had been
compelled to give way. Fairfax resolutely refused to be a
party to it, and withdrew from all association with the
regicide republic. It was an act of suicidal lunacy which
made the ultimate restoration of the Stuarts all but inevitable. Charles I. alive would have been impotent and
harmless—as insignificant and innocuous as the runaway
kaiser, William II., at Doorn after 1918. He was so
thoroughly discredited by his futilities and failures; so
deeply distrusted owing to his shameless duplicities; so

thoroughly disliked by reason of his numerous treacheries
and betrayals, that scarcely a cavalier would have lifted a
finger to put him back into a position for which he was so
manifestly unfit. His execution, however, changed the
whole situation. On the one hand, it transferred the
titular kingship, and with it the loyalty of all the cavaliers,
and of the immense mass of the nation outside their ranks,
to the young Charles II., a boy of eighteen, innocent of
his father's follies, and concerning whom nothing but good
was known. On the other hand, it conferred upon the
murdered Charles I. the crown of martyrdom, thus re-
deeming him from all his faults, covering his iniquities,
purging him from his offences, and making him an object
of pity and adoration. He had so obviously sacrificed his
life for the church—since the Scots were prepared to
restore him any moment at the price of presbyterianism—
that his intrigues with Irish catholics and English independents were forgotten, and he became the beatified
model of anglican loyalty. Moreover, during the later
days of his adversity he displayed so fine a courage, so
lofty a dignity, so profound a piety, so serene a refine-
ment of character, so charming a grace of behaviour, that
he seemed to reach the ideal standard of both the great
gentleman and the suffering saint. Finally, on the scaffold
he met death with so superb a heroism that he commanded
the admiration even of his enemies. As Marvell magnificently wrote :

> " He nothing common did or mean
> Upon that memorable scene,
>   But with his keener eye
>   The axe's edge did try;
> Nor called the gods with vulgar spite
> To vindicate his helpless right;
>   But bowed his comely head
>   Down as upon a bed."

Thus he became the centre of a cult ; and the *Eikon Basilike*,
which was confidently (although erroneously) attributed to
him, grew to be the Bible of cavalier devotion. Charles
transformed and glorified in death was immeasurably more
potent than he had ever been in life. His ghostly power made

the permanent establishment of the puritan republic at once and for ever impossible. No self-respecting nation could continue, except under irresistible military pressure, to obey a government set up by the murderers of the royal martyr. The persecuted anglican church for which he shed his blood acquired a new hold on the affections of the people. Even the constitution, for which he had shown in life so little regard, came to be associated with his sacred memory; for the injuries which he had inflicted appeared to be the trivial wounds of paternal love compared with the destructive operations of the ideologues of the puritan army. Nay, more, if after the Revolution of 1688, during the eighteenth century, and even into the nineteenth, jacobitism remained a living force, its strange and pathetic vitality was due far more to the idealised memory of the martyred Charles I. than to any reverence for the tradition of the execrable James II. The doctrine of the divine right of kings, which had been an intolerable incubus to the cavaliers of the early seventeenth century, became a source of perennial inspiration to the tories and the jacobites of the later age. Such was the influence of the martyrdom of Charles I.

A martyr's death is, indeed, one of heaven's divinest gifts to man; a crown investing him with a superhuman majesty; a baptism of fire purging all imperfections; the completer and consummator of his life-work. However long a man of noble deeds may live, unless he have outlasted his powers, we always feel, when at length death claims him, that his life has been cut short and that his work is unfinished. On the other hand, however short and however faulty a life may have been, martyrdom gives to it the completeness of the eternal, and a perfection beyond that bestowed even by a long series of great achievements. The martyr utilises death, and economises where nature is prodigally wasteful. For ordinary men there is a struggle always humiliating, often wearisomely protracted, with disease and circumstance—the blind forces of the universe —and when death, the inevitable end, comes, it is defeat. For the martyr there is a contest, stern but glorious, not with inanimate powers, but with men his living equals, and when they have done their utmost it is on them there falls the paralysis of failure; but for him death is victory.

Although, however, the death of Charles ensured the ultimate triumph of the cause for which he died, nevertheless for eleven long years the triumph was delayed. During those eleven years the church was proscribed, the constitution suspended, the crown driven into exile. The period, it is true, was not without its glories. So long as Cromwell lived and with his strong and patriotic hand conducted affairs, England played a part in the politics of Europe more conspicuous and splendid than any she had played since the closing years of the great Elizabeth. Her invincible army and her formidable navy—each well equipped at a cost treble that which it had been within the power of the Stuarts to afford—enabled her to crush the Dutch and the Spaniards, to dictate terms to the Duke of Savoy, and to force the reluctant Mazarin into an alliance. But at home all was seething discontent. The pious anglicans loathed the ministrations of the tinkers and tailors who were placed in the pulpits of their desecrated churches; the magistrates and constables refused to administer the republican ordinances which supplanted the ancient common and statute law of England; the populace at large declined to recognise the authority of the councils and committees which usurped the functions of the crown and its officers. In particular the loyal cavaliers resolutely withheld payment of the heavy and wholly illegal exactions by means of which was maintained the military power that alone made possible the continuance of the rickety republic. The extortions of ship-money and the oppressions of the star chamber, galling as they had been during the eleven years of Charles's arbitrary rule (1629-40), were but as dust in the balance compared with the systematic confiscations and deliberate tyrannies of the eleven years of the arbitrary rule of the soldiers and the saints (1649-60). Even Cromwell, who sincerely desired to bring back the country to something like the old constitution, was compelled ultimately (1655-58) to give up all attempts at civil administration, to divide England up into military districts, each under a major-general, and to rule by naked coercion. The sufferings of the ejected clergy, the humiliations of the superseded magistracy, the privations of the plundered royalists, were extreme in their intensity. Not, however, until Cromwell passed away (September 3, 1658), and not until, following his death, the army by means of which he had held England in subjection split into wrangling fragments, was it possible for the longing desire of the nation to be fulfilled, and the king to be recalled.

Meantime, during those eleven weary years—apart from the exciting but disastrous adventure which had culminated at Worcester in 1651—the exiled court had perambulated the Continent, amid circumstances of poverty and peril which had for ever more than satisfied any desire for foreign travel that the young king may have at any time felt. Paris, Spa, Cologne, Bruges, Brussels—those were in turn the principal seats of his shadowy and impecunious court. The good news, however, that reached Brussels from England in the spring of 1660 caused Charles and his cavalier companions to move to Breda, near the Dutch coast. There the invitation to return reached him, and thence he set forth for The Hague and Dover towards the end of May.*

* Among those who accompanied Charles from Breda to The Hague, where he embarked, were his brother James (aged 26) and his nephew, William of Orange (aged 9).

CHAPTER V

COURT PARTY VERSUS COUNTRY PARTY
1660–1679

" We desire and ordain that henceforth all notes of discord, separation, and difference of parties be utterly abolished among all our subjects, whom we invite and conjure to a perfect union among themselves, under our protection, for the re-settlement of our just rights and theirs in a free parliament, by which upon the word of a king we will be advised."—CHARLES II., *Declaration of Breda, April 4, 1660.*

" The king is a suitor to you . . . that you will join with him in restoring the whole nation to its primitive temper and integrity, its old good manners, its old good humour, and its old good nature."—HYDE, *To the Convention, September,* 1660.

" I have a most zealous esteem and reverence for the constitution."—CLARENDON.

§ 21. THE RESTORATION

THE Restoration of Charles II. has justly been described as the most popular event recorded in English history. The journey of the young king from Dover, by way of Canterbury and Rochester, to London, amid the springtime glory of the Kentish fields and orchards, evoked so general an outburst of loyal enthusiasm that the returning monarch, with that genial cynicism which was one of his peculiar graces, remarked that it must have been his own fault that he had not come back years earlier. The wild rejoicings, however, that marked that regal progress were only in part due to pleasure at seeing the young king himself. They were due far more to the almost universal delight at the restoration of those old English institutions that naturally and inevitably came back with him. The return of Charles meant that the ghastly attempt of the puritan zealots to establish by force an Old Testament theocracy in England was over. With the vanishing protectorate went the " triers and ejecters," the

intruded preachers, the major-generals, the army councils,
the sequestrations and confiscations, the inquisitions and
excises, that had made the eleven years of the commonwealth régime a nightmare of gloomy oppression. With
the returning king came back the church and the constitution. Once more the evicted bishops occupied their
palaces and the ejected clergy their livings; once again
the familiar services of the Elizabethan liturgy were heard
throughout the chapels of the land. The house of lords
was re-established, and a freely elected house of commons
reoccupied the hall of Westminster. The long-suspended
justices of the peace resumed their venerable and beneficent rule; the county militias were revived, and the " new
model " army was disbanded. The maypoles were re-
erected; the theatres were reopened; the land re-echoed
with the long-suppressed laughter of the old English sports.

Never before—not even at the Norman Conquest—had
there been so complete a break in the continuity of the
national life as that which had marked the years 1649-60.
And the utter bankruptcy of political puritanism at
the end of that period was primarily due to the fact
that it had broken so entirely from the past. It had tried,
with fanatical violence, to remake the nation anew on
Hebrew and not Anglo-Saxon lines. It had outraged,
with reckless disregard of consequences, all the conservative instincts of a proud and ancient people. Only the
might of the invincible army and the genius of the great
Cromwell had maintained it at all, after the death of
Charles I., against the execration of the overwhelming
majority of the nation.

Nevertheless the puritan interlude, though a period of
painful discipline for those doomed to pass through it,
did not come to an end without bequeathing some permanent benefits upon the nation. It left behind it a tradition of profound personal religion, of high moral integrity,
of austere virtue, of lofty idealism. True, none of the
institutions which it had set up were allowed to survive
its fall : all its innovations in church and state were ruthlessly swept away. But, on the other hand, its negative
results were permanent. Most of the worst abuses that

had flourished under Charles I. and Laud had been abolished never to recur. Hardly the most extreme reactionary who came back to power in 1660, having learned nothing and forgotten nothing, dreamed of attempting to restore ship-money or impositions, the star chamber or the high commission court. The work of the conservative reformers of 1641 had been confirmed beyond all possibility of doubt. The problem of the seat of sovereignty in the constitution had been settled once for all: in case of conflict it was the will of parliament and not the will of the monarch that should prevail. Charles II. recognised from the first that neither he nor any successor of his would ever be in a position to resist the authority of parliament as a whole. Nevertheless, he had a strong desire, and even a fixed determination, to get his own way—his own way in the matter of religion, in the matter of foreign policy, and so on. But he perceived that in the new circumstances the only means by which he could accomplish his purpose would be, not by challenging parliament to a new struggle for supremacy, but by forming within parliament itself a " court party " subject to his personal control, and capable of using the machinery of parliament to achieve the royal designs. Hence in the reign of Charles II. the organisation of permanent political parties began. The cavaliers of the civil war period formed the nucleus of the " court party " pledged to maintain the anglican church, the constitution as reformed in 1641, and the prerogatives of the crown as they existed at the Restoration. Over against this " court party " gradually formed itself, largely from the relics of the roundhead régime, a " country party " which demanded legal recognition for orthodox protestant dissent, the further reform of the constitution, and the steady increase of parliamentary control over the monarchy and executive generally.

It was, of course, only by slow degrees that the parties took shape during the reign of Charles II. In the early years of the reign, particularly, much confusion was caused by the fact that the ideals of the " court party " were not quite the same as those of either the king or his chief minister, the earl of Clarendon. The " court party "

was primarily the party of the Church of England, but
Charles secretly leaned towards Roman Catholicism; the
" court party " accepted the reforms of 1641, but Charles
was secretly resolved to rescind them; the " court party "
was content with the limited monarchy which had survived
the catastrophe of the commonwealth, but Charles was
secretly determined to recover all his father's lost prerogatives and to restore effective sovereignty to the
crown.   The real aims of Charles were not such as he
dared publicly to proclaim.   The avowed aims of his
supporters in parliament were not such as he privately
approved.   As for Clarendon, he was a true Elizabethan
who did not believe in parties at all.   He stood for the
united nation; for the national church as including and
representing the whole community; for the patriotic
monarchy as symbolising the solidarity of the state; for
the privy council as the concentration of the nation's
highest wisdom; for the parliament as the support of
the throne and the protection of the people's liberties.
Clarendon, then, was out of sympathy with both the king
and the " court party "; in 1667, indeed, the two combined to overthrow him and drive him into exile.   Nevertheless for the seven years that followed the Restoration
he played so prominent a part in politics, and did so
much to steer conservatism safely between the Scylla of
reaction and the Charybdis of revolution, that it is necessary for us to study his character and career more in
detail.   Probably he did more than any other man to
give the English conservatism its mark of moderation and
judicious compromise.   Mr. Keith Feiling rightly describes
him as " the most important single figure in the history
of the party."*

§ 22. Edward Hyde, Earl of Clarendon

Edward Hyde was one of the first of Englishmen to
rise by sheer strength of character and ability from comparatively lowly rank to the highest offices of state
and to commanding political influence.   Born in 1609,

* Feiling, K., *History of the Tory Party* (1924), p. 68.

the third son of a Wiltshire squire, he took up the law as a career, came to London, married judiciously, made important friendships, and built up a practice that rendered it possible for him at the age of thirty to devote himself wholly to affairs of state. He entered the Short Parliament of April, 1640, as a strong conservative reformer, and he threw such weight as he had on to the side of Strafford when that great man tried to dissuade the king from the fatal mistake of dissolving the parliament in anger (May, 1640). In the autumn of the same year he sat as member for Saltash, and from the first took a prominent part in attacking the abuses which had grown up and flourished during the eleven years of Charles's arbitary and unparliamentary rule. The reforms of 1641 were to no small extent moulded and kept within the bounds of constitutional moderation by his legal knowledge, sound judgment, and debating skill. With these reforms, as completed at the end of the first session of the parliament, he was content. He had no wish to see the church made presbyterian, the constitution republican, or the crown less than sovereign. Hence, together with Falkland and Colepeper, he resisted the puritan attacks on the bishops, and the attempts of the revolutionaries to secure annual parliaments. The presentation of the Grand Remonstrance to the king (December, 1641) carried him wholly and openly on to the royalist side. He saw that the integrity of the church, the continuity of the constitution, the unity of the nation, and the proper authority of the crown were all gravely menaced. The parliamentary majority had ceased to be conservative and had become revolutionary.

From December, 1641, to March, 1645, he faithfully and laboriously served the king, carefully keeping him within the limits of legality and maintaining his fidelity to the church; in 1643 he was knighted, sworn to the privy council, and made titular chancellor of the exchequer. He drew up most of the king's manifestos and conducted his negotiations with the enemy. In March, 1645, when the royalist cause was obviously on the decline, the king placed the young prince Charles (*æt.* 15) in his charge,

and when it became necessary for the prince to take to
flight, it was Edward Hyde who secured his escape from
Bristol to Truro, from Truro to the Scilly Islands, and
from the Scilly Islands to Jersey, where he arrived in
April, 1646. The prince soon (July, 1646) left Jersey to
join his mother in France, and for more than two years
he and Hyde were separated. But in the summer of
1648 the prince called him to his side, and from that date
to the Restoration, with masterly prudence and circum-
spection, he conducted the main business of the exiled
and impecunious court. It was, indeed, through him,
and through him almost alone, that the Restoration was
possible. Three things he recognised clearly, and these
three things determined his policy during the commonwealth period. They were, first, that, if Charles was to
be restored, his restoration must come from the free invitation of the English nation, and not from foreign
invasion; second, that the free invitation would come only
if the English nation had satisfactory guarantees respecting indemnities for the past and constitutional government for the future; and third, that of all the guarantees
for the future the most vital was that of the maintenance
of the Church of England as by law established. Hyde
was absent on an embassy when Charles committed the
all but fatal error of taking the covenant and becoming
a presbyterian in order to recover his throne by Scottish
aid. After the disastrous termination of this escapade at
Worcester (September, 1651), Hyde was able, though with
much difficulty, to prevent him from avowing himself a
catholic in order to secure the assistance of Spain and
the pope. Charles little realised where lay the sources of
his strength : he was, indeed, through all his life a very
imperfect conservative. If with sceptical levity he had
during his exile twice betrayed the church of his father,
he most certainly would never have been recalled to the
throne in 1660.

At the Restoration Charles recognised the immensity
of the debt which he owed to Edward Hyde by conferring
upon him a barony together with a gift of £20,000 (November, 1660) and by elevating him a little later to the earldom

of Clarendon (April, 1661). Clarendon continued to serve the king as lord chancellor and virtual prime minister until November, 1667. His policy was one of eminent sanity and moderation—conservative in the best sense of the term. He had, however, to pursue his conservative course of wise conciliation and compromise amid the vehement upbraidings of both resentful roundheads who lamented the fall of the commonwealth, and revengeful cavaliers who wished to return to the full autocracy of Charles I. His prime concern was to restore the religious unity of the nation in the anglican church. In order to do this he was willing, as was the king, to broaden the basis of the church so as to make it easy for presbyterians to remain within its compass. This wise and benevolent design was, however, frustrated partly by the unreasonableness of the presbyterian leaders, who asked for too many concessions, and partly by the intolerance of the " cavalier parliament," which would make no concessions at all. Hence the so-called " Clarendon Code " (1661-65), which drove the presbyterians out of the church, and converted both them and the anglican residue into sects, was so far from representing Clarendon's own policy that it marked the definite frustration of his great design of comprehension and unification. It made ultimately inevitable a new policy of toleration which at that date did not enter into the schemes either of Clarendon or of any other responsible statesman. We shall later on have to see how it was left for Halifax and Bolingbroke to make it a part of the conservative programme.

Next to the unity of the nation in the church, the maintenance of the Elizabethan constitution, as restored and defined in 1641, was Clarendon's guiding purpose. On the one hand, he resisted any further attempts to limit the king's authority : for example, he opposed the demand of parliament for the appropriation of supplies and the audit of the royal accounts. On the other hand, he kept the king faithful to his oaths, opposed his efforts to secure toleration for catholics, rebuked him for his laziness and immorality, and deliberately kept him short of money and dependent on parliament for supplies.

By 1667 he had but few friends left. The king was thoroughly tired of him, and resentful of his tutelage; the cavaliers hated him because he had baulked them of their revenge, and had prevented them from recovering their estates; the roundheads blamed him for the persecution that they were enduring under the Act of Uniformity; the parliament as a whole was angry at his attitude towards appropriation and audit; the whole nation condemned him for the sale of Dunkirk to the French and for the disasters of the Dutch War (1665-67). Hence when Charles dismissed him in November, 1667, and advised him to go abroad so as to escape impeachment, he found none to plead his cause or lessen the catastrophe of his fall. He had, it is true, developed faults of temper and behaviour which had made him a difficult man to deal with during the later years of his power. Nevertheless, with austere and almost puritanical virtue he had served both his king and his country well. In particular, he had laid down once for all the main lines of sound and constitutional conservatism—the conservatism that combines pious continuity with moderate reform.*

§ 23. Thomas Osborne, Earl of Danby

The fall of Clarendon allowed Charles to take the supreme power into his own hands. For six years he conducted affairs himself, with the aid of a clique of political schemers to whom the collective name of " cabal " has been for ever attached. Not one of them—Clifford, Arlington, Buckingham, Ashley, Lauderdale—can by any stretch of imagination be called a conservative. Most of them were unscrupulous, self-seeking, and time-serving scoundrels. They placed no check on Charles's unconstitutional and nefarious designs. Now the three chief designs that the king had in his mind were, first, the recovery of the lost royal prerogative by the aid of Louis XIV.; secondly, the obtaining of a revenue independent of par-

* Clarendon retired to France, and devoted himself to the writing of his autobiography and to various other literary works. He died at Rouen on December 9, 1674.

liamentary grant by means of French subsidies; and thirdly, the re-establishment of catholicism by foreign aid, as a cement to the Anglo-French alliance, and as a support to the revived autocracy of the monarchy. The king's efforts to achieve his purposes were specially signalised by the conclusion of the Secret Treaty of Dover with Louis XIV. (1670), and by the issue of the Declaration of Indulgence (1672). The secret terms of the treaty were widely suspected, and were deeply resented when they drew England on to the French side in a disastrous war with the Dutch in 1672; the issue of the Declaration of Indulgence called forth from the angry parliament the smashing anti-catholic Test Act (1673), the first operation of which was to break up the cabal administration and to drive from the office of lord high admiral the king's brother, James, Duke of York, who had openly professed catholicism in 1669.

The political crisis of 1673 brought into prominence and soon into temporary power a man who stood for the two dominant principles of the conservatism of the day— namely, (1) the maintenance of the monopoly of the established church against both the toleration for catholics desired by the king and his brother, and the toleration for protestant nonconformists (but not for catholics) advocated by Shaftesbury and the " country party "; (2) the emancipation of both king and country from dependence upon Louis XIV., and the provision of a national revenue sufficient to enable Charles to carry on the government without the aid of French subsidies. This man was Sir Thomas Osborne, baronet, of Kiveton in Yorkshire, who was later to be known as earl of Danby (1674), marquis of Carmarthen (1689), and duke of Leeds (1694). He had first come to court and entered parliament (for York, 1665) as a protégé of the cabalistic duke of Buckingham, his neighbour in Yorkshire. But after 1673 he shook off his dependence on a leader whose policy he disliked and whose abilities he despised. A man of strong will, high administrative capacity, soaring ambition, and immense energy, he attained to the supreme office of lord high treasurer, and virtual prime minister, rather in

spite of, than as the choice of, Charles II. The power
behind him was that of the high anglican and proudly
patriotic majority of the Cavalier Parliament, which for
four years and more sustained him alike against the
intrigues of Charles and Louis, and the open attacks of the "country party" led and organised by
Shaftesbury, Russell, and Sidney. Danby, then, was
primarily a parliamentarian. Under him the party—no
longer appropriately called the "court party," and not
yet nicknamed the "tory party"—the party which stood
for the established church, the old constitution of the
government, and the proper prerogatives of the crown,
first acquired a definite organisation and a corporate consciousness. Hence with some justification Danby has
been described as "after Clarendon the greatest tory
statesman of his time";* and has been called "the first
tory prime minister" and, "with the exception of Bolingbroke and Disraeli, the greatest of tory leaders."†

The most complete embodiment of Danby's high
anglican domestic policy was the Non-Resisting Test Bill
of 1675, in which "the anglicans were offered complete
political supremacy on the understanding that they would
use their power in the interests of the crown."‡ This bill
passed the house of lords, but was lost in the commons
amid a quarrel between the two houses ingeniously engineered by Shaftesbury. Danby's anti-gallican foreign
policy achieved its supreme triumph in the marriage between William of Orange and Mary, daughter of James,
Duke of York, which he carried through in 1677, against
the wishes of James, and without the knowledge of
Louis XIV. He was already anxiously pondering the
problem of the protestant succession to the English
throne.

At the time of the Orange marriage Louis XIV. was still
at war with the Dutch. The English parliament, in its
eager protestantism, wished to follow up the marriage by

* Kent, C. B. R., *Early History of the Tories* (1908), p. 236.
† Woods, M., *History of the Tory Party* (1924), pp. 24 and 72.
Cf. also Feiling, K., *History of the Tory Party* (1924), p. 165.
‡ Browning, A., *Thomas Osborne* (1913), p. 25.

active intervention on the Dutch side, and early in 1678 it declared for war and voted subsidies for its prosecution. Then Danby made the mistake which brought his ministry to an end and involved himself in mortal peril. He for his own part did not want war : he saw no advantage in it for England, and he realised that the country could not long finance it. Charles, of course, with the Treaty of Dover still in existence, was anxious above all things to avoid it. Hence he easily persuaded Danby to write a secret letter to Paris promising that, in spite of the parliamentary vote, no war should take place, provided that Louis would supply him with sufficient money to carry on the government without the aid of the house of commons. The letter was a godsend to Louis. He judiciously made its existence and its contents known to Danby's enemies, and its disclosure brought down upon the head of the prevaricating minister the execrations of both parliament and people. In order to save Danby from impeachment and possible execution, Charles—whose signature accompanied that of Danby on the incriminating letter—had to dissolve his once enthusiastically loyal, but now intensely hostile, Cavalier Parliament—the "Long Parliament of the Restoration"—which had sat for eighteen years (January, 1679). As for Danby, the impeachment hung over his head for five years, during which period he was kept as a prisoner in the Tower. And even when (February, 1684) he was released, he merely came out under a bail of £40,000. Both Charles and James were glad to be rid of him. Neither his anti-catholicism nor his anti-gallicism fitted in with their cryptic designs.

§ 24. The Popish Plot Frenzy

At the time when Danby fell, the air was thick with rumours of "popish plots" and catholic conspiracies. The fanatical fury of the attack which overthrew Danby was, indeed, due to the atmosphere of suspicion and alarm that prevailed. Behind these rumours there was a certain amount of truth. Charles and James were known to be in collusion with Louis XIV., and Louis in France was inaugurating that policy of frightful persecution of the protestants which culminated in the Revocation of the Edict of Nantes (1685). Louis was also involved in intrigues against Danby with the leaders of the country party, some of whom (*e.g.*, Algernon Sidney) he had in his pay. Moreover, it is certain that Edward Coleman, secretary to the duchess of York, was deeply committed to some subterranean design which (in his own words) was to give " the greatest blow to the protestant religion it has received since its birth." But, whatever this design was, it bore no relation to the monstrous fabrications of the execrable Titus Oates and his associates, by means of which the country was driven mad with irrational terror, and mesmerised into the perpetration of acts of gross cruelty and fiendish iniquity—acts concerning which, on its return to sanity, it had cause to repent in dust and ashes. The house of commons well expressed the general credulity and trepidation when, on October 21, 1678, it passed the resolution that " there hath been and still is a damnable and hellish plot carried on by papist recusants for assassinating the king, subverting the government, and rooting out the protestant religion."

The leading politicians kept their heads, though not their consciences, in the midst of the all-but-universal panic. Charles laughed at the whole ridiculous scare, until it became too serious for laughter; he himself exposed some of the baseless fictions that Oates advanced as evidences of his accusations; but he soon found that it would be dangerous for him to express his incredulity too openly, and realised that if he should exert his royal authority to save the innocent victims of Oates's malignity, he himself might be involved in the catholic ruin. Hence he let things take their course, using his regal power only when the flood of suspicion seemed likely to overwhelm his wife or his brother. His policy was prudent, if not heroic; but Charles never pretended to be a hero: the heroic tended to be uncomfortable. As for Danby, at first, when the frenzy was mild and manageable, he rather welcomed it. He thought that it might assist him in his chronic struggle with his perpetual opponent,

James, duke of York; that it might diminish the influence of Louis XIV. in England; that it might in general further his anti-catholic and anti-gallic policy.   He soon discovered, however, that he had miscalculated.   He had underestimated the height to which the frenzy would rise; he had not realised that the revelation of his improper letter to Paris would involve himself in suspicion of catholicity; he had not taken into account the diabolical unscrupulousness and cleverness of his arch-enemy Shaftesbury, head of the country party, or of Shaftesbury's bucolic comrades Russell and Sidney.   Shaftesbury, in particular, with remorseless malignity deliberately fanned the flame of anti-papal passion, in the hope that it might finally consume catholicism in. England, secure the exclusion of James from the succession, destroy Danby, and win for himself a place of power whence he might restore sovereignty to parliament, obtain toleration for protestant nonconformists, and carry his long-cogitated Habeas Corpus Bill.

For a time the designs of Shaftesbury seemed to prosper. So great was the insensate terror which held the populace in its grip that no fabrication of Oates and his confederates was too gross to command credulity.   The first statutory result of the disgraceful panic was the passing of the Parliamentary Test Act (November, 1678), by which catholics were excluded from both houses of the legislature.*   Danby, not yet overthrown, managed to carry an amendment in the Lords (by two votes only) exempting James, duke of York (against whom the measure had been primarily directed), from the operation of the bill. This courageous act, carried out at the king's command, helped to seal Danby's own fate.   It seemed to make it obvious—if any evidence beyond his letter to Paris were needed—that he was on the catholic side, and that he was a dangerous traitor to protestantism.   Hence the impeachment, which caused Charles hastily to dissolve his Cavalier Parliament in January, 1679.   Never since the days of the civil war had political passions raged so furiously.

* This disability was not removed until 1829.

CHAPTER VI

ABHORRERS VERSUS PETITIONERS
1679-1681

" That the said James, duke of York, should be incapable of inheriting the crowns of England, Scotland, and Ireland, with their dependencies, and of enjoying any of the titles, rights, prerogatives, and revenues belonging to the said crowns."—THE EXCLUSION BILL, *May,* 1679.

" I am of opinion that the kings of England have their right from God alone, and that no power on earth can deprive them of it."—SIR LEOLINE JENKINS.

§ 25. THE EXCLUSION BILL STRUGGLE

The exemption of James, duke of York, brother and heir presumptive of Charles II., from the operation of the Parliamentary Test Act, made it necessary for Shaftesbury to come out into the open and formally to throw down his challenge to the duke, the king, the upholders of divine right, and all the conservative forces in the country. He realised that England was not large enough to hold both himself and the proud, resentful duke whose religion he was denouncing, whose friends he was destroying, and whose rights he was seeking to take away. He believed, moreover, that as leader of the London mob,* whose protestant passions were at the moment inflamed to a fury bordering upon delirious insanity, he could impose his will upon both court and commonalty. The prospects of civil war and revolution had for him no terrors : he felt himself capable of rising to Cromwellian heights of dictatorship. His confidence was still further confirmed by the results of the election which followed the dissolution of the Cavalier Parliament (February, 1679): they showed that the anti-popish panic had seized the country as well as the town.

* The term " mob " first came into use at this time. It is, of course, an abbreviation of the Latin *mobile vulgus,* the fickle crowd.

98

Danby's supporters were reduced to a pitiful and impotent thirty; Shaftesbury, completely dominant, seemed to be in a position to "ride the whirlwind and control the storm." Charles II., roused from his usual easy-going carelessness by the extremity of the peril in which both his brother and himself—not to mention the unloved and much-compromised Danby—were placed, recognised that it would be impossible at the moment directly to resist the fanatical parliament or the frenzied populace. With consummate prudence he played for time, waiting until the people should recover their sanity : he prepared himself to make any concessions to the Shaftesbury faction that did not involve irrevocably any fundamental questions of principle. Thus when Shaftesbury demanded that James should be excluded from the privy council, Charles advised his brother voluntarily to stop away; when Shaftesbury urged the exile of James, Charles sent his brother across the Channel to Brussels; but when the Shaftesbury party brought in and carried through the house of commons a bill to exclude James from the throne, on the ground that he was a man whom the agents of the pope had "seduced to the communion of the Church of Rome" (May, 1679), then Charles realised that the limit of concession had been reached and passed. On May 27, 1679, he prorogued, and a few weeks later dissolved, the parliament. The elections to the second parliament of 1679 took place in August amid scenes of unprecedented excitement. If Charles had hoped that the events of the spring and summer had conduced to popular sobriety, he was disappointed. The Shaftesbury faction came back from the constituencies with unimpaired strength and even enhanced ferocity. The king, realising that the meeting of such a parliament at such a time would inevitably precipitate a crisis of the first magnitude, prorogued the houses before they actually assembled (October, 1679); and the prorogation was renewed periodically until twelve months in all were passed. Not until October, 1680, did the House of Commons, elected in August, 1679, actually come together.

This year of repeated prorogations was one of prodigious agitation and activity. Charles, for his part, cleared the field for battle by dismissing Shaftesbury from his council, and by calling to his side such safe and loyal men as Halifax, Sunderland, Essex, Laurence Hyde (Clarendon's second son), and Sidney Godolphin. He then appealed to Louis XIV. of France for a substantial pension in order to save him from the necessity of summoning parliament. Louis, although he had no love for Charles and little faith in him, felt that it would be worth his while to pay a certain amount of blackmail; for he realised that the parliament, if summoned, would probably demand war with France, and would certainly pass an Exclusion Act that would place the English crown on the head of some person —whether William of Orange, or Mary Stuart, or Monmouth—whose policy would not be amenable to French influence. Nevertheless, the sums that he paid were small and irregular, and Charles had to depend mainly on his own resources, which consisted primarily of an unlimited capacity for running into debt. Having made the best provision possible in the circumstances, he withdrew into the background of administration, and left Shaftesbury with his associates to do their worst. They speedily did it, and, as Charles had foreseen, undid themselves. "Give these men but rope enough, and they will hang themselves," was a remark frequently on his lips at this time. Shaftesbury's prodigious and cumulatively fatal mistakes can easily be discerned and briefly tabulated. First, he selected as his nominee for the throne in place of James, not James's protestant daughter Mary, or her husband William of Orange, but Charles's illegitimate son, the duke of Monmouth, a weak and unprincipled youth whom no sober constitutionalist could possibly contemplate as king; moreover, he encouraged Monmouth to defy his father's commands and make a semi-royal and semi-rebellious progress through the western counties. Secondly, he rashly started a prosecution of James as a popish recusant before a grand jury in the court of king's bench, a prosecution which the lord chief justice countered by dismissing the jury. Thirdly, he organised gigantic and tumultuary processions of protestants in London and elsewhere, in order to strike terror into all pro-papist breasts, a proceeding that alarmed many besides the catholics aimed at. Fourthly, he tried to revive the dying embers of the plot panic by bringing forward new fabricators, such as the execrable Dangerfield, with fresh fictions respecting catholic conspiracies; but although their short stories were better constructed than the primitive dreadfuls of Oates, they were received with a growing incredulity. Finally, he organised and stimulated a bombardment of petitions from all parts of the country, demanding the assembly of the oft-prorogued parliament.

§ 26. THE ORGANISATION OF PARTIES

In 1680, however, Shaftesbury no longer got things all his own way. The petitions which from every county and town were poured in upon Charles, often with but little pretence of respect to his office or civility to himself, evoked a growing stream of counter-petitions expressing abhorrence of the pressure brought to bear upon his majesty, and detestation of the violence in the behaviour of those who presented them. Hence the country speedily divided itself once again into two sections. Those who in the days of the old troubles would have been called " roundheads," and in the early years of Charles II. the " country party," now acquired the designation of " petitioners." On the other hand, those who inherited the spirit and the traditions of the " cavaliers " and the " court party " came to be called " abhorrers." The two names " petitioners " and " abhorrers " were not good party names. They were too long, and their obvious abbreviations into " pets " and " horrors " conveyed different and inappropriate ideas; they were, moreover, purely ephemeral in their significance—that is to say, they connoted merely a passing detail of a momentary brawl, not any difference respecting a vital principle; finally, and worst of all, they were not abusive enough, they did not sufficiently relieve the feelings of those who hurled them against the foe, they did not carry sufficient weight of anger and contempt.

Two other terms gained vogue for a short time as party

designations—namely, " brummagem protestants," due to the fact that Birmingham was a centre of violent petitioners, and " tantivies," from the hard-riding fox-hunting squires whose rustic minds seemed peculiarly subject to abhorrence of the urban petitioners, and whose equine vocabulary most effectively expressed that abhorrence. These terms, however, equally with the terms " petitioners " and " abhorrers," lacked the elements of brevity, universality, and scurrility. Before the close of that eventful year, 1680, however, the much-desired labels had been found. The " petitioners " had become " *whigs* " and the " abhorrers" had become " *tories.*" Here were names that were at once memorably short and highly abusive : they slipped off the tongue easily ; they hit the enemy hard ; they relieved the feelings inexpressibly. For " whigs " were Scottish covenanting rebels, and " tories " were Irish bog-trotting thieves.* The " whigs " were the scum of revolutionary calvinism, the " tories " the dregs of reactionary catholicism.

The fixing of party names, however, in 1680 was but the outward and visible sign of the organisation of political parties themselves. Danby had in his day done a great deal to keep together, largely by means of systematic bribery, the " court party " in parliament. But Shaftesbury went far beyond Danby in working the constituencies and in stirring up passion in the proletariat. " Shaftesbury," says Dr. J. R. Tanner, " is the first great party leader of modern politics. He is also the first party organiser and wire-puller, the modern demagogue."† North in his *Examen* describes him as the " prompter-general " of revolutionary clubs in London and in the other great cities and towns. On the conservative side there was no one who quite corresponded to the fiery and indefatigable Shaftesbury. The counter-petitions of the abhorrers were for the most part generated locally by the spontaneous combustion of the fury of independent lords-lieutenant, indignant sheriffs, and outraged justices of the peace. But the person who at this time more and more came to the

* For a fuller discussion of these terms, see above, pp. 50-2.
† Tanner, J. R., *English Constitutional Conflicts* (1928), p. 289.

fore as the opponent of Shaftesbury was the eminently sane and moderate George Savile, successively viscount, earl, and marquis of Halifax. To him we shall have to return again, for he played the prime part in the drama of 1688. For the present it is enough to note that in 1680 he embodied the very genius of sound conservatism. He held no brief for James. For he realised the difficulty of having a catholic king as the official head of a protestant church, and he was well aware that James's political ideas were far from accordant with the principles of the reformed English constitution. Nevertheless, he perceived that it would be a grave misfortune if the line of succession were to be broken, and he believed that safeguards could be provided by law which would suffice to protect the church and constitution during their temporary obscuration by a catholic despot. As to Shaftesbury's proposal to advance Monmouth as a substitute for James, he opposed it with a weight of argument and an energy of restrained passion that made its adoption for ever impossible. He steadily and effectively maintained that if James were to die, and therefore if he were to be declared incapable as a catholic of succeeding to the throne, his claim would pass unimpaired to his protestant daughter Mary, princess of Orange.

When Charles, driven by financial necessity, at length assembled his oft-prorogued parliament (October 21, 1680), a second, more stringent, and more offensively worded Exclusion Bill was speedily brought in. It asserted concerning James that " if the said duke should succeed to the imperial crown of this realm, nothing is more manifest than that a total change of religion within these kingdoms would ensue." Moreover, not only did it demand his exclusion from the succession; it required his immediate and permanent departure from the kingdom, subject to the penalties of high treason if he should ever return. The whigs were plainly over-reaching themselves in their passionate animosity to James. Charles put them still more in the wrong when he astutely offered to them safeguards for both church and constitution that would have left James with little more than the name of sovereign. All ecclesiastical control should be taken out of his hands; all papists should be excluded from both council and parliament; all officers in both army and navy should be subject to parliamentary approval. The rejection of such terms showed that Shaftesbury and his whig associates had cut themselves adrift from all reason. The only possible excuse for their violence and irrationality is that they put no trust in the word of either Charles or James, and felt that to bind either of them by means of legal restraints was like binding the unshorn Samson with withes. Be that as it may, they carried their Exclusion Bill through the commons by such overwhelming majorities, and with such extreme violence, that the conservative minority did not on the third reading challenge a division. In the lords, however, things went very differently. There Shaftesbury and Halifax confronted one another face to face, and a tremendous oratorical duel supervened. With Halifax the unquestionable victory remained. Not only did he demolish the sophistries of his opponent; he carried the house with him and secured the rejection of the bill by 63 votes to 30 (November, 1680). The house of commons, goaded to madness by this unexpected rebuff, passed resolutions that were a clear challenge to civil war. In vain Halifax tried to conciliate the insensate whigs by offering, in the king's name, to accept the banishment of James, and his exclusion from everything except the title of king. Shaftesbury and his party would be content with nothing less than the bill and the whole bill. In January, 1681, they voted that no supplies should be granted until the bill had been passed. In those circumstances Charles, greatly daring and wisely disregarding the timid counsels of his terrified advisers, prorogued (January 10) and dissolved (January 16) the impossible parliament. He believed, and rightly believed, that his hour had struck.

§ 27. The Crisis of 1681

In February, 1681, for the third time within a space of twenty-five months, a general election took place. For the third time an overwhelming majority in favour of exclusion was returned. But Charles was prepared for the emergency : many signs had convinced him that the popish plot frenzy had exhausted itself, that the country as a whole was thoroughly ashamed of its temporary but lamentable lapse from sanity, and that the whigs had passed the zenith of their power. On the one hand, by a stroke of political genius—of which Danby was probably the inspirer—he summoned the parliament to meet, not at Westminster, but at Oxford. This completely upset the machinations of Shaftesbury, who had been confidently counting on the London mob to reinforce his partisans in the house of commons. It, moreover, vividly recalled to the consciousness of the country the last sad occasion, at the outbreak of the great civil war, on which a doomed monarch had fled from his rebellious capital to the loyal shelter of Oxford's devoted halls. The painful parallel was still more deeply impressed upon the minds of thoughtful and anxious observers when the injudicious whigs, at the direction of their reckless leader Shaftesbury, made their way to " the city of the dreaming spires " armed to the teeth, and accompanied by bands of militant attendants. Old men whose memories went back forty years said that the circumstances of the 'forties were repeating themselves in every detail. War rather than debate was in the air. And the one thing above all others that the country as a whole was anxious to avoid was a repetition of the agonies of 1642-46.

On the other hand, while parliament was preparing to eliminate the king, the king was making more practical and effective arrangements for the elimination of the parliament. He came to a definite though secret arrangement with Louis XIV. to the effect that, on condition (1) of ceasing to support Spain against France, and (2) of dismissing parliament and calling no other for three years, he should have during that period a large and regular subsidy from the French government.

With considerable confidence, and in a spirit of exceptional cheerfulness—a spirit markedly contrasting with that of Halifax and others who were unaware of the Anglo-French bargain—Charles proceeded from Windsor to Oxford to open the new parliament on March 21, 1681.

He took with him a large company of guards, in order to neutralise the whig companies that infested the city, and in order to frustrate a plot to kidnap him that was strongly suspected.

At Oxford events ran their predestined course in seven hectic days. The commons, assembled in the convocation house, began hopefully and characteristically by trying to revive the anti-popish panic. They proceeded to impeach a certain Irish catholic, Fitzharris by name, of complicity in some plot or other. The lords, on technical grounds, refused to accept the impeachment, and so precipitated a furious wrangle between the two houses. Then the irritated commons proceeded to re-open the exclusion business. Halifax repeated his offer of large concessions and ample safeguards, but they were all contemptuously rejected. He was prepared to go even so far as to leave James with no more than the titular kingship, placing all effective power in the hands of a protestant regent. But the whigs insisted on their full pound of flesh. A third Exclusion Bill was prepared for presentation to the house, and at all costs it was to be forced on to the statute book. Then the king struck his premeditated, skilfully prepared, and admirably engineered blow. On March 28, with a suddenness and secrecy that took friends as well as foes by surprise, he made his way to the lords, summoned the commons, and dissolved the parliament. Having done so, he withdrew with his guards to Windsor, and left his enemies to decide what next to attempt.

If Shaftesbury had followed the precedent of the Scots in 1639, or had anticipated the action of the French in 1789, he would have declined to accept the dissolution, would have continued the session of parliament, and would have carried his Exclusion Bill through all its stages. This, of course, would have been rebellion, and it would certainly have led to civil war. Oxford, no doubt, was a bad place in which to effect a *coup d'état*. But Shaftesbury lacked either the wits or the guts to take the decisive step. He hired a horse and rode away, and that was the end of him.

§ 28. The Triumph of Charles II.

The whigs by their violence and unreasonableness had brought well-merited ruin upon their cause and upon themselves in 1681. Their offences, indeed, were many and great. They had menaced the established church by their ferocious attacks upon the royal supremacy and upon the bishops; they had gravely increased the religious disunion of the nation by their intrigues with the sectaries, from among the more extreme of whom the majority of Shaftesbury's " brisk boys " were drawn. Then, again, they had threatened the constitution by the gross intimidation that they had employed in the constituencies; by the remorseless pressure that they had exerted throughout the country in order to procure signatures to their petitions; by the violence of their tumultuary processions and demonstrations; and by their constant incitements to civil war and revolution. Further, they had flagrantly and persistently flouted the king, insulted the queen, denounced with mendacious calumnies the duke of York, and brought the whole royal family into suspicion and contempt; they had challenged the doctrine of the divine authority of the crown; they had sought to diminish the ancient prerogatives of the sovereign; they had endeavoured to break the sacred line of succession, and to place in the seat of the legitimate heir a weak and degenerate bastard. Finally, in addition to these offences against church and constitution and crown—the three institutions that conservatism was most concerned to defend—they had incurred the execration of all humane and honourable men by the diabolic iniquity with which they had fomented and used for their own political ends the wild passions of the popish plot frenzy. The blood of the innocent victims of the great illusion, from the youthful Father Coleman to the aged Lord Stafford, cried aloud for expiation and revenge.

Charles, having by his cool courage and his tactical skill routed his enemies at Oxford, did not give them an opportunity to re-form their forces. He pursued them and broke them up. Most of them, indeed, by reason of their plottings and their perjuries, were at the mercy of the law.

Shaftesbury himself was arrested and accused of high treason. Clear, however, as was the evidence of his guilt, the grand jury of the city (drawn entirely from his partisans) refused to return a true bill, and he had to be released. He at once used his recovered liberty to plan with Russell and Sidney a violent revolution. His designs, of course, soon became known to the government, and since he could not hope a second time to evade justice, he thought it prudent to flee to Holland (November, 1682). There, within two months, his restless spirit passed away.

" The whigs," says Hallam when describing this crisis in English constitutional history, " the whigs, so late in the heyday of their pride, lay like fallen angels prostrate upon the fiery lake." The veiled reference is, of course, to Milton's *Paradise Lost*, and it naïvely suggests that Shaftesbury was the arch-fiend himself. This is a surprising suggestion to come from Hallam; for Hallam himself was a whig (of the mild nineteenth-century sort), and much disposed to see the best in the whig cause of the Exclusion Bill period. It is a suggestion, however, that entirely accords with a saying that Lord Acton (himself a strong liberal in his sympathies) used to be very fond of quoting, namely, that the devil—and not, as some people asserted, St. Thomas Aquinas—was the first whig. However that may be, this at least is made clear by Milton, that " fallen angels " by the mere fact of their fall are speedily converted into aggressive fiends who at once commence fresh conspiracies against the majesty of heaven and the peace of earth. Charles in 1682 realised that whiggism, though for the moment " prostrate on the fiery lake," would soon, if left undisturbed, rise again to pursue new schemes of subversive violence. He therefore determined to destroy it in those centres whence hitherto it had drawn the main sources of its power—namely, the corporations of the cities and towns of England. Its possession of the corporations not only gave it control of much local administration, it also enabled it to return a solid phalanx of whig members to parliament. Charles, therefore, by means of *quo warranto* proceedings, called in and rescinded the governing charters of London and many other whig strongholds, thus opening the way to the remodelling of the corporations in the tory interest. It was a highly arbitrary act, of which conservative opinion decidedly disapproved; and it would not have been possible if the whigs had not put themselves entirely in the wrong by their excesses.

If anything, however, was needed to give justification to Charles for his pursuit of the whigs to their very lairs, that justification was provided in 1683 by the Rye House Plot—a plot to murder both Charles and James on their way from Newmarket to London, and to place Monmouth on the throne; a plot frustrated only by the accident of a great fire at Newmarket (started by a spark from the pipe of a careless groom) which caused the king and his brother to return to town slightly sooner than they had intended. The discovery of this plot, and the process of its unravelment, brought to light a further conspiracy of the whig leaders for the subversion of the Government. Its prime movers, Russell and Sidney, were condemned for high treason and sent to the block (July and November, 1683).

For the short remainder of his reign Charles was no more troubled by whigs. Moreover, in spite of the Triennial Act—and in the face of the earnest appeals of Halifax, the great conservative constitutionalist—he called no parliament together. Never since the halcyon days of Charles I.'s absolute government had the English monarch enjoyed so tranquil and unchallenged an exercise of sovereignty. In the midst, however, of peace and power, the immensely able but extremely enigmatical king, suddenly stricken with apoplexy, passed away (February 6, 1685). On his deathbed he was received into the Roman church.

CHAPTER VII

TORIES VERSUS WHIGS
1681–1689

" Upon the day of Monmouth's execution James renounced his alliance with the tories. Henceforth, until his expulsion, we are to regard him, not as the head of one of the political parties, but as the enemy of both."—G. W. COOKE.

" The petition of the bishops against the Declaration of Indulgence deserves attention as the formal recantation of the old high church extravagances, and the first public indication of the transition from the old toryism to the new."—F. E. SMITH [LORD BIRKENHEAD].

§ 29. THE ENIGMATICAL CHARLES

CHARLES II. was not a good conservative. The great causes for which seventeenth-century conservatism—the conservatism of Strafford, Clarendon, Danby, and Halifax—stood were not those that he had at heart. First and foremost, he was not loyal to the Church of England, of which he was the official head. It is doubtful whether, until he was stricken with apoplexy, he had any serious religious convictions at all : certainly he had no convictions strong enough to restrain the lusts of his evil and undisciplined nature. He had no sympathy with the ideals of archbishop Sheldon and his colleagues, who hoped to restore the ecclesiastical unity of England by means of the rigours of the so-called " Clarendon Code." He would rather have broadened the basis of the church so as to have included both moderate catholics and moderate presbyterians. In so far as he himself had any religious predilections, he leaned towards Rome : it was the church of his mother and her family; it was the church of Richelieu, Mazarin, and Louis XIV.—the men who in France had established a form of absolute government that was his constant object of envy and imitation; it was the church of all the continental powers that were likely to aid him in his great task of recovering his lost royal prerogatives. For, secondly, he was not loyal to the constitution as it had been restored to him in 1660. He resented the limitations imposed upon his sovereignty. He objected to the control of parliament over his ministers; he protested against the poverty in which he was kept, and against the audit of his accounts on which parliament insisted; he longed to be free from the shackles of Test Acts and Habeas Corpus Acts; he ardently desired to have at his disposal the old instruments of royal authority, the star chamber, the high commission court, and the writs *per speciale mandatum regis*. He wished to go back behind the legislation of 1641, and to regain the autocracy enjoyed by Henry VIII. But, thirdly, although he desired a revival of the royal autocracy, he was not really loyal to the crown. He was willing, as Clarendon discovered to his dismay, to make damaging surrenders of power and dreadful abandonments of principle in order to secure temporary advantages. Above all, he was ready to sell the independence of England to the French king; to become his pensioner; to accommodate English policy to French requirements; and recklessly to sacrifice English interests in order to achieve personal ends.

During the four closing years of Charles's reign (1681-85) the fact that the English government was the helpless and submissive parasite of France, kept alive by annual doles of French money, had momentous and disastrous consequences. It left Louis free to pursue his remorseless persecution of the Huguenots; and, still worse from the European point of view, it left him unchecked to develop his "reunion" policy by which he secured possession of the key fortresses of Strasbourg and Luxemburg. The seeds were sown of many future wars.

The policy of Charles during the closing years of his reign was, indeed, almost as alien from sound conservatism as it was from whiggism in all its forms. Nevertheless, so extreme was the popular reaction against the violent and revolutionary whiggism of Shaftesbury, Russell, and Sidney, that Charles was able to do anything he liked without fear of opposition. A wave of high-toryism swept over the country. The doctrine of the divine right of kings was proclaimed in its most unqualified form: Filmer's *Patriarcha* (published 1680) became a textbook for devoted royalists. The duty of passive obedience, and the sinfulness of all resistance to kingly authority, were preached from countless anglican pulpits. For those who preferred non-theological arguments for absolutism, the *Leviathan* and the *Behemoth* of Thomas Hobbes provided a storehouse of potent principles. The political satires of Dryden, written for the occasion, and the older *Hudibras* of Butler poured ridicule and contempt upon roundheads, puritans, republicans, and whigs. The universities of Cambridge and Oxford vied with one another in manifestos of ultra-royalism. "Kings," proclaimed the university of Cambridge, " derive not their titles from the people, but from God; to Him only are they accountable: it belongs not to subjects either to create or censure, but to honour and obey their sovereign who comes to be so by a fundamental hereditary right of succession which no religion, no law, no fault or forfeiture, can alter or diminish." It must have seemed difficult to go any further than that in exaltation of divine right or in reprobation of rebellion. Yet the university of Oxford achieved the incredible in a manifesto of July, 1683, which may be regarded as registering the high-water mark of the tory reaction. After making a solemn holocaust of the works of Buchanan, Languet, Bellarmine, Milton, Baxter, and others who had combated the theory of divine right, or advocated the rival contract theory, the university authorities formally denounced and condemned twenty-seven propositions embodying the whig conception of the state and the church.

The king readily fell in with the humour of his ultra-loyal subjects, to whom (thanks to the reaction from the revolutionary violence of the whigs) the duty of defending the crown seemed to be the first and foremost of conservative obligations. He revived on an unprecedented scale the practice—extremely displeasing to his fastidious taste—of touching for the king's evil: it was a practice which demonstrated to the credulous populace as nothing else could the divine virtue which resided in the monarch as the consequence of his hereditary right. Within twenty-four days, at the close of 1682, Charles touched no fewer than 3,535 persons, among whom some miraculous cures seemed to be effected.

Truly, when Charles died in February, 1685, he passed on to his brother James a goodly heritage of superstitious and unmitigated loyalty.

§ 30. THE INJUDICIOUS JAMES

James II. began his reign well. He had largely recovered his popularity. For he had passed very creditably (thanks to his brother's restraining hand) through the frightful and terrifying ordeal of the " popish plot " mania of 1679-81. The country, now that it had recovered its sanity, felt sympathy with the man who had been subjected to so cruel and malignant an attack, together with respect for a confessor who, rather than abandon his religion, was prepared to face exclusion from the throne, exile from the kingdom, and possible death. He had, indeed, behaved extremely well in the face of gross provocation, and when peace and power had come back to him, he had displayed no disposition to wreak his vengeance upon his prostrate enemies. His brother, in spite of the Test Act, had recalled him to the privy council, and had reinstated him in his office of lord high admiral —an office in which, as Pepys bears ample witness, he did excellent administrative work. The voice of protest was stilled, and real popularity took the place of the former hatred and suspicion.

James, then, succeeded to the throne in February 1685 without opposition and amid the plaudits of the multitude. His early acts enhanced his popularity, and calmed the fears both of conservatives (such as Sir Edward Seymour), who doubted whether it could be possible for a catholic to be the official head of a protestant church, and of constitutionalists (such as Halifax), who questioned whether a Stuart could conceivably be persuaded to govern according to law. On the one hand, he gave a

formal and public pledge to maintain the Church of
England : " I know," he said to his privy council, " that
the principles of the Church of England are for monarchy,
and that the members of it have shown themselves good
and loyal subjects ; therefore I shall always take good
care to defend and support it." The declaration gave
immense satisfaction and caused intense relief. " We
have the word of a king," said one jubilant anglican,
" and of a king who was never worse than his word." On
the other hand, James actually summoned a parliament,
after a four years' interval, which under Charles II. had
seemed likely to be indefinitely prolonged. He had his
reward in the return of a house of commons overwhelm-
ingly tory and exuberant in its expressions of devoted
loyalty. He further inspired confidence by retaining
among his chief ministers Rochester, Halifax, and Sunderland. Rochester (Laurence Hyde, second son of the great
Clarendon, and therefore James's brother-in-law), " was
the staunchest of tories, and of the church party," says
Roger North, " he had the honour for many years to be
accounted the head " : of his loyalty to anglican protestantism there could be no doubt. Halifax was the great
constitutionalist of the day ; Sunderland was a devotee of
the crown. Hence all the three great conservative causes
seemed to be secure.

Unfortunately, however, the golden promise of this
halcyon dawn was soon overcast. Even within the short
three months (February to May, 1685) that elapsed between
James's accession and the meeting of his parliament, some
amazement and apprehension were caused by the fact that
he continued to levy customs duties, together with ton-
nage and poundage, without legal warrant ; by the fact
that he hunted out and punished with ferocious severity
Titus Oates and other relics of the " popish plot " era ;
and by the fact that he pardoned and released on his own
authority a number of recusants and other dissenters who
were suffering imprisonment under the Clarendon Code.
The next six months, however (May to November, 1685),
which comprised the one and only session of this ultra-
loyal but speedily disillusioned parliament, witnessed the

complete alienation of the king from the bulk of his subjects. And what alienated them was the king's obvious intention to subvert both the church and the constitution. The king, indeed, was gracious and injudicious enough to explain that when he promised to maintain the church and constitution he did so on the implied condition that both convocation and parliament would do as he told them: he introduced the whig idea of contract into his relations with his subjects.

But the things that he told his subjects to do, together with the things that he himself did, during the summer and autumn of 1685, caused the widest alarm throughout the country, and completely destroyed all confidence in James himself. He made an ostentatious display of catholicism at court; he brought pressure to bear upon his ministers—a pressure to which Sunderland and others ultimately yielded—to cause them to abandon protestantism; he invited a papal nuncio to England and received him with an immense display of pageantry; he ordered Archbishop Sancroft and the other bishops to silence preachers who held forth in their pulpits against catholicism; he sounded both his ministers and members of parliament in general as to their willingness to procure for him the repeal of the Test Acts and the Habeas Corpus Act; he steadily increased his standing army, and, in defiance of the Test Acts, granted most of the new commissions to papists. This last flagrant violation of the law caused even this ultra-loyal parliament to protest. For its primary devotion was to the Church of England. The king took the protests very ill. He dismissed Halifax from his office, and Compton, bishop of London, from the privy council; on November 20 he prorogued the parliament itself, which in fact never met again.* In order to carry on the government, James, like his predecessor, became a pensioner of Louis XIV.

The same summer and autumn as witnessed this breach between James and his parliament saw also the ill-starred rebellions and invasions of Monmouth and Argyll, followed

* The prorogation, originally for three months, was twice renewed in 1686. Finally, the parliament was dissolved in 1687.

by their merciless suppression. The country as a whole
had no sympathy with these silly and incompetent re-
crudescences of Shaftesbury's unscrupulous whiggism. It
loathed the thought of civil war, and rejoiced when the
capture of Argyll in Scotland, and the defeat of Monmouth at Sedgmoor (July 5, 1685), put an end to the disturbance. But it was horrified at the brutal and unnecessary ferocity with which these futile and not formidable risings were stamped out. The dragonades of Colonel
Kirke and the subsequent judicial massacres effected by
the abominable Jeffreys filled the land with horror, and
destroyed whatever vestiges of respect and popularity
James still retained. November, 1685, was the turning
point of the reign.

§ 31. A Conflict of Loyalties

For three years—during which no parliament was
called—by means of complacent ministers, corrupt judges,
subservient courts, and French subsidies, James strove
with resolute determination to carry through the three
great designs upon which his mind was bent—namely, first,
the abrogation of the Test Acts and the Habeas Corpus
Act; secondly, the building up of a strong and devoted
standing army, officered by catholics; and thirdly, the re-
establishment of catholicism in England. His policy has
been well described, by a writer not unsympathetic towards
toryism, as " a blend of popery, absolutism, and an ignoble
and corrupt subservience to the French court."*

The rapid increase in the numbers of the standing army;
the steady recruitment of Irish papists; the almost exclusive appointment and promotion of catholic officers; the
concentration of the forces in a camp at Hounslow Heath
—all these things caused widespread alarm. They seemed
to portend a military dictatorship on the Bourbon model.
But still more disturbing both to whigs and to tories was
James's persistent attack upon the protestant Church of
England. First, he used his admitted " dispensing power "
to exempt catholics from the penalties of the Test Acts

* Kent, C. B. R., *Early History of the Tories* (1908), p. 324.

when they accepted offices for which they were by law in-
eligible. A collusive action brought by a servant, Godden,
against his master, Sir Edward Hales, who under a dis-
pensation from James held a colonelcy without having
taken the required oaths, was decided by a packed bench
in James's favour (1686), and from that time onward none
but catholics found it worth while to apply for military
posts. In virtue, too, of the same dispensing power, and
on the strength of his position as head of the established
church, James proceeded to intrude papists into the
universities and even into the church itself: a catholic
(Massey) was made Dean of Christ Church, and a crypto-
catholic (Parker), Bishop of Oxford. Secondly, James
employed his alleged "suspending power" to stop the
enforcement, against both catholics and protestant nonconformists, of those Acts of the Clarendon Code that restricted freedom of worship. In April, 1687, he issued
a Declaration of Indulgence granting, in defiance of the
law, freedom of worship to all, while at the same time
expressing a hearty wish "that all the people of our
dominions were members of the catholic church."
Hitherto he had tried to keep on terms with the anglican
church, presuming on its ostentatious loyalty, and trust-
ing to its adherence to those doctrines of divine right
and passive obedience which it had been proclaiming in
season and out of season ever since the Restoration. Now,
in anger at the anglican protests to which his actions
gave rise, he definitely broke with anglicanism, and made
a bid to get his way by the joint aid of hopeful catholics
and grateful dissenters. He purged his council of protestants: Rochester, whose large charity had for two
years hoped all things and endured all things, was dismissed early in 1687, and his elder brother Clarendon was
shortly afterwards compelled to surrender his Irish lord-
lieutenancy to the catholic Tyrconnel. Power passed into
the hands of the extreme papal faction, led by the Jesuit
Edward Petre—a fashion to which the renegade Sunderland gave his venal support.

James calculated that the anglicans would remain true
to their political principles, and the dissenters to their

religious interests.   In both calculations he was mistaken.
Loudly as the anglicans had preached the duty of passive
obedience to the king, they maintained still more strongly
the obligation of fidelity to the protestant Church of
England as by law established : it had apparently never
occurred to them till then that church and crown could
come into irreconcilable conflict.   They learned a lesson on
this occasion which they did not speedily forget—namely,
the peril that lurks in the too emphatic and unqualified
assertion of any principle whatsoever.   The dissenters, on
the other hand, were sorely tempted to accept the relief
which James offered them, even if it were contrary to the
law.   For the law was morally indefensible in their eyes,
and they had long begged for its repeal.   Since the fall of
the whigs in 1681, moreover, their sufferings had been very
seriously aggravated.

Now, in 1687, however, when the king and the tories
were at loggerheads, the dissenters held the key position.
If they accepted relief under the Declaration of Indulgence, the Clarendon Code would become a dead letter.
If, on the other hand, they refused to recognise the validity
of the Indulgences it would remain inoperative and the
authority of parliament would be vindicated.   The constitutional Halifax saw the urgency of the crisis and also the
way of its resolution : he wrote his famous *Letter to a Dis-
senter*, virtually promising, in the name of the dominant
section of the tory party, that if the dissenters would maintain the sanctity of the law, they should receive by Act of
Parliament the freedom of worship which James offered
them under his arbitrary Declaration.   They preferred the
good faith of the great conservative statesman to the
doubtful honesty of the cruel and fanatical king, and in
general they declined to avail themselves of the means of
relief which James seemed to offer to them.

The general disregard of the Declaration of Indulgence
roused James to fury.   When twelve months had elapsed
he reissued it, accompanying it on this occasion with a
command that it should be publicly read from the pulpits
of all anglican churches.   Thus he forced the issue between
church and crown.   It was an act of suicidal folly.   For,

when faced by this dilemma, neither anglican clergy nor conservative laity had the slightest hesitation as to which horn they should take. The protestant Church of England was their prime concern, and the integrity of the constitution was their second concern; the king (except in so far as he stood for the church and the constitution) came a clear third. The clergy almost to a man refused to obey the king's command. Seven bishops, headed by the primate, petitioned the king to withdraw the offensive document; and when the king, in high amazement and indignation, had them accused of seditious libel, they were acquitted by a London jury amid demonstrations of the wildest rejoicing. This trial was the prelude to the revolution. On the very day on which the bishops were acquitted (June 30, 1688), a trusty emissary, representing both whigs and tories, crossed from England to Holland, inviting William of Orange to come and deliver from destruction the anglican church and the English constitution.

The sending of this decisive invitation was precipitated by a new factor of cardinal importance. On June 10 Mary of Modena, James's catholic queen, had given birth to a son. His advent destroyed the hope of the succession of the protestant Mary of Orange, the prospect of which had buoyed up anglicans and constitutionalists during the trials of the three preceding years. The probability that a James III. would succeed to a James II. was more than either whigs or tories could stand. The chiefs of the two parties united to summon the Prince of Orange to their aid. He landed on November 5, 1688, and before the end of the year James was in headlong and pusillanimous flight to France.

§ 32. The " Glorious Revolution "

The revolution of 1688 was a conservative revolution. This is a point on which Bolingbroke, Burke, and Beaconsfield all strongly insisted. James was the innovator; he was the person who sought to undermine the church which he had pledged himself to maintain, and to subvert the

constitution which it was his duty to support.* The lead
in the movement which resulted in his expulsion was taken
by the great conservative statesman Danby, who met the
powerful whig lord Devonshire at Whittington, in Derby-
shire, and there held counsel with him as to how the two
parties could combine to save church and state from
destruction.   The invitation to William was signed by
Danby and Devonshire, and by five others drawn from
both parties.   After William had landed, and when James
was marching as though to meet him and stop him on
Salisbury Plain, the revolt of the north, planned con-
jointly by Danby and Devonshire, and organised with
Danby's extraordinary practical ability, turned the scale
against James and caused him to retreat to London.
When he was hesitating in London as to what to do next,
a judicious letter from the trimmer Halifax kindled his
fears for his own personal safety, and caused him to ease
the situation incalculably by running away.

But, although the revolution was carried through by a
combination of the leaders of both parties, it is clear that
the tories entered into it with feelings very different from
those of the whigs.   To the tories it was a painful necessity; to the whigs it was a glorious opportunity.   The
whigs were able to rise against James with whole-hearted
enthusiasm : their exclusion policy was vindicated and
revived; their contractual conception of monarchy was
confirmed; their ideal of parliamentary sovereignty was
realised; their policy of wide toleration for protestants
was triumphantly advanced.   The tories, on the other
hand, were torn by conflicting loyalties and distracted by
diverging policies.   They were, of course, virtually unani-
mous in their desire to secure the Church of England from
subversion, whether by royal dispensations, high commissions, or declarations of indulgence; they were equally
agreed among themselves, and with the whigs, as to the
need of maintaining freedom of elections, liberty of debate
in parliament, control of taxation, independence of judges
and juries, the right of presenting petitions, and so on;
but they were dreadfully distressed that their defence of

* *Cf.* Jones, J. Deane, *The English Revolution,* pp. 156, 162, 344.

church and constitution brought them into violent conflict with their sovereign lord, the son of that martyred saint Charles I., the wielder of the sceptre *jure divino*, and the man to whom they had sworn heartfelt allegiance. When, early in 1689, the time came to decide what form the government should take in the new circumstances, they were desperately eager to find some solution of the problem that would still leave inviolate—at any rate in theory—their loyalty to James.

Three various schemes, each more or less consonant with the principle of hereditary divine right, were propounded by troubled tories. First was the true full-blooded jacobite scheme, advocated by Sherlock, that James should be brought back and restored, on the best terms that he could be persuaded to concede; few were there who dared to contemplate that heroic adherence to principle. Secondly came Nottingham's less impossible proposal—namely, that James should be allowed to retain the titular kingship, but that he should not be permitted to enter his kingdoms or to exercise any authority over them; but that all actual power should be conferred upon a regent—*e.g.*, William of Orange: the obvious inconveniences of having a line of *de jure* sovereigns in France, and another hostile line of *de facto* sovereigns in England, were so great as to cause Nottingham's proposal to be decisively rejected. Then, thirdly, came Danby's suggestion that James's flight should be regarded as equivalent to abdication or death, and that therefore December 23, 1688, should be taken to be the date of the automatic accession of his daughter Mary, Princess of Orange: William's emphatic objection to the rank and status of prince consort—his wife's " gentleman usher " he called it—caused this scheme to be abandoned. There remained, then, nothing but the whig solution of the problem—namely, the declaration that the throne was vacant, and the election of William and Mary jointly to fill the vacancy. With infinite misgiving and unwillingness the tories in a body accepted the motion, carefully framed so as to offend their sensibilities as little as possible : " That King James II., having endeavoured to subvert the con-

stitution of the kingdom by breaking the original contract between the king and people, and by the advice of
jesuits and other wicked persons having violated the
fundamental laws, and having withdrawn himself out of
the kingdom, has abdicated the government, and that the
throne has thereby become vacant." This admirably
illogical, inconsistent, and inconsequential resolution con-
tains a tit-bit for all: the Jesuits for the church; the
fundamental laws for the constitutionalists; the abdication for the tories, and so on.   But the whigs had most
of the plums; in particular they got their contract theory
recognised, and they secured the incomparably important
admission that the throne was vacant.   That meant that
the line of hereditary descent was broken; that the royal
claim to divine right was for ever rendered invalid; and
that a new monarchy remained to be created, deriving all
its powers and prerogatives from parliament.   In accordance with that popular principle a Declaration of Right
was drawn up, enumerating the evil deeds of James and
providing against their repetition; it was presented to
William and Mary, and on their acceptance of its terms,
they jointly and severally received the offer of the crown.
They accepted the offer and the six weeks' interregnum
was at an end (February 13, 1689).

CHAPTER VIII

TRIMMERS VERSUS ZEALOTS

1689-1714

" The substitution of the contract theory for that of divine right was the central fact, the pivot, upon which the Revolution turned. It placed the monarchy on a new basis: it shifted, so to speak, the mental perspective of the nation."—C. B. ROYLANCE KENT.

" In 1689 the succession to the Crown was changed, in order to preserve the Church."—J. DEANE JONES.

" No logical process could reconcile the tories' political theory with their constitutional sense or their religious convictions."— KEITH FEILING.

§ 33. THE WHIG TRIUMPH

THE revolution of 1688-89 was an event of outstanding importance in the history of England. It brought to an end the long conflict for sovereignty which had been waged between monarch and parliament ever since the closing days of the great Elizabeth; it established once for all the supremacy of parliament, making the crown henceforth the creature of statute. Further, it assured, in so far as civil law could do so, the protestant ascendancy in England, formally excluding from the throne all claimants either themselves papists or married to papists. Again, it modified and reformed the constitution, strengthening parliamentary control over the dispensing and suspending powers, the levying of money, the enrolling of a standing army, the setting up of ecclesiastical courts, and so on; and at the same time securing freedom of debate in parliament and freedom of election in the constituencies. Thus it was a revolution of considerable magnitude, and yet it was a peaceful revolution, effected with the minimum of noise and violence. It embodied and expressed, indeed, the very genius of English conservatism—namely, unbroken continuity coupled with cautious reform.

But though the continuity of the constitution was pre-
served, none the less the consequences of the revolution
were far-reaching and profound. The substitution of
William for James inaugurated a new era in our foreign
policy, plunging England into hostilities with France that
lasted, with intervals, until 1815. Similarly, it opened a
new period of imperial development—namely, expansion
by conquest, coupled with loss owing to French-aided
rebellion. But what more particularly concerns us in our
present study is the fact that the revolution not only
changed the crown by making it patently statutory, and
transformed the constitution by making it definitely parliamentary, it also greatly modified the position both of
the established church and of the two political parties.
On the one hand, the church had to accommodate itself to
the principle of religious toleration, to recognise the legal
existence of dissent, and to abandon its ideal of the
respublica christiana. The Toleration Act of 1689 imple-
mented the promise made by Halifax to the protestant
nonconformists—namely, that if they would refuse to
receive the improper relief offered to them by James in
his Declarations of Indulgence, they should be granted
freedom of worship by statute. This formal abandonment
of the old conservative principle of the ideal identity of the
Anglican church and the English nation, although highly
gratifying to the whigs, was a source of profound regret
and alarm to the tories. The deep underlying cause of the
non-juring schism was, indeed, not so much adherence on
the part of the non-jurors to the doctrine of the divine
right of kings, as their devotion to the conception of the
religious unity of the nation and the sanctity of the state
as being also a church.

Hence, if, on the one hand, the church was distressed by
the diminution of its status, and by its legal reduction to
the rank of a sect, on the other hand the two political
parties were each of them profoundly affected by the
change of dynasty. To the tories, as we have remarked,
the revolution was a painful necessity ; to the whigs it was
a glorious opportunity. In 1681 nothing seemed less likely
than a whig revival : the whigs by their abominable ex-

ploitation of the popish plot frenzy, and by their fury concerning the Exclusion Bill, had put themselves beyond the
pale of civilisation. But the fates were kind to them :
first, providence relieved them of the incubus of the
violent and unscrupulous Shaftesbury, who died in
Holland early in 1683; secondly, James kindly, though
with ineffable folly, removed the distracting Monmouth
from their midst, and so enabled them to reunite round
the Orange tree; finally, the same injudicious king, by his
attacks on the church and the universities (the two institutions most closely identified with the royalism of the
day) split the tory party into fragments, and opened the
way to the unexpected and almost incredible whig triumph
of 1689.

The settlement of 1689 was unquestionably whig and
not tory in its essential features; equally in respect of
church, constitution, and crown it registered grave devia-
tions from tory ideals. As a whig settlement it was distinctly unwelcome to William, who had high notions of royal
prerogative and no willingness whatsoever to be the mere
doge of a Venetian oligarchy. He resented the restrictions
placed upon him by the Bill of Rights; he was aggrieved
at the inadequacy of the revenue assigned to him by parliament, and at the novel safeguards by which it was
accompanied; he assented with extreme reluctance and
under strong protest to the new Triennial Bill of 1694.
Above all, he struggled to escape from whig dictation; he
wished to be effective king of the nation, not nominal
leader of a political party; and he greatly preferred his
tory supporters to the whig "junto" which claimed him
as its own. His first ministry, therefore, was plentifully
leavened with tories. Danby (who was created marquis
of Carmarthen) became lord president of the council and
virtual prime minister; Nottingham, the most faithful of
custodians of the Anglican church, received one of the two
secretaryships of state; Godolphin was placed at the head
of the treasury; Torrington and Lowther, two unmitigated
tories, went to the admiralty; while that influential
"trimmer," George Savile, marquis of Halifax, was made
lord privy seal. This powerful conservative element in

William's first ministry was strengthened and confirmed by the general election of 1690, which returned a tory majority. The privileges of the church, the continuity of the constitution, and the prerogatives of the crown, were all carefully maintained against both the innovations demanded by the more progressive whigs and the reactions threatened by the more uncompromising tories.

§ 34. JACOBITES AND NON-JURORS

The years 1690-95 during which the tories retained their ascendancy in parliament, and during which the veteran Carmarthen remained virtual prime minister, were, unfortunately, years of conflict both at home and abroad. The revolutionary change of government, peacefully effected in England and Wales, had to be imposed by force of arms on Scotland and on Ireland. Still more serious, the placing of the Prince of Orange on the English throne plunged this country as a principal into the great war which Louis XIV. was waging on the Continent against William's ponderous "grand alliance." And the war, which lasted eight years (1689-97) without bringing either glory or profit to England, involved the country in enormous expense, necessitated the inauguration of the national debt, compelled the continuance of the existence of the hated and dreaded standing army, and flooded both the court and the capital with Dutch and Germans. Hence a number of the more cautious and moderate whigs, headed by Robert Harley—who under Queen Anne became earl of Oxford and lord treasurer—satisfied with the new securities that had been established for religious toleration and parliamentary sovereignty, began to draw away from their leaders and to advocate freedom from continental entanglements; the separation of the interests of England from those of the Dutch Netherlands; peace and retrenchment; the abolition of the standing army; the liquidation of the national debt; resistance to the growing power of the moneyed interest; emancipation from alien control; return to the Elizabethan policy of insularity, sea-power, and the dominance of land over gold.

The whig seceders inevitably drifted in the direction of toryism. For the tories, even more than they, were dissatisfied with the way that things were going. They regretted, even when they accepted, the necessary implications of the revolution—namely, recognition of protestant nonconformity, establishment of parliamentary sovereignty, and diminution of royal prerogative; but they emphatically rejected, repudiated, and detested the war, the standing army, the foreign favourites of the king, the subordination of English interests to those of the Continent in general and of Holland in particular, the insolence and unreasonableness of the grand allies abroad, and at home the growing aggressiveness of dissenters, financiers, and lawyers. Their allegiance was given to Mary rather than to her Dutch husband, whom they regarded with mingled apprehension and dislike. Hence, when in 1694 Mary died, at the early age of thirty-two, tory enthusiasm for the new régime was much cooled. William, indeed, found it increasingly necessary to get rid of his tory ministers, and to place his affairs exclusively in the keeping of the whigs.

Some tories, however, were compelled by their consciences to go much farther than the trimmers who, whether willingly or reluctantly, followed Carmarthen, Nottingham, Godolphin, and Halifax in accepting the revolutionary settlement. They were unable to accept it. They could not recognise the validity of the title of the new monarchy; they could not approve the new encroachments of the parliament on the executive; above all, they could not tolerate the new toleration of dissenters. Hence they had to withhold their allegiance and to proclaim themselves supporters of the cause of the exiled Stuarts. Such were the non-jurors and the jacobites. The two groups were by no means identical, and within each of them there were many shades of difference. (1) *The non-jurors* were mainly clergy of the Church of England who, having sworn the oaths of allegiance and supremacy to James II., felt themselves unable to repudiate these oaths and to swear new ones to William and Mary. They realised that they had so completely committed themselves to the doctrines of divine right, non-resistance, and passive obedience that they could not without grave scandal recognise a settlement based on the negation of these doctrines. Strong efforts were made to conciliate and win over these conscientious objectors, and in some cases these efforts were successful. But, when all had been done, more than four hundred stalwarts, including Archbishop Sancroft and five other bishops, had to be deprived of their offices and driven into the wilderness. The non-jurors—who claimed to be the only true authentic Church of England—continued as a distinct religious organisation well into the nineteenth century. (2) *The jacobites* were the much larger and more general company of those who looked for, and worked for, the restoration of the exiled Stuarts. By no means all of them were non-jurors. Many, not being public servants, were not called upon to take any oaths at all. Others, including generally some fifty members of parliament, found it possible (according to the principles of an interim-ethic) to make the necessary professions of loyalty to the new régime, clearly admitting that they left themselves free, and felt themselves in duty bound, to labour for the restoration of the old. But of course the majority, relics of the old cavalier party inspired by devotion to the memory of the martyr-king, or catholics faithful to the interests of Rome, held sternly aloof from the revolutionary government, and ceaselessly plotted for its overthrow. Jacobitism remained a serious and powerful political cause until 1746. Even after that date it survived as a tragi-comedy all through the eighteenth and nineteenth centuries. Indeed, it is not wholly defunct at the present day : there are still some devotees of the dogma of hereditary divine right who regard Ruprecht of Bavaria (descendant of Henrietta of Orleans, sister of Charles II.) as legitimate king of Great Britain and Ireland.

Thus it will be seen that during the reign of William and Mary, under the disintegrating influence of the problems of a new age, a three-party system came into existence. On the one side were the thorough-going whigs, led by the famous " junto " (Somers, Montagu, Russell, and Wharton), who gloried in the revolution, who supported William in his continental diplomacy and his incessant wars, and who joined themselves in intimate alliance with the dissenters and with the bankers and other city magnates. At the opposite pole to these were the jacobites and non-jurors, who stood for the vanished England of Charles I. or Henry VIII. In between the two grew up the true conservative party, the party of the trimmers, formed by the union of (1) the tories led by Carmarthen, who accepted the revolution; (2) non-party men led by Halifax, who maintained the continuity of the constitution; and (3) dissentient whigs led by Harley, who increasingly disapproved of the policy of William and the junto.

As to William, in spite of his preference for tory views of royal prerogative, he found himself compelled, in order to get support for the continental enterprises which were his prime concern, gradually to shed all his tory ministers and to give himself wholly to the whig junto. The trimmer Halifax (who could never get on with Carmarthen) went so early as October, 1689; Nottingham was driven to resign in 1693; Carmarthen himself (who became duke of Leeds in 1694) was virtually superseded as chief minister by Somers in 1695; finally Godolphin was driven out in 1697, and so a purely whig ministry was constituted.

The election of 1695, moreover, returned a whig house of commons, so during the year 1697-98 the whigs had it all their own way both at home and abroad. In 1698, however, a tory reaction occurred, and during the closing years of the reign William and his whig ministers (who did not resign) were involved in conflicts with a hostile parliament that must have called up in their minds sympathetic pictures of St. Paul's combats with wild beasts at Ephesus. The leading members of the junto were impeached; William's Dutch guards were dismissed; the army was reduced from 80,000 men to 7,000; many royal grants of land were rescinded; above all, an Act of Settlement was passed (1701) which, after making new arrangements for the succession to the crown,* was converted

---

* The Act of Settlement decreed that failing heirs to William and to Anne the crown should pass to the Electress Sophia of Hanover, daughter of Elizabeth of Bohemia, and therefore granddaughter of James I., and to her successors, being protestants.

into a prolonged vote of censure on William and his
administration. The tories, in fact, in their blind detestation of the Dutchmen and the whigs, inflicted permanent
injuries upon that very royal prerogative which it was
their special province to preserve. So high did party
passion flame in 1701.

Before the end of the year, however, and six months
before the death of William, a slight revulsion took place.
In September, 1701, James II. passed away in France,
and at once Louis XIV. recognised his son, "the pretender," as king of England under the title of James III.
This act of impudent interference with English affairs
(which also violated the recently concluded treaty of
Ryswick) caused Englishmen of all parties to rally to
William's side, and enabled him to get what he had for
many months vainly striven for—namely, the entry of
England into the war of the Spanish Succession.

§ 35. THE RECONSTRUCTION OF CONSERVATISM

The war of the Spanish Succession did not interest the
people of England directly; it was fought to decide the
question whether a grandson of Louis XIV. or a grandson
of the emperor Leopold should be established on the
tottering throne of Madrid. The English entered it only
because the aggressions of Louis XIV. menaced the independence of the Netherlands, the balance of power in
Europe, and the protestant succession in Great Britain.
They entered it as auxiliaries; for, when they came in, it
had already been in process for more than a year. But
they soon found themselves involved in it as principals on
whom fell the main burden of the fighting and the major
part of the cost. Hence very speedily tory opinion turned
against it, and throughout the reign of Anne (1702-14) the
prime question dividing the two great parties was that of
the continuance and the conduct of the war. The trimmers
and non-party men oscillated: in particular Godolphin
(who was lord treasurer and virtual prime minister from
1702 to 1710) and Marlborough (the great commander-in-

chief) were compelled by the exigencies of the conflict to migrate slowly from the tory side to the whig. Other questions, several of them connected with the war, also became bones of party contention. In the sphere of foreign policy the whigs wished to continue William's active intervention in continental affairs, while the tories desired a return to England's comfortable insularity. Hence the whigs stood for a strong aggressive army; the tories for a powerful protective navy. When the war dragged its weary length into the second decade of the century, the tories became ardent advocates of peace at almost any price; the whigs demanded the continuance of the conflict until all the original aims of the allies should have been realised. The tories made and defended the treaty of Utrecht; the whigs opposed and denounced it as a gross betrayal of the allied cause. When during the course of the war the problem of union with, or complete separation from, Scotland was raised in an acute form by the passing of the Scottish Act of Security (1704), the leading whigs became the chief advocates of the union, while the tories tended to oppose it, partly because of their almost instinctive dislike of presbyterians, and partly because of the formidable obstacle which union would place in the way of a Stuart restoration. In the prolonged negotiations that preceded the Act of Union (1707) matters of money and merchandise were of prime concern both to the Scots as a nation and to the whigs as a party. The tories were perturbed by the growing prominence of commerce and finance in politics, and by the increasing ascendancy of the moneyed and mercantile class. Hence the maintenance of the old agricultural England became one of their preoccupations. In order to secure the dominance of the landed interest in parliament, they carried during the period of their power at the close of Queen Anne's reign (1711) a *Property Qualification Act*, which made the possession of an estate in land worth £600 a year a necessary condition of county membership, and even for borough membership an estate worth at least half that amount. Of course, the whig lawyers soon found means to circumvent this statute; nevertheless, it re-

mained an incubus upon parliamentary representation
down to a time so late as 1858.

Thus it will be seen that new problems and new interests
began to divide English politicians at the opening of the
eighteenth century. But it must not be assumed that
the old lines of division were wholly obliterated. On the
contrary, church, constitution, and crown continued to be
major subjects of controversy, although in each case the
nature of the controversy had been changed by the revolution of 1688. In the sphere of the church, the thorough-
going tory—e.g., Nottingham, whose prime concern was
the maintenance of anglicanism—was much disturbed by
the rapid spread of dissent; by the ease with which nonconformists evaded the test acts and qualified themselves
for office by means of the subterfuge of "occasional conformity"—that is, by a formal taking of the sacrament,
under protest, once a year in an anglican church; and also
by the portentous growth of eminently efficient dissenting
"academies," or secondary schools. The high-water mark
of the tory reaction of the closing years of Anne was
registered by the passing of the *Occasional Conformity
Act*, 1711, and the *Schism Act*, 1714 (which provided that
no person other than a member of the anglican church
should keep a school or act as a tutor).* In the sphere of
the constitution, the tories were eager to defend the
ancient rights and privileges of the privy council—a body
dependent on the monarch, sworn to his service, anterior
to and aloof from political parties—as against the whig
device of the cabinet—a body drawn from one political
party, dependent on a majority in the house of commons,
and the master rather than the servant of the crown. One
of the provisions of the tory *Act of Settlement* (1701) was
intended to establish the authority of the privy council as
against the cabinet after the death of Anne; the whigs,
however, secured its repeal in 1705 before ever it had come
into operation. As to the crown, the tories were loyal and
eager in their support of the powers and prerogatives of
Anne, whose devotion to the Church of England won their
enthusiastic applause. But as to the succession to the

* Both these Acts were repealed in 1719.

throne after the death of the queen (who, though not old, was, according to the standards of insurance companies, a very bad life) they were gravely divided. The moderates, the trimmers, the ex-whigs, followed Harley in firm adhesion to the protestant succession, as determined by the *Bill of Rights* and the *Act of Settlement*. The extremists, however, the high-fliers, and *a fortiori* the non-jurors and the jacobites leaned to the side of divine hereditary right and the exiled house of Stuart. If " the pretender "— whom, following Louis XIV., they called " James III."— would have turned anglican, his succession to his half-sister's throne would have been as certain as anything human can be.

§ 36. The Return of the Tories, 1710-14

As we have already observed, the growing embroilment of England as a principal combatant in the war of the Spanish Succession made it necessary for Queen Anne (much against her inclination) to place power more and more in the hands of whig ministers. One by one the tories had to go—*e.g.*, Rochester (the queen's uncle), 1703 ; Nottingham, 1704 ; Wright, the tory lord chancellor, 1705 ; and in 1708 even the moderate ex-whig Harley with his young protégé Henry St. John (of whom more anon)— and for two years the whigs in cabinet and parliament were supreme (1708-10). The whigs, however, not yet purged of their seventeenth-century violence, greatly abused their power. For party purposes they needlessly prolonged the war, rejecting in 1709 terms of peace far more favourable to the allied cause than those actually secured four years later at Utrecht. In order to persuade the reluctant Dutch to continue the fighting, they concluded with them a *Barrier Treaty* in which permanent English interests were recklessly bartered away. Heavy and vexatious taxation exhausted and irritated the country, while the depredations of the press-gang by means of which the necessary supply of cannon-fodder was provided caused widespread resentment. The queen was exasperated almost beyond endurance by constant minis-

terial opposition to her will, and by incessant efforts on
the part of the whig leaders to force their obnoxious supporters into her service. ": The question is this," she
finally said, " whether I shall submit to the five tyran-
nising lords or they to me." It was indeed a *Machtfrage*,
that most fundamental of political problems. Then, to
crown all, the whigs repeated the suicidal folly of
James II. : they attacked the Church of England. They
attacked it, of course, from the opposite side to that from
which James had launched his assault. They undermined
it by appointing low church and erastian bishops (such as
Burnet, Hoadley, and Wake); they debased its sacraments
by encouraging " occasional conformity "; they challenged its function as the educator of the nation by fostering dissenting academies; they broadened the limits of the
Toleration Act by stretching it to include unitarians and
deists; they recognised presbyterianism as the state
religion of Scotland, and they even connived at its endow-
ment in Ireland. Hence all the anglicanism of the tory
party was roused to a fury of protest, and a " high church "
movement, partly political and partly ecclesiastical, stimulated and acerbated by the jibes of non-jurors and
catholics, commenced. It was a romantic reaction recall-
ing, on a petty scale, the grand features of the counter-
reformation, and anticipating, on a lower plane, the ten-
dencies of the Oxford movement of a century later. High-
anglican pulpits began to pour forth long-silenced strains
concerning the celestial source of sovereignty, the divine
right of kings, the duty of passive obedience, and so on—
strains extremely pleasing to the ear of Anne, who was
always keenly conscious of her descent from the royal
martyr, Charles I. She started touching for the " king's
evil " with apoplectic energy—among her patients being
the infantile Samuel Johnson, who, if not cured of the
scrofula, was permanently inoculated against whiggery.

Among the high-fliers of the anglican reaction, Dr.
Henry Sacheverell, a vehement and irrational agitator,
distinguished himself by the violence of his denunciation
of political rebellion and religious toleration : he included
the revolution of 1688 and the *Toleration Act* of 1689

among the objects of his unmitigated condemnation. A
sermon of his, preached at St. Paul's before the lord mayor
and the city corporation on November 5, 1709, caused so
great a sensation that the whig ministry injudiciously
determined to impeach the agitating divine, and to take
the occasion of the impeachment to re-assert in the most
public and emphatic manner possible the principles of
1688-9. In coming to this conclusion the whigs gravely
miscalculated the power of the church, the passion of the
queen, the strength of toryism in the country, and the
generality of the detestation with which they themselves
had come to be regarded. The trial of Dr. Sacheverell,
1710, precipitated a first-class political crisis, in the midst
of which the queen seized the opportunity to dismiss the
whig tyrants with ignominy and to recall the tories to
office. A general election in the autumn completed the
whig debacle. The tories were returned in an overwhelming majority, under the leadership of Robert Harley and
his brilliant young disciple Henry St. John.

To Robert Harley more than to any other single individual the overthrow of the whigs was due. He had
worked in the court through his cousin, Mrs. Masham; he
had won over the moderates in the cabinet; he had intrigued with the economical Scots; he had reunited by a
subtle diplomacy which secured for him later the name of
"Robin the Trickster" the discordant sections of the
tories; he had made himself master of both St. John and
the queen. He was not by nature a strong party man.
He was, indeed, anxious to unite moderate tories with
moderate whigs in a central conservative block, devoted to
the best interests of the nation. But circumstances were
against him, and even if they had not been so, he was not
the man to realise his ideal. He was too shifty, too in-
sincere, too much addicted to treachery and intrigue, too
jealous of colleagues, too obviously lacking in integrity
and in strength of character. In 1710 he was carried away
against his will into extreme measures by the vehemence
and violence of the reactionary host whom, as he wished
to remain their leader, he was compelled to follow.

Henry St. John, also, by inheritance and by early

association was a moderate. Born in 1678, he was a great-grandson of Oliver St. John, defender of John Hampden, colleague of Cromwell, and member of the commonwealth council of state. His maternal grandfather, too, Robert Rich, second earl of Warwick, had been a strong parliamentarian in the civil war, one of whose grandchildren (Henry St. John's first cousin) had married Cromwell's daughter Frances. Henry himself had received, in the manor house of Battersea where he had been born, a sternly puritan education at the hands of a dissenting divine, Dr. Daniel Burgess. Eton, Oxford, and the Continent had, however, effectually eradicated puritanism from his constitution, and he had entered parliament in 1701 as an irresponsible debauchee. For three years he had displayed a wild and factious toryism; but he had also manifested so great an ability and so brilliant a power of oratory that Harley (together with Marlborough) had set to work and had temporarily salved him for sanity and moderation. He had entered the Godolphin government with Harley in 1704, had worked with him, and in friendly collaboration with the moderate whigs, for four years, and had retired with him in 1708. Two years later he came back with Harley in triumph, as secretary of state, and obviously second only to his leader in importance.

Henry St. John, like Robert Harley, was carried away in 1710 by the flood of extreme tory reaction; but, unlike his leader, he did not attempt to stem it or to struggle against it. On the contrary, he flung himself into it in the hope that it would carry him to supreme power. In the interests of personal ambition he became the extreme party man, putting party before country, and humanity nowhere. He made it his business during the four critical years that closed the reign of Anne, first, to terminate the war of the Spanish Succession at any cost, so as to enable the ministers to concentrate their attention on the English succession problem, and so as to make it possible to discuss the problem with the courts of Versailles and St. Germain; secondly, so completely to crush the whigs both in parliament and throughout the country that whenever the queen should die the tories would control the situation;

thirdly, to re-establish the ascendancy of the Church of England as a political institution, at the expense of both catholics and dissenters; and, finally, to replace the landed interest in its old position of supremacy. Hence he took a lead in such measures as the harsh dismissal of Marlborough and the scandalous Treaty of Utrecht; the expulsion of Walpole from the house of commons and his commitment to the Tower; the carrying of the *Occasional Conformity* and *Schism Acts*; and the requirement of a high property qualification from all members of parliament. Rarely had there been such an orgy of riotous partisanship.

Toryism seemed well on the way to achieve by violence the utter ruin of its rivals, and its own permanent establishment in power.

Sed dîs aliter visum.

CHAPTER IX

WHIMSICALS VERSUS WHIGS AND JACOBITES
1714–1760

" Bolingbroke is, with the exception of Disraeli, the greatest shining light of toryism."—MAURICE WOODS.

" Whatever is permanent in Bolingbroke's teaching had long been anticipated in Harley's practice."—KEITH FEILING.

" I abhorred Oxford [Harley] to that degree that I could not bear to be joined with him in any case."—BOLINGBROKE.

§ 37. THE SUCCESSION CRISIS, 1714

THE tory debacle of 1714 was one of the most unexpected and amazing phenomena recorded in English history. It exceeded both in its completeness and in its suddenness even the whig catastrophe of 1681. And it was all the more remarkable because the whigs were notoriously a minority of the nation, and because only four years earlier they had been at the very nadir of unpopularity. But this quadrennium of severe adversity had welded them together, had compelled them to formulate a clear line of policy, and above all had taught them the invaluable lesson of the virtue of moderation and restraint in the conduct of affairs. Robert Walpole, in particular, had learnt from his arch-enemy, Henry St. John, on the one hand the science and art of party government, but, on the other hand, the mistake of excessive partisanship in a country of common sense, where the ultimate sovereignty rests with a largely free and not wholly unpatriotic electorate. There can be no doubt that St. John—who in 1712 became viscount Bolingbroke—went far to ruin himself, his party, and his country by his violence and unreason during the years 1710-14.

While, however, the whigs were being consolidated by persecution and purified by suffering, the tories, on the other hand, were being distracted by excess of power, torn

by schisms, and incapacitated by divergent policies. The
"whimsicals," or hanoverian tories, stood by the *Act of
Settlement*, maintained with firm determination the principle of the protestant succession, and asserted the claim
of the electress Sophia (sister of prince Rupert and granddaughter of James I.) to be regarded as heir-presumptive
of Anne. The jacobite tories repudiated the *Act of Settlement*, reaffirmed the doctrine of the divine right of kings,
and urged the recognition of the pretender as heir.
Between these rival bands of logicians oscillated the queen
and most of the ministers. If the pretender would have
abandoned his religion they would have given him their
whole-hearted support and his succession would have been
secure. But their prime devotion was to the Church of
England as by law established, and they were not prepared
a second time to run the appalling risk of placing a protestant church under the headship of a catholic king. So
long, however, as the pretender seemed to be hesitating
between the recovery of his kingdom and the salvation of
his soul they remained in an agony of hesitation.

Meanwhile the two tory leaders, Harley (who in 1711
became earl of Oxford) and Bolingbroke (who was greatly
incensed because next year he secured a mere viscounty)—
the two tory leaders, who should have united to give a
clear lead to their party—drifted apart in irreconcilable
disagreement, insensate jealousy, and mutual suspicion.
In 1712 they became obvious rivals, and two years later
their rivalry developed into open and blatant enmity. In
1714 the council chamber, and even the welkin, rang with
the clamours of their mortal animosities. Oxford, always
at heart a trimmer and a "whimsical," stood for accommodation with the moderate whigs; for the *Act of Settlement* (which, indeed, was peculiarly his own creation);
for the Church of England as a national institution which
should include all the sects that lay between the extreme
poles of catholicism and deism; for the ending of the party
system of government; and for a return to the Elizabethan
unity of the people. Bolingbroke, on the other hand, as
we have seen, had at this period of his career embarked
on a course of pure partisanship which necessitated the

destruction of the whigs, and which almost inevitably involved the adoption of jacobitism. No one laboured harder than Bolingbroke to ·persuade the pretender to make the necessary profession. He could not comprehend the conscientiousness that could sacrifice a crown to religious scruples. He himself, an avowed unbeliever, found no difficulty in attending his parish church with decorous regularity, or even in taking the communion required as a qualification for office. He was no " occasional conformist." When, then, the pretender proved to be unpervertible, Bolingbroke was bewildered. He decided, however, that his proper course would be to oust Oxford; get control of the government; fill every office both central and local with tories; and thus put toryism so strongly in possession of power that it could confidently offer the crown to the pretender on condition of his becoming protestant, and, if he refused, could confer it upon the hanoverian candidate on terms that would leave the tories in effective and permanent control of the administration.

On July 27, 1714, Bolingbroke completed the first item on his programme : he secured the dismissal of Oxford. But the operation was a painful and a noisy one, and it had to be carried on in the presence of, and through the agency of, the queen. Intense agitation and disgust, working on a constitution already weakened by disease, precipitated the unhappy queen into an apoplectic fit, of which she died on Sunday, August 1. Thus the realisation of the rest of Bolingbroke's programme was for ever frustrated. For the queen did not like or trust Bolingbroke : she knew him to be a violent and irresponsible politician, as well as an irreligious and grossly immoral man. Hence, on her death-bed, she refused to confer upon him the white staff which would have made him virtual regent of the kingdom. She conferred it, instead, upon the great whig duke of Shrewsbury, and thus made the hanoverian succession a certainty. The whig lords, who had all their plans ready, set up a provisional government and sent off post-haste for the elector George, who in Hanover had succeeded his mother, the aged Sophia, a few months previously. He promptly came, and the distracted and divided tories passed into opposition and impotence for nearly half a century. Queen Anne had in the last resort, true to the basal principle of English conservatism, preferred the church to the crown. As for Bolingbroke, his supersession was the appropriate penalty of his violence and vice. But his failure to function at this crisis of his fate, and his final fall from power, were irretrievable tragedies not only for himself, but for his party and his country. If only his character had matched his abilities he would have occupied in politics a place akin to that which Marlborough occupies in war. For in the realm of ideas, as we shall later see, he was the supreme genius of English conservatism.

§ 38. THE WHIG ASCENDANCY, 1714-60

George I. was placed upon the English throne not so much as the king of the nation as the executive agent of the whig party. He was content that this should be so. For he realised that he owed his crown to the whigs, and he was convinced that if the tories had had their way he would either have been excluded altogether or would have been accepted under conditions such as would have made his position intolerable. Hence he dismissed the tory ministers from their offices: Bolingbroke in particular he treated with marked hostility and contumely. Oxford suffered his fate with easy indifference; underwent an impeachment as part of the natural order of events; spent two comfortable years in prison, and then emerged to become a notable collector of books and manuscripts. Bolingbroke, whose courage and whose wits equally deserted him at this hinge of affairs, was scared into an act of folly fatal to himself and ruinous to his party. In March, 1715, he fled to France, joined himself to the pretender (July), and helped him to organise the 'fifteen rebellion which marked the close of the year. If anything were needed indelibly to associate toryism with jacobitism in the slow mind of George I., that thing was thus achieved by Bolingbroke. His hasty and incredibly foolish action for ever prevented his own rehabilitation in England, and it involved the tory party in nearly fifty years' exclusion from power. It was all the more mad because Bolingbroke was not, and never had been, a jacobite. He found himself both at the pretender's court in Lorraine and at the jacobite headquarters in Paris wholly alien from the superstitious, fanatical, unintelligent, and unpractical crowd that constituted the pretender's following. He did not even profess to believe in the doctrine of hereditary divine right : he was a utilitarian before that name was invented. He loathed and detested the intolerant priests who kept the pretender from apostasy by the constant exhibition of the horrors of hell. He was soon at daggers drawn with the pretender's entourage, and it required only the humiliating failure of the 'fifteen rebellion (due entirely to the abnormal incompetence of its so-called leaders) to provide an excuse for his ignominious dismissal from the jacobite service. He experienced the unique but embarrassing distinction of lying at one and the same time under the attainder or impeachment of both the king *de humano facto* and the king *de divino jure*. As for the pretender, never did even he, whose long and lethargic career was an unbroken catalogue of errors, make a more fatal mistake than he did when he dismissed Bolingbroke in 1716. For he turned his ablest servant into an implacable enemy, not only of jacobitism, but of the whole Stuart line from Mary Queen of Scots onward. And nothing—not even the fiasco of the 'fifteen and the tragedy of the 'forty-five—did so much to purge toryism, not merely from its jacobite taint, but also from its pathetic devotion to the memory of the royal martyr, as did Bolingbroke's writings during the remaining thirty-five years of his life.

While, however, Bolingbroke in exile and adversity was slowly constructing a new ideal toryism out of the ruins of the old, the whigs were enjoying the plenitude of power. From 1714 to 1762 they held a monopoly of office. If we ask what were the causes of the long continuance of their ascendancy, the reply lies on the surface of the history of the period. They had the open and whole-hearted support of the hanoverian rulers, who regarded all tories as either avowed or concealed jacobites; they had the support of the moneyed classes, who feared that a tory government would repudiate the national debt and rescind the charter of the Bank of England. They had the support of the dissenters, who dreaded a tory repeal of the *Toleration Act* and a return to the policy of the later years of Anne. Further, they were favoured by the disintegration of the tories into " whimsicals," led by Windham, and jacobites, who looked to William Shippen as their head.* A similar schism weakened the Church of England, which was no longer the nation in its religious aspect, but merely the tory party conforming to the Clarendon Code. The lower clergy—that is, the rural rectors and vicars—were jacobite almost to a man; but the higher clergy—that is, the bishops, the deans, the holders of rich crown livings, and the urban incumbents—were whigs or " whimsicals," primarily concerned to maintain the hanoverian régime. Again, the decline of the old landed gentry, and the acquisition of their estates by city magnates, transferred many tory strongholds into whig hands.

But these external and adventitious causes were not the only explanations of the prolonged ascendancy of the whigs. They developed an excellent party organisation, both in parliament and in the constituencies, under the direction and control of the great " revolution families "— Russells, Cavendishes, Grenvilles, Manners, Campbells, Bentincks, and others. Moreover, they possessed great wealth (drawn from commerce, stock-jobbing, and banking), and they used it prodigally for the purchase of power ; and to the same end they employed the extensive patronage of the crown. But over and above party management, bribery, and corruption, they had, it must be admitted, a policy in the main sound and suited to the conditions of the country at the time. They stood for political moderation ; for religious toleration ; for freedom of the press, freedom of commerce, freedom of colonisation ; for peace and for a firm refusal to become involved in the entanglements of continental politics.

* Bolingbroke, who was allowed to return to England in 1723, of course supported Windham.

Now there was, it will be observed, nothing radical or revolutionary about this programme. Indeed, the policy of peace and of freedom from foreign complications was precisely the policy for which Harley and Bolingbroke had stood under Queen Anne. Speaking generally, in fact, we may say that while the crisis of 1714 turned the bulk of the tories into jacobites, it turned the bulk of the whigs into conservatives. They ceased to attack the Church of England, for all its major patronage was in their hands; they maintained the *status quo* of the constitution, opposing all substantial reform, because they had all the machinery of government completely in their own control; they defended the hanoverian crown because it was in their pocket, and they had no desire to have it degraded or diminished. It was not easy, indeed, for a "whimsical" tory seriously to criticise the sound conservatism of Walpole and his cabinet, any more than, a century later, it was easy for Disraeli to pick holes in the seamless conservatism of Palmerston and his so-called "liberal" ministry. Nevertheless, the task of criticising whig policy and of overthrowing Walpole was the task to which Bolingbroke devoted the second half of his life.

§ 89. Henry St. John, Viscount Bolingbroke

The whigs had become conservative, but they had not ceased to be corrupt. Under their long immobile régime it is true the country became peaceful and prosperous: it is, indeed, to their credit that beneath their sway, however lethargic and bibulous it may have been, religious animosities died down, political passions cooled, and all fears of either civil wars or ministerial decapitations passed away. But, on the other hand, it is equally true that during the continuance of their power all generous enthusiasms expired, and that the country sank into a condition of gross and semi-comatose sensuality unparalleled in our history. Whiggism, as represented by the first two hanoverian kings, with their sordid courts, their sodden cabinets, their venal parliaments, and their corrupt constituencies, showed itself indifferent to religion and morality, hostile to the church as a spiritual (as opposed to a political) institution, erastian, materialistic, devoted to the service of mammon; it degraded and depressed the monarchy, establishing what Disraeli well described as a Venetian oligarchy in which the king occupied but the inoperative elevation of a doge; it was unfriendly to the landed interest and excessively favourable to the moneyed class; it lamentably hastened the transformation of the old rural England—the England of lovely villages and peaceful hamlets—into the England of factories and slums; it was indifferent to sea-power, neglectful of the navy, careless of the national honour, too much subservient to hanoverian commands; it was narrow and unimaginative, selfish and exclusive, hostile to reform, keeping people as well as king from due influence in the state.

All these truths were pointed out and emphasised by Bolingbroke during the quarter-century of incessant activity that followed his return from exile after 1723. He had, as we have observed, completely shed and discarded his jacobitism. He came back to England a " whimsical " or hanoverian tory, eager to be reconciled to the Georges, and anxious if possible to secure complete rehabilitation at their hands. But he was filled with the most intense hatred of Walpole, his old antagonist, his supplanter, the purloiner of his ideas, the man who blocked all his efforts to attain entire restoration to property, peerage, parliament, and power. His attack upon his enemy was twofold. On the one hand, he laboured to organise an overwhelming coalition against him. It was to consist of jacobites such as Shippen; " whimsicals " such as Windham; dissentient whigs such as Pulteney, Carteret, and Chesterfield; and patriotic " boys " such as William Pitt (not yet " the elder " or earl of Chatham). He actually did form some sort of coalition—a chronic opposition to Walpole's government. But the bond that united its constituent members was too slender to stand the strain of success : its only unifying principle was the negative one of detestation of the prime minister and desire to compass his destruction. On all the high positive problems of politics and religion there was too wide a

divergence of opinion among the coalitionists to allow of
any real cordiality or effective co-operation. In vain
Bolingbroke tried to formulate an agreed programme
and to propound a common coalition policy. Being
excluded from parliament, he was compelled to make
the attempt by means of the press. Hence, as the
second mode of assault upon his strongly entrenched foe,
he launched a tremendous and long-sustained literary
attack. In *The Craftsman*, published periodically during
the decade 1726-36, he and his associates poured forth
masses of miscellaneous missiles upon their immobile and
contemptuous antagonist. The most ponderous and formidable were Bolingbroke's *Remarks on the History of
England* (1730-31) and his *Dissertation upon Parties*
(1733-34). In the former he subtly suggested that Walpole combined all the evil qualities of all the bad
ministers of English kings from Becket to Buckingham;
in the latter he argued that the distinction between the
two parties, whigs and tories, which had been valid under
Charles II. and James II., had lost all rational meaning
since the Revolution of 1688-89, in the achievement
whereof the two parties had combined. In the course of
his disquisitions, and in his search for a political platform,
Bolingbroke succeeded in committing himself and his
" whimsical " associates to a good many constitutional
reforms. So that under George II., while the whigs in
office stood for the maintenance of the *status quo*, the
tories in opposition appeared as the radical reformers!
Bolingbroke advocated *inter alia* the repeal of the *Sep-
tennial Act*, the shortening of parliaments, the holding
of more frequent elections, the introduction of vote by
ballot, the disqualification of interested voters, the exclusion of placemen and pensioners from the legislature,
the limitation of the powers of the cabinet, the publication
of voting lists, and the reporting of debates in the two
houses. But not all Bolingbroke's organising, all his in-
triguing, all his writing, all his programmes and pledges,
sufficed to dislodge Walpole from his fortified office. Things
looked most hopeful for the coalition in 1733-34 when Walpole's *Excise Bill* provoked an unexpected (and wholly

irrational) outburst of popular hostility; but Walpole placidly withdrew the obnoxious measure, and calmly continued as before. Bolingbroke in disappointment and disgust retired once more to France, gave himself up to historical and philosophical study, and allowed the ineffective coalition to collapse.

Bolingbroke remained abroad, with occasional visits to England, from 1735 to 1744. During this period, aloof from the political arena, he formulated a new policy for the opponents of the whigs. It was the policy of what he called " patriotism " as opposed to partisanship. It implied the personal government of a popular prince, the fusion of parties, the abolition of the cabinet system, the restoration of the privy council to power, and the general return to the happy condition of national unity that prevailed under Elizabeth. The figure round whom Bolingbroke's patriotic hopes centred was Frederick, prince of Wales, eldest son and heir-apparent of George II. The prince, as was the custom with the Hanoverian hopefuls, was on the worst possible terms with his father and his father's ministers. Hence he seemed to be the proper leader for a national opposition. To prepare the way for a general attack on the party system of government, Bolingbroke wrote his *Spirit of Patriotism* (1736), in which he called his fellow-countrymen to the service of the commonwealth as a whole. This he followed up with his more famous *Idea of a Patriot King* (1739), in which he framed a programme for Frederick, and for himself as Frederick's chief minister, in the coming new age. 'Twas all in vain. Frederick, in any case, was a knave and a fool, totally incapable either mentally or morally of returning to Elizabeth. Moreover, he died in 1751. And towards the close of the same year Bolingbroke himself passed away.

§ 40. THE DECLINE OF JACOBITISM AND WHIGGISM

Bolingbroke was a man of varied and splendid abilities. He had considerable learning and a prodigious memory, combined with remarkable power of original thought and a conspicuous freedom from convention. He was endowed, too, with a splendid eloquence that made him a master of assemblies, and he had a natural capacity for leadership. But his fine abilities were marred, especially in his early life, by fatal moral weaknesses. In private life he was a drunkard and a debauchee; in public life he tended to be violent, unscrupulous, and factious. There can, indeed, be little doubt that his personal vices so undermined his constitution and so weakened his will that in the crisis of his fate in 1714 he displayed an irresolution and a cowardice that ruined both himself and his party. There can be equally little doubt that his violence and factiousness defeated their own ends and reduced him ultimately to impotence. He did not succeed in any of his great designs : he failed to become prime minister; he failed to establish the tories in power; he failed to construct an effective coalition against the whigs; he failed both to destroy the party system of government and to find a patriot king.

He did, however, succeed, albeit posthumously, in one great task, perhaps more difficult than all the rest. He succeeded in educating, and indeed in transforming, the tory party. His teachings, of course, accorded with the needs of the times, or they would not have been effective. Nevertheless, to have made them effective at all was a remarkable achievement. For it meant educating a large and devoted body of men out of doctrines which, though erroneous, they held with a passionate enthusiasm, and out of loyalties which, though obsolete, were dearer to them than life itself. In the first place, he educated them out of jacobitism, and out of much more than jacobitism. For he was not content merely to expose and denounce the pretensions of the pretenders; he exposed and denounced the doings and the dogmas of the whole alien and disastrous house of Stuart from its accession onwards. Not even the royal martyr himself escaped condemnation : he was held responsible for the civil war, and his doctrines of divine right and passive obedience were declared to be false. The revolution of 1688 was defended, declared to be necessary, and claimed as a model of conservative resistance to royal encroachments. His cry was "Back to Elizabeth." In the second place, he educated the tories out of religious intolerance. He showed them that the age of persecution was past; that it was plain that neither roman catholicism nor protestant nonconformity could be stamped out; that it was not proper to attempt to stamp them out; but that the ideal policy would be to incorporate them all in a single national institution, wholly undogmatic and rational.

But Bolingbroke, in conjunction with the *Zeit Geist*, did not merely purge toryism of jacobite sentimentality and religious exclusiveness; he gave it a positive creed. He taught it to strive, first and foremost, for a monarchy strong-based on popular goodwill and wholly above political party; a monarchy, also, restored to its proper powers and prerogatives; a monarchy representative of the unity of the nation on its secular side. He taught it, secondly, to seek to re-establish a national church representative of the unity of the people of England on the spiritual side; a church so broad as to include all schools of thought; a church so tolerant that not even deists, dissenters, and catholics need feel themselves outside it. He taught it, thirdly, to labour for a reform of the constitution, and in particular of the representative system; a reform that would secure more frequent appeals to the electorate, the exclusion of placemen and pensioners from parliament, the suppression of bribery and corruption, and the diminution of the influence of the peerage in the constituencies. He taught it, fourthly, to safeguard the interests of the landed classes; to maintain the amenities of rural England; to resist the encroachments of commercial wealth, and to discountenance the spread of upstart towns. Finally, he taught it—and this was a new gospel—to turn its eyes away from continental conflict and military glory, and to devote its energy and will to the building of an invincible fleet, the securing of the command of the sea, and the development of a world-wide empire. In the positive message of Bolingbroke to the young men who surrounded him in his old age—among whom the first William Pitt was by no means the least eminent—can be clearly heard the preliminary cadences of both tory democracy and conservative imperialism.

And the age was ready to receive the message that Bolingbroke had to deliver. The time for the revival of toryism was fully come—not, of course, the old toryism of the Stuart period, but the new toryism that freely accepted the *Bill of Rights* and the *Act of Settlement*; that frankly recognised religious dissent; and that was genuinely loyal to the hanoverian crown. For both the once formidable rivals to this new toryism were by the middle of the eighteenth century discredited and decadent. Jacobitism, on the one hand, had, with the failure of the 'forty-five invasion, passed beyond the pale of practical politics. The old pretender, James Edward, although he lingered on earth till 1766, sank into hopeless lethargy in Rome; the young pretender, Charles Edward, who survived till 1788, became an irreclaimable dipsomaniac and debauchee; the last member of the family, Henry, intimated his abandonment of the Stuart claims by taking orders in the Roman church and becoming cardinal bishop of Frascati, where he died in 1807, a pensioner of the British Government. On the other hand, whiggism had outlived both its usefulness and its popularity. It had in its day done good service by its policy of laissez-faire : it had allowed the country to settle down to peaceful money-making after the distracting religious and political conflicts of the idealistic seventeenth century. But it had become otiose and reactionary, purposeless and corrupt. Moreover, after the peril of jacobitism had passed away, it had increasingly tended to split into factions, wholly unprincipled, divided simply by the desire for office and emolument. When George II. died in 1760 the hour for the overthrow of the long dominance of the whig oligarchy had also struck.

CHAPTER X

KING'S FRIENDS VERSUS KING'S FOES
1760–1794

"A disposition to preserve and an ability to improve, taken together, would be my standard of a statesman."—EDMUND BURKE.

"Burke at one time or another expressed almost the whole faith of modern conservatism."—*Spectator*, July 23, 1927.

"Burke's writings are the political Bible of all who are on the side of law, religion, property, and order."—A. A. BAUMANN.

§ 41. THE REVIVAL OF ROYALISM

IN 1760 both whigs and tories were conservative. The whigs, however, were more than conservative: they were reactionary. They wished to maintain unchanged the revolutionary settlement of 1688–89. They were satisfied with things as they existed—that is to say, with an erastian church, an oligarchic constitution, and a merely ornamental crown. They were opposed to all substantial reforms. The tories, on the other hand (as educated by the great triumvirate Harley, Swift, and Bolingbroke) were less reactionary and therefore more genuinely conservative. True, their cry was "Back to Elizabeth," and their ideal date was 1588 rather than 1688. But they did not construe their slogan in any too literal sense: it did not mean to them back to Elizabethan institutions so much as back to the Elizabethan spirit; back to the united people; back to the national church; back to the living and adaptable constitution; back to the active and patriotic monarchy; back to the England of prosperous manors and peaceful villages; back to the Britain that in those spacious days ruled the waves.

Bolingbroke, the prime inspirer of the new toryism, had in 1760 been nine years dead. But he had left behind him two men pledged to the perpetuation of his policy—

151

namely, the first Pitt and the third George. Most unhappily, the two did not for six critical years (1760-66)
learn to work together, and even then their co-operation
was rendered ineffective by Pitt's failing health and
George's obstinate unintelligence. They soon, moreover,
after 1766, drifted apart again in respect of important
matters of practical administration—matters involving
immediate decision, if not fundamental principle—such
as American taxation, Indian government, and Continental war. Hence what might have been one of the most
powerful partnerships in our annals was deprived of half
its virtue and efficacy. Nevertheless, each of the two
"patriots," though generally insulated from the other,
had a notable influence on the course of events—an
influence in Pitt's case almost wholly to the good, by
reason of his lofty character, high ability, and pure
devotion to his country's cause; an influence in George's
case almost wholly to the bad, by reason of his craft and
guile, his feeble intellect, and his devotion to selfish and
sectional ends.

William Pitt the elder,* Bolingbroke's greatest disciple, was in 1760 at the height of his fame and his power.
A dissentient whig, he had, from his first entry into parliament a quarter of a century earlier, rebelled against the
sordid domination of Walpole and his satellites : he had
opposed Walpole's Hanoverian subsidies (thereby in-
curring George II.'s fierce detestation); he had condemned
the Spanish convention of 1739; he had denounced the
chronic corruption of the government; he had assailed the
very bases of the whig monopoly of power in speeches
directed against the party system in general and cabinet
administration in particular. By 1746 so great had become the influence of his torrential eloquence that
George II. was compelled, much against his will, to admit
him to the ministry. His great chance had come in 1757,
during the course of the Seven Years' War, when his
inspiring courage and organising genius had snatched victory from humiliation and defeat, and within two years

* Born 1708, entered parliament 1735, created earl of Chatham
1766, died 1778.

had given to Britain undisputed command of the sea, complete possession of Canada, and secure ascendancy in India. Thus, as we have observed, in 1760 he was at the height of his fame and power. So famous and powerful, indeed, was he that the young George III., who wholly failed to appreciate his greatness, was jealous of him, and never rested till he secured his resignation (October, 1761). For five years Pitt remained in retirement, and then, recalled by George, he (as earl of Chatham) constructed a ministry on the pattern displayed in Bolingbroke's *Patriot King*—that is to say, a ministry framed on non-party lines. It included whigs such as Grafton, tories such as North, independents such as Shelburne and Townshend—a hotchpotch of incongruities and incompatibles which Burke in a famous passage compared to "a tessellated pavement without cement." It is doubtful whether in any circumstances Chatham could have got it to hold together. As it happened, his health broke down, his mind gave way, he withdrew from affairs, and before he recovered and returned to public life his crazy ministry disintegrated "in hideous ruin and perdition." Its failure demonstrated one truth with conclusive clarity, at any rate to the observant eye of Burke—namely, that if you want parliamentary government you must have a cabinet, and if you want a cabinet you must have strongly organised, sharply defined, and mutually exclusive political parties. Chatham, then, failed—spectacularly and fortunately failed—in his attempt to abolish the party system of government. But, before he died in 1778, he did much to break the power of the whig oligarchy, to purify politics of its worst corruptions, to rouse the patriotism of the people, to revive the prestige of the monarchy, to make the British name respected throughout the globe, and to turn British energies to the establishment of a secure command of the sea and the development of a world-wide empire. It was, in particular, he who—under the inspiration of Bolingbroke's idea—introduced into conservatism the noble strain of a large and lofty imperialism.

George III., Bolingbroke's other disciple, was quite incapable of appreciating, or even comprehending, the finer and more permanently important elements of Chatham's policy—meticulous purity in politics, unselfish patriotism, establishment of a secure command of the sea, expansion of empire. He was, however, whole-heartedly with him in his detestation of the party system; in his determination to end the whig domination; in his dislike of cabinet government; and in his desire to revive the monarchy on a popular basis. The textbook of his limited and imperfect education had been that manual of personal rule which Bolingbroke had written for the guidance of his defunct father, Frederick, prince of Wales. His tutor, the marquis of Bute, and his mother, Augusta of Saxe-Gotha, combined to impress upon his retentive unintelligence the simple but devastating maxim : " George, be king." Circumstances, too, at the time of his accession conspicuously favoured a royal attempt to return to Elizabeth. The whigs, devoid of ideas, bankrupt of principles, obese with prosperity and corruption, were hopelessly divided into gangs struggling for office and emolument—the Newcastle gang, the Bedford gang, the Grenville gang, and so on. On the other hand, the tories, chastened by adversity, purged of jacobitism, inspired by new ideals, were ready as a strong united body to rally round a young monarch who " gloried in the name of Briton," who was devoted to the anglican church, who hated the whigs and the oligarchic system that the whigs had set up, and who professed himself resolute to revert to the tudor constitution under which England in the old days had become prosperous at home and respected abroad. The rising tide of royalism was further swelled by various powerful literary influences—*e.g.*, by the writings of Jonathan Swift, Alexander Pope, and Samuel Johnson; by the strong monarchism of Blackstone's *Commentaries on the Laws of England*; and by the sustained bias in favour of kingly authority displayed in Hume's *History of England*. Altogether in 1760 the stars in their courses seemed to combine to foster and further George's design to re-establish personal government in Great Britain.

§ 42. REACTION AND RADICALISM

If George III. had been an abler man, or if, alternatively, he had been lucky enough to make his experiment in royal autocracy during less troublous times, he might very well have achieved his purpose. For the crown in the middle of the eighteenth century had still immense reserves of undistributed prerogative—*e.g.*, it still had power to control ministers, determine policy, bestow patronage, grant pensions, influence elections, create peerages, fill places, exert social pressure, and in countless other ways exercise a subterranean sovereignty. But, on the one hand, George III. was, although exceptionally brave and resolute, a very ignorant and stupid man, with an insane jealousy of men cleverer than himself, and with a peculiar faculty for selecting dull mediocrities as his ministers. On the other hand, he and his satellites were called upon during the twenty years of their ascendancy (1760-80) to face problems of unprecedented magnitude and difficulty, including the problems produced by the revolt of the American colonies; the transformation of the East India Company from a commercial to a political organisation; the demand of the Irish for a repeal of the penal laws; the conclusion of a great peace and the waging of a world-wide war; the rise of a new radical party with insistent demands for parliamentary and other reforms; and the beginning of the industrial revolution with its vast social and economic disturbances. Not unnaturally the attempt of abnormal incapacity to deal with abnormal complexity resulted in chaos. Rarely has a great nation, in the absence of any sudden catastrophe, sunk so rapidly or so completely from the summit of prosperity and glory to the abyss of humiliation and disaster as did the British peoples during the two decades of George's personal misrule.

Rarely, moreover, has there been a period within the compass of British history when the voice of sane conservatism was less listened to. Edmund Burke, it is true —the man in whom the very genius of sane conservatism was incarnated—entered public life in 1765 and began then

to play his part in great affairs. But during all this heyday of George III.'s effort to establish benevolent despotism
throughout his three kingdoms and their dependencies,
he was but a voice crying, with scarce an echo, in the
wilderness. The political battles of the period were waged
by rival armies of extremists. Rigid reactionaries were
faced by a new and alarming rabble of rabid radicals.

The reactionaries who rallied to the side of George, and
supported him in his endeavour to "dish the whigs,"
destroy the cabinet, and revive the royal authority, became known collectively as the "king's friends." They
were a miscellaneous and unconcatenated crowd. They
included ex-jacobites (such as Murray) and whimsicals
(such as North), disgruntled whigs (such as Bedford), and
mere courtiers (such as Bute); but the bulk of them were
placemen and pensioners attached to the king's cause by
personal interests and by the prospect of titles, emoluments, and power. They were resisted, of course, by the
official whig party, which at the time of George's accession, under the leadership of Newcastle, shared power with
a handful of patriots headed by the elder Pitt. But the
official whigs, as we have seen, had by this date entirely
exhausted their mandate; they had long since given the
country such political and religious benefits as they had
been able to bestow, and they were, oligarchically, at least
as reactionary as the "king's friends" were monarchically.
And the circumstances of the time urgently called for
movement and for reform. The growth of population,
the spread of education, the development of industry, the
concentration of artisans in towns, the collapse of the
Elizabethan apprenticeship system, the breakdown of the
mediæval machinery for the joint regulation of prices and
wages, made some measure of parliamentary reform imperative. The vast increase of the American colonies,
together with the discovery of the limitless economic resources of the New World, made the mercantile system of
English imperial administration wholly obsolete and intolerable, and clearly indicated the need of large concessions of colonial self-government. Similarly, reforms
in both the Indian and the Irish executives were obviously

overdue, as also was the general relaxation of the penal laws directed against catholic and protestant dissenters.

Since the " king's friends " and the whig oligarchs in their conflict for office and for power were almost wholly engrossed with the problem of the restoration or the restriction of the royal prerogative, the new problems of the new age had—until Burke by the magic of his genius showed the way of safe solution—to find expression in the raucous clamour of ignorant and violent, yet suffering and pitiful, mobs of radicals and revolutionaries.   Since they had no direct representatives in parliament, they were driven to give voice to their grievances and demands by means of the comparatively novel and extremely disconcerting devices of press agitation, pulpit declamation, and public meeting.   Hence American rebels, Indian revolutionaries, Irish bog-trotters, and English radicals made the political welkin (already resonant with the clash of " king's friends " and whig oligarchs) echo with the roar of novel controversy.

Particularly noteworthy was the formation, in and around 1769, of the new radical party in England.   It was generated in the wild agitation that centred in John Wilkes and his Middlesex election struggle of 1768-69; it received the effective formulation of its principles from the vitriolic pen of the mysterious and still unidentified " Junius," who poured forth his epoch-making letters during the period November, 1768, to May, 1772; it finally formulated its immediate programme at the hands of Charles James Fox and the Westminster Reform Committee—a programme which in the nineteenth century provided the famous " six points " of the people's charter.

To the radical proclamation of the sovereignty of the people, the " king's friends " could merely reassert the divine institution of monarchy, and the whig oligarchs the sanctity of the original contract.   To the popular demand for parliamentary and other reform neither the government nor the official opposition could do more than reaffirm the perfection of the constitution as established in 1689.   To the requests of the Americans, the Indians, and the Irish for concessions—requests, it is true, that were frequently both offensive in form and immoderate in substance—the king and his ministers were disposed to make no response save a flat and indignant negative.

§ 43. Reform and Revolution

The king's ministers during the first decade of the period of George's personal misgovernment (1760-70) were numerous and ephemeral. With great adroitness George broke up the powerful Newcastle-Pitt coalition which he found in office on his accession, compelling Pitt to resign in October, 1761, and Newcastle in the following May. Then he appointed a ministry after his own heart under his own old tutor, Lord Bute. By means of bribery on a scale that made the disbursements of Walpole or of New-castle appear both economical and ethical, the king secured support for his ministry in parliament; but—an omen of the dawn of democracy—Bute's ministry was speedily driven out of office by its intense unpopularity throughout the country. Bute personally was hated as a " North Briton " and as a royal favourite possessing a sinister influence over both the young king and his mother. As a minister he was widely denounced both for the ferocity of his attack upon the whigs and for the betrayal of the national interests in the Peace of Paris, with which he apologetically concluded the glorious Seven Years' War. Before he had been a year in office he dared not go about without a strong bodyguard. At last the strain of con-stant terror became too much for him; he handed in his resignation and fled (April, 1763). For three years George was compelled to jog along with one or another of the various combinations or permutations of whigs—ministers whom he intensely disliked, and against whom he con-tinually plotted and intrigued. Then he came to terms with the elder Pitt, and together they made their disas-trous experiment in non-party government (1766-68)—an experiment continued after Pitt's resignation, with even more tragic failure, by the duke of Grafton (1768-70). Finally, in 1770, George found his *fidus Achates* in his foster-brother, Lord North, and the twelve years of their association as autocratic monarch and servile minister all but achieved the ruin of Britain and its dominions. The year 1780, as we have already remarked, may be taken as the date of the depth of British degradation. That year witnessed the Gordon riots wherein London remained for a week at the mercy of plundering and incendiary mobs; it saw the loss of the British command of the sea and the consequent disruption of the first British Empire; it beheld America virtually independent, South-East India ravaged by Hyder Ali of Mysore, Gibraltar invested by the Spaniards, the North Sea infested by hostile Dutch men-of-war and Yankee privateers, and the island of Jersey in French occupation. That the king was himself personally responsible for this condition of disaster and disgrace was clearly indicated by the motion which Mr. John Dunning (afterwards Lord Ashburton) proposed and carried through the House of Commons on April 6, 1780: "That the influence of the crown has increased, is increasing, and ought to be diminished." The mere fact that he could carry such a motion through a venal assembly nearly one-half of whose members were tied creatures of the court indicates the intensity of the rage and despair that filled the nation as a whole.

Lord North, terrified by the associated spectres of invasion, disruption, and revolution, implored the king to let him resign. But for two more years George compelled him to remain and to work the royal will. But then the crowning catastrophe of Yorktown (October, 1781) and the ineluctable necessity to make peace at any price with the victorious Americans and their European allies, compelled George to let him go and to recall the whigs to office (April, 1782). The belated and almost fatal experiment of the Hanovarian monarch to revive the Tudor autocracy was over.

The whigs came back under their chosen chief, the marquis of Rockingham, who was happy in having the supreme genius of Burke to guide and direct him. Unfortunately, however, Rockingham lived for only three months after his appointment; and then commenced a struggle which raged for a year and a half (July, 1782, to

December, 1788) as to whether the king should present a
prime minister to parliament, or parliament should impose one upon the king. The king selected Shelburne as
Rockingham's successor, and rejected Portland, the whig
nominee. The whigs by themselves were not strong
enough to turn Shelburne out, and before seeking for
allies they allowed him to complete the necessary (and
necessarily unpopular) preliminaries for peace with
America, France, and Spain. Then, when early in 1783
these were achieved, they (led by Fox) made an amazing
and wholly scandalous coalition with the tories (under
North) to drive Shelburne from office and compel the
king to accept Portland as prime minister, with Fox and
North as his two secretaries of state. Since Shelburne,
an able but enigmatical and ineffective man, could not be
persuaded or compelled by George to fight, the king was
forced for the moment to accept the negligible Portland,
the abominable Fox, and the treacherous North (no longer
the king's friend, but his declared enemy). But he never
rested until he had found a champion to overthrow them.
And this champion he discovered in the young William
Pitt, second son of the great Chatham, a youth of twenty-
four, who had been in parliament but three years.

William Pitt was imposed by the king on a hostile parliament, and for three months (December, 1783, to March,
1784) he was continually defeated in all his motions and
measures. But he held on, strong, first, in the support
of the king, and, secondly, in the conviction that the corrupt and unprincipled Fox-North coalition did not repre-
sent the opinion of the electorate or the general will of the
country. The election of March, 1784, amply confirmed
the justice of his conviction. The supporters of Fox and
North were defeated with unprecedented thoroughness, and
Pitt came back at the head of an overwhelming majority.

If George had expected to find in the youthful Pitt
a complacent tool, he was speedily disillusioned. Pitt
emphatically repudiated royal interference in policy. He
reasserted with Walpolian emphasis the dignity and
authority of the prime minister. He restored the cabinet
system of government, and he built up in parliament and

the constituencies a new middle party, essentially conservative in its character, pledged to support him in a
policy of moderate and cautious reform. His great
ministry lasted for no fewer than seventeen years. Its
fruitful period was the initial ten years of peace (1783-93).
In that halcyon decade Pitt attempted to tackle the thorny
problem of parliamentary reform; he supported his friend
Wilberforce in his efforts to secure the suppression of the
slave trade; he concluded an important commercial treaty
with France; he restored British prestige abroad; he re-
moulded the government of both India and Canada; above
all, he effected with masterly ability a complete reorganisation of the financial system of the country. He showed
himself, in short, to be an almost perfect exemplar of the
principles of conservative reform—that is to say, reform
which improves operation without destroying continuity.

But in the midst of his beneficent and pacific career the
French Revolution broke out. Its immediate effect in
this country was to put a stop to reform. Its ulterior
effect was to plunge Great Britain into a war that caused
reaction to resume its sway for a whole generation.

§ 44. THE NEW CONSERVATIVE COALITION

To treat of the French Revolution—that theme of multi-
tudinous monographs—is fortunately beyond the scope of
this essay. We are concerned with the great upheaval—
the most momentous and portentous event in modern
European history prior to the war of 1914—only as it
affected British parties. On them, indeed, it had a profound and permanent influence. No doubt, even apart
from the French Revolution, they would soon have had to
be reconstructed. For both the old parties—whigs and
tories—were obsolete parties. They were divided on defunct issues. They were out of touch with the realities of
the changing eighteenth century. They were both of
them, in a narrow sense, conservative parties, differing
only as to what they wished to conserve. Both of them,
however, were dominated by sections that were more than
conservative—namely, distinctly reactionary and obstin-

ately opposed to even necessary reform.   Hence they were
alien from the true spirit of conservatism, which is progressive as well as retentive.   They needed to be revitalised,
rejuvenated, reconstructed, re-energised.   Over against
them, abounding in licentious vitality and lawless energy,
the forces of the coming democracy, denied legitimate expression and representation, were constrained to use
irregular and dangerous means of manifestation.   This
was the day of secret and subversive societies.   Even
before the outbreak of the French Revolution there arose
in England such organisations as " The Society for Supporting the Bill of Rights " (1769); " The Constitutional
Society " (1771); " The Society for Constitutional In-
formation " (1780), and " The Quintuple Alliance "
(1782).   But it was the French Revolution that precipitated the political transformation and made it spectacular.
On the one hand, it stirred up the exultant democrats to
new and prodigious activity; the existing societies
doubled their propaganda; many fresh societies, each
more revolutionary than its predecessors, came into
being.*   On the other hand, it forced the whigs and the
tories to face reality.   They were brought into the valley
of decision, and were compelled to align themselves on
this side or on that.   For the French Revolution was one
of those cardinal events which admit of no half-and-half
views.   It was either very good or very bad; either the
dawn of a new and better day or the beginning of the
end of Christian civilisation.   The radicals, of course, as
represented on the platform and in the press by such men
as Thomas Paine, Joseph Priestley, and Richard Price,
welcomed it with enthusiastic fervour : it seemed to herald
the speedy recognition of the sovereignty of the people,
and the establishment in Britain of secularist repub-
licanism.   But, as we have seen, the radicals at this date

---

* Prominent among the new societies were " The Society for
Free Debate " (1791), " The Corresponding Society " (1792), and
" The Friends of the People " (1792).   One of the urgent needs
of historical scholarship at the present moment is a good account
of the constitutions, the aims, and the developments of these
revolutionary organisations.

had but little representation in parliament: they lay outside the pale of the estates of the realm. Within that
pale the tories were solid in their antagonism to the revolution. It menaced the existence of all the institutions
that they held most dear; it challenged all the principles
which to them were most sacred and authoritative; it
threatened the destruction of the church, the subversion
of the constitution, the abolition of the crown, the confiscation of the land, the schism of the community, the
ruin of all the respectable classes. The whigs, however,
were divided: it was through their ranks that the line of
schism ran. A small minority, led by Charles James Fox,
joined themselves to the radicals, and glorified the revolution in such apostrophes as: "How much the greatest
event it is that ever happened in the world, and how much
the best." They fraternised with the French, palliated
their worst excesses, and exalted their achievements as
models for English imitation. The immense majority of
the whigs, however, under the masterly and enlightened
guidance of Edmund Burke, remained on the other side
of the dividing line. As sound conservatives they aligned
themselves with the tories in defence of the principles
which the disciples of Rousseau repudiated, and of the
institutions which the followers of Robespierre threatened.
In October 1790 Burke published his epoch-making *Reflections on the Revolution in France*: within twelve
months it passed through eleven editions in England, and
before long it was translated into most of the European
languages, and widely disseminated throughout the Continent. Few works have had a more immediate and
decisive influence upon public opinion.

In May 1791 occurred, amid dramatic circumstances
in the House of Commons, the final and irreparable breach
between Fox and Burke: Burke crossed the floor of the
house and took his seat between his old antagonists, Pitt
and Dundas. In July 1791 he issued his famous *Appeal
from the New Whigs to the Old*, in which he showed con-
clusively that he with his cautious conservatism, and not
Fox with his reckless radicalism, represented the genuine
and original whiggism of the days of William III. and

Anne.   Three years later (July 1794) the leaders of the
Old Whig majority — Portland, Fitzwilliam, Spencer,
Windham, Grenville—accepted Pitt's invitation to join
his administration. The formation of this coalition, which
remained permanent and became a complete fusion,
marked the creation of a new and composite conservative
party. Its strength lay in the landed interest, the back-
bone of the old toryism, combined with the moneyed
interest, the sinew of the old whiggism. For more than a
quarter of a century it controlled the destinies of Britain,
rendering to the United Kingdom and the Empire the
inestimable services of saving them alike from the horrors
of sanguinary revolution from within and of destructive
conquest from without.

The major prophet of this new conservatism was
Edmund Burke, and as his works still remain the supreme
expositors of conservative principles, it is necessary for
us to pause to contemplate his career and his teachings
as a whole.

CHAPTER XI

THE CONSERVATIVE COALITION VERSUS REVOLUTIONARIES
1794–1822

" The true conservative party is that which Burke formed in the last decade of the eighteenth century by drawing after him to join Pitt the best of the whigs, leaving the remainder under the care of Fox and Sheridan."—A. A. BAUMANN.

" In the conservative party we must have those who are essentially reactionary, who think that the world is perfectly good as it is, and who do not desire to make any improvement. That element must always be in our party; but it would be a bad thing for the party, and a bad thing for the country, if it ever became the dominating influence."—A. BONAR LAW.

§ 45. EDMUND BURKE

HENRY THOMAS BUCKLE speaks of Burke as " one of the greatest men, and, Bacon alone excepted, the greatest thinker who has ever devoted himself to the practice of English politics." Buckle rightly discerns the secret of Burke's pre-eminent distinction : he was at once a philosopher and a man of affairs. He wrote no abstract treatises on political theory, but he investigated and expounded, in the light of fundamental principles, every practical problem as it arose. He was of course an " old whig "—that is to say, an eighteenth-century conservative, who believed that the Bill of Rights and the Toleration Act of 1689 had established in the British Isles and for the British peoples a system of government in all essentials as near perfection as the wit of man could devise. He was devoted to the maintenance of a tolerant church, an aristocratic constitution, and a limited monarchy. He entered the arena of high politics in 1765, at the age of thirty-six, having made a name for himself in the world of literature, and having served a painful apprenticeship to administration in the service of " single-speech Hamilton." In 1765 he became secretary to Lord Rockingham, the " old whig " prime minister, who soon found for him a seat in parliament. In parliament he remained for nearly thirty years, and during that long period he was called upon to formulate the " old whig " policy—that is to say the sound conservative policy, midway between the reactionary obscurantism of the " king's friends " and the revolutionary illuminism of the radicals and the " new whigs "—respecting five problems of prime magnitude. These problems were, first, the government of Ireland (his native country, and the scene of his sufferings under Hamilton); secondly, the American rebellion; thirdly, the king's personal misrule in England; fourthly, the administration of the East India Company; and, finally, the French Revolution.* In respect of Ireland, America, England, and India, he stood forth definitely and prominently as a conservative reformer: he advocated with unparalleled power and persuasiveness toleration for Ireland, conciliation in America, the purification of English politics from corruption, the purging of Indian administration from fraud and tyranny; he was the avowed opponent of the evil and unintelligent Court and of its parasitic ministers. He traced most of the political evils of the day to the supersession by the king and his friends of the cabinet system of government, as developed by the whig aristocracy of the post-Stuart period. In respect of France, however, he was compelled to show himself as a convinced anti-revolutionary. He had to change his front, though

* Concerning Ireland, see the admirable collection of Burke's *Letters, Speeches, and Tracts on Irish Affairs*, edited by Matthew Arnold (Macmillan, 1881). Concerning America, specially note Burke's two great speeches, April 19, 1774, and March 22, 1775, together with his letter to the sheriffs of Bristol, April 3, 1777. Concerning George's misgovernment, read Burke's *Observations* (1769) and *Thoughts on the Cause of the Present Discontent* (1770). Concerning India, see Burke's speeches on Fox's India Bill, 1783, the Nabob of Arcot's Debts, 1785, and the impeachment of Warren Hastings, 1788-95. Concerning the French Revolution, consult Burke's *Reflections* (1790), his *Appeal from the New Whigs to the Old* (1791), and his *Letters on the Regicide Peace* (1795-97).

not his ground. The principles on which he denounced the destructive enormities of the French jacobins, and the subversive propaganda of their English sympathisers, were precisely the same as those which had led him to support the pleas of Irish catholics, American colonists, English economic reformers, and oppressed Bengalese. No man was ever more fully and profoundly consistent throughout the whole of his career. He was always a conservative even when most emphatically a reformer; always a believer in evolutionary progress even when most vehemently a condemner of revolutionary change.

If we ask what were the foundation principles of Burke's conservatism, the answer, I think, can be summarised in the two expressions, first, the religious basis of society, and, second, the organic nature of the state. As to the first, Professor John MacCunn, in his admirable work on *The Political Philosophy of Burke*, thus states and expounds it: "Burke's political religion has its roots deep in three convictions. The first is that civil society rests on spiritual foundations, being indeed nothing less than a product of a divine will; the second, that this is a fact of significance so profound that the recognition of it is of vital moment, both for the corporate life of the state and for the lives of each and all of its members; and the third, that whilst all forms of religion within the nation may play their part in bearing witness to religion, this is peculiarly the function of an established church, in which the consecration of the state finds its appropriate symbol, expression, and support."* Burke formally and openly resumed the position taken up by Hooker in his *Ecclesiastical Polity*, and asserted that " in a Christian commonwealth the church and the state are one and the same thing, being different integral parts of the same whole."† It will be observed that this reversion to Hooker marked on the one hand a distinct departure from Locke, whose works on *Civil Government* and *Religious Toleration* were still regarded as the scriptures of official whiggism, and,

* MacCunn, J., *Political Philosophy of Burke* (1913), p. 122.
† Burke's speech in the House of Commons on Fox's motion for the repeal of the penal statutes, May 11, 1792.

on the other hand, a clear advance on Bolingbroke, with whom, rather than with Locke, Burke was ideally akin. Locke regarded society as natural, the state as contractual, and the church as an institution wholly separate from the state, concerned entirely with the affairs of the other world beyond the grave. Bolingbroke, on the contrary, maintained the intimate association of church and state, but to him, as a non-believer in the Christian revelation, the church was merely a political institution established and supported for reasons of state. He, like Hobbes before him, attended church in the same spirit, and with the same reservation, as that with which Naaman bowed down in the house of Rimmon. Burke, however, was a profound and convinced believer, who regarded his membership of the established church as of the very essence of his citizenship. He was, nevertheless—as became a man whose mother was a catholic, and whose schoolmaster had been a quaker—widely tolerant. If he held that every country should have an established church, he was quite prepared to admit that that church might properly be presbyterian in Scotland and catholic in Ireland.

Burke's second great political principle was the organic nature of the state. He habitually regarded it as a living entity, subject to growth and liable to decay and death. This view was entirely accordant with the political philosophy of Bolingbroke; but it was strikingly alien from the contractual, legal, mechanical, and inorganic conception of Locke. This organic view of the state gives us the key to Burke's specific doctrines, both as a reformer and as an anti-revolutionary. On the one hand, he held and taught that if an organism is to live and thrive it must continually adapt itself to its environment; so that if in Ireland, in America, in England, or in India circumstances materially changed, it was suicidal to retain unaltered the obsolete administrative system of an earlier day. On the other hand, he proclaimed the truth—specially applicable to revolutionary France—that changes too rapid and too complete, changes made without respect for tradition or prescription, resembled not a surgical operation conducive to restored health, but a decapitation fatal to continued existence. He condemned the French because, instead of reforming their ancient and venerable constitution, they swept it all away—church, aristocracy, monarchy, provincial estates, feudal law, the whole social, political, and ecclesiastical system—and tried, with deplorable results, to start everything afresh on mechanical lines, according to the abstract formulæ of Rousseau's *Social Contract.**

§ 46. THE REVOLUTIONARY AND NAPOLEONIC WAR

The British Government, warned by Burke as to the true nature of the French upheaval, watched the proceedings of the revolutionists with growing disgust and apprehension. They saw constitutional monarchists, such as Mirabeau, give place to the visionary republicans of the Gironde, and these again speedily superseded and exterminated by the sanguinary savages of the Jacobin Club. Nevertheless, in spite of their increasing horror and alarm, for some three years (1789-92) they had no serious thought of war, and no intention whatsoever of intervening in the French tragedy. Pitt, in particular, was pacific. He was engaged in many projects—financial, commercial, colonial, philanthropic, diplomatic—which imperatively demanded tranquillity and international goodwill. At first, indeed, he rather welcomed the revolution, for by limiting the power of the Bourbon monarch it relieved him from the menace of an inveterate foe: in 1790, for instance, when he became involved in a dispute with Spain concerning Nootka Sound, he was grateful to the French ministers who refused, as their predecessors of the old régime would not have done, the appeal of Spain for help. So peaceful, in fact, were his purposes that in 1792 he actually (in the interests of economy) reduced both the army and the navy, and in a budget speech on February 17 of that year uttered the remarkable words: " Unquestionably there never was a time in the history of this country when from the situation of Europe we

* For a fuller treatment of Burke by the present writer, see *Social and Political Ideas of the Revolutionary Era* (1930, Harrap and Co.).

might more reasonably expect fifteen years of peace than at the present moment."

Even as Pitt uttered those false-prophetic words the French republicans of the Gironde were spoiling for war, and no more than sixty-three days elapsed before they compelled the unhappy and reluctant Louis XVI. to declare it. The flame of conflict thus kindled on April 20, 1792, spread until it covered the whole of the European continent, and it raged with scarcely any intermission for more than twenty-three years. Yet, even so, Britain was not dragged into the fray until the early part of 1793. The causes which ultimately made the maintenance of peace impracticable were primarily the French occupation of Belgium; the opening of the Scheldt in violation of recently concluded treaties; the horrible massacres of September, 1792; the decrees of the following November wherein the jacobins of France incited their correspondents in all countries to follow the French example and overthrow their monarchies, promising them aid in their enterprise; and, finally, the execution of Louis XVI., which automatically terminated diplomatic relations between the two countries. It was the French who took the last step by formally declaring war on February 1—less than twelve months after the promulgation of Pitt's amazing false prophecy.

The effect of the outbreak of the war upon British parties and politics was immediate and profound. We have already noted how it broke the whigs into two irreconcilable sections, causing the majority to ally themselves with the tories in a permanent conservative coalition. Further, it put an instant stop to Pitt's reform projects, and converted Pitt himself from a highly successful successor of Walpole to an extremely incompetent imitator of his own father, that inspired war minister, the earl of Chatham; it also transformed him from a rigid economist to a reckless spendthrift, who saddled the country with a national debt which it has never been possible to pay off. Thirdly, as the war prolonged itself, and as one continental coalition after another was broken up by the apparently unconquerable might of the emancipated French, Britain found herself on no fewer than three occasions* alone in face of the overwhelming military ascendancy of her enemy : Ireland was threatened ; India was menaced ; England herself had to face the prospect of imminent invasion. Hence everything had to be sacrificed—men, money, and, worse still, cherished rights and liberties—under the imperative need to safeguard mere existence. And what made the peril more extreme, everywhere throughout Britain and the Empire were zealots and traitors who openly advocated revolution, fraternised with the French, and sought their country's destruction. Ireland broke into overt rebellion ; in India the powerful ruler of Mysore accepted French citizenship and plotted for the expulsion of the English ; in Britain herself the subversive societies spread disaffection and fostered mutiny in army and navy. In the circumstances both government and nation were seized by a not unreasonable alarm : the danger was, indeed, formidable and pressing. They did not, however, like their jacobin enemies in similar conditions, entirely lose control of themselves, and give themselves up to the panic-stricken cruelty of a " reign of terror." They did, however, rightly and necessarily, pass and enforce a series of precautionary and repressive measures. Not to have done so would have been to betray their trust. Among the most important of these was an Alien Act (1793), which excluded foreign immigrants, a Traitorous Correspondence Act (1793) which punished those found in communication with the enemy, a Habeas Corpus Suspension Act (1794) which enabled the administration, when it felt it necessary, to refuse speedy trial to political suspects, and finally a Seditious Meetings Act, a Treasonable Practices Act, and an Anti-Combination Act (all 1799), which marked the limit of curtailed liberty.

Most conspicuous, however, of all Pitt's war measures was the Act of Union which brought Ireland's much-abused independence to an end, and fused the two realms of Great Britain and Hibernia into a single United Kingdom (as from January 1st, 1801). After the deadly Irish

* 1797-99, 1800-01, and 1804-05.

rebellion of 1798 had been suppressed, and the French force which landed to assist it heavily defeated, Pitt realised that the only alternatives before the two countries were either entire separation or complete union. The risks of separation seemed at the moment to be too great, hence he decided for union, and, with the help of his able and devoted disciple, Lord Castlereagh, carried it through with a high hand. The means that he adopted in order to persuade the Irish Parliament to vote its own extinction were such as could be justified only in a time of war and when national existence is at stake. But even in the critical state of war which then prevailed he did one thing which cannot be defended. He held out to the Irish as part of the price of fusion the hope of catholic emancipation. No doubt he meant to fulfil his half-promise; but he had not taken the trouble to consult the king, and when the inopportunely and obstinately conscientious George positively refused his assent to any Catholic Emancipation bill, Pitt did not enforce his will, but merely resigned. Pitt's failure and default in the Irish crisis of 1801 was a fruitful source of subsequent woe. It undermined the foundations of good faith, and substituted a quicksand of suspicion and resentment.

§ 47. The War Ministries

The untimely and lamentable death of Pitt in his forty-seventh year, when once again he was prime minister (January 23, 1806), left the conduct of the war and the government of Britain to a band of smaller men who in the anxious circumstances of the time could do little more than haltingly follow in his footsteps. It is true that they included men of character like Castlereagh, and men of genius like Canning, but none combined those high qualities of mind and heart which made Pitt the greatest of all English prime ministers. He had not, of course, the dynamic intensity of his father; but Chatham was at his worst in a cabinet; he was the wrecker not the maker of ministries, the destroyer not the creator of parties. Pitt, on the other hand, was supreme in the art of the management of men. He could lead, could accompany, could follow, as circumstances demanded. He had power to conciliate or to crush as occasion required. Above all, he had the faculty of inspiring confidence, of generating courage, of securing co-operation, of compassing coalition. He shared with Burke the glory of creating and consolidating that great conservative combination of loyal and patriotic whigs and tories under whom Britain and the Empire were saved from foreign conquest and internal disruption. That day in March, 1794, which saw Burke in the house of commons leave his seat near Fox and Sheridan and cross to the side of Pitt and Dundas was a cardinal date in the history of English political parties. Burke was pre-eminent in intellect and emotion: he brought with him a wealth of principle and passion. Pitt was dominant in will and administrative capacity. Together they formed an alliance of unprecedented stability and power. It is sad that they were destined to work with one another for so short a period of time. Had they lived longer the whole complexion of the nineteenth-century history of England might have been different. They would never have made the mistakes which their smaller successors made in respect of catholic emancipation, parliamentary reform, the corn laws, and the government of Ireland. Burke, however, died in 1797, leaving the dissemination of his ideas to men like Southey and Coleridge; Pitt, although thirty years younger than Burke, survived him less than nine years, bequeathing his policy to a group of disciples among whom Castlereagh and Canning, Peel and Palmerston, Huskisson and Melbourne were the most prominent.

But, although Pitt died in middle age, on the twenty-fifth anniversary of his entry into parliament, he had accomplished a great and enduring work. He had purified the administration from some of its worst corruptions; he had immeasurably elevated the tone of public life; he had re-established the cabinet form of government; he had revived the office of prime·minister, and had raised it to incontestable pre-eminence; he had transformed the house of lords, making it representative of money as well as of land; he had rehabilitated the party system, and had taken the leading share in the work of reconstructing the old and obsolescent factions in accordance with the needs and the problems of the new revolutionary age.

He was succeeded as head of the government by his cousin William, Lord Grenville, who, even more than Pitt himself, was a disciple and devotee of Burke. Grenville in particular was an enthusiast, beyond either Pitt or Burke, for the cause of catholic emancipation, and it was because he could not refrain from pressing his obnoxious principle on the consecrated George that he was soon compelled to resign (March, 1807). Grenville's ministry had been broad-based; it had been called euphemistically the "ministry of all the talents"; its policy had been distinctly progressive and liberal. It was succeeded by a ministry that was markedly more reactionary and less enlightened. This ministry remained substantially unchanged for the long period of twenty years (1807-27). During that time it was controlled in turn by three premiers—namely, Portland (1807-9), Perceval (1809-12), and Liverpool (1912-27)—all of whom were conspicuous by their opposition to catholic emancipation and parliamentary reform, the two matters of prime prominence in the domestic politics of the day.

Until 1815, however, no problems of domestic policy compared in importance with the problem of the conduct of the war and the deliverance of Europe from the tyranny of Napoleon. In dealing with these great matters the ministry showed itself to be extremely energetic and successful. It is not, indeed, too much to say that Canning and Castlereagh fell hardly short of Nelson and Wellington themselves in the prominence of the parts they played in the overthrow of the Napoleonic hegemony and the restoration of the European balance of power. Canning, as secretary of state for foreign affairs, 1807-9, achieved the decisive coup of the seizure of the Danish fleet, countered Napoleon's Berlin and Milan decrees by means of the masterly Orders in Council, and, above all, initiated the Peninsular War, which marked the beginning of the end of Napoleon's career of conquest. Castlereagh—

less spectacular than Canning, but superior to him in the drudgery of administration—as secretary for war, 1807-9, made Wellington's successes in Portugal and Spain possible by his admirable military organisation; while later, as secretary for foreign affairs, 1812-22, he was the main factor in the building up of the decisive fourth and fifth coalitions against Napoleon. He was also one of the " big four " whose policies and wills determined the general lines of the European resettlement made at Vienna in 1815.

To the brilliance and fascination of the pantomimic Canning justice, and more than justice, has been done by an interested posterity. To the solid worth, the superb courage, the high executive ability, and the masterly achievement of the tongue-tied Castlereagh only recently has adequate recognition been given. It is safe to say, however, that the researches of Mr. Arthur Hassall and Professor C. K. Webster have for ever rendered his reputation secure from the aspersions of his prejudiced contemporaries Shelley, Byron, and Brougham, and from the ill-informed abuse of their uncritical successors. Among great and noble patriots, and among statesmen of wide European outlook, Castlereagh deserves a high and honourable place.

§ 48. THE DISTRESSFUL YEARS 1815-22

The long continuance of the Revolutionary and Napoleonic wars, together with the constant recrudescence of subversive violence at home, had the natural and almost inevitable results, first, that the majority of the progressive and reformative movements evident before 1789 were stopped,* and, secondly, that power passed into the hands of the more reactionary members of the conservative coalition. During the war this did not matter much. It was, indeed, to some extent an advantage. For the reaction-

---

* It must not be forgotten, however, that it was during the war period that the first Factory Act was passed (1802); that the Slave Trade was abolished (1807); and that both educational and missionary enterprise was most vigorous and successful.

aries were precisely those who were most firmly resolved
to perform the necessary tasks of breaking the power of
Napoleon abroad, and of crushing incipient revolution at
home.

After 1815, however, circumstances materially changed.
A new England had arisen during the preceding quarter-
century of tumult; novel conditions imperatively called
for an adjustment of the constitution and a revision of the
law. The time for mere reaction was past; the time for
cautious reformation had come. In particular, English
industries, abnormally stimulated by the demands of the
belligerent nations, had caused the growth of mushroom
factory towns and the aggregation of large and squalid
artisan populations. And at the same time the imperative
need to make the British Isles self-sufficing in the matter
of food had kept multitudes of normally unnecessary
labourers on the land. Hence the re-establishment of
peace conditions, coupled with the disbanding of the war-
time armies and navies, produced a problem of unemployment and destitution unprecedented in its magnitude.
Never before had England known so distressful a period
as the seven years that followed the triumph of Waterloo
and the pacification of Vienna (1815-22).

A wise conservative government—that is, one in which
the pioneers of cautious reform were dominant—would
have recognised the impossibility of maintaining unchanged the laws and institutions of the sparsely popu-
lated rural England of the Tudors and Stuarts. There
was urgent need of new and stringent factory laws, sani-
tary laws, housing laws, poor laws, to counter the evils of
the new industrial system. There was need to repeal or
modify many of the old statutes relating to apprenticeship, settlements, and combinations of working-men, that
were unsuited to the novel conditions. There was also a
need to resume in a new and sympathetic spirit those projects of parliamentary reform and religious emancipation,
those schemes for the better government of Ireland and
India, those suggestions for the modification of the mercantile system and the navigation laws, those financial
and administrative reforms, which had occupied the atten-

tion of Pitt and Burke during the years preceding the
lamentable catastrophe of the French Revolution. The
natural evolution of the British polity had been arrested
in 1789, precisely at the moment when social and economic
changes demanded an exceptionally rapid and complete
re-adaptation of the civic organism to the novel environment. Incomparably more urgent, therefore, was the
need of progressive statesmanship when the return of
peace in 1815 once more made it possible for ministers to
turn their thoughts to domestic affairs.

Unfortunately, most unfortunately, during the critical
seven years 1815-22 the leaders of reaction reigned
supreme in the ranks of the conservative administration.
Liverpool, Castlereagh, Eldon, Sidmouth, and even the
great Wellington himself, all of them, filled with dread of
" the revolution," seemed to think that the only function
of government was the maintenance of order and the suppression of rebellion. Their view, it is true, was not mere
obscurantism and perversity. They were all of them able
men, patriotic citizens, Christian gentlemen, and sincere
humanitarians. They were right in supposing that the
triumph of lawlessness in England would be the greatest
of all possible disasters to the labouring and suffering
classes. And those who were demanding reform—radicals,
republicans, communists, atheists, anarchists—were busy
making the cause of reform hateful and intolerable by
associating it with wild revolutionary dogmas and with
outbreaks of sanguinary violence. The Spa Field riots of
1816, the march of the " blanketeers " of 1817, the election disturbances of 1818, the " Peterloo " tumult at
Manchester in 1819, all combined to convince the venerable reactionaries at Whitehall that the country was
tottering on the verge of a catastrophe similar to that
which had lately wrecked the French monarchy and involved Europe in a quarter-century of bloodshed. It
must be remembered, too, that there was no professional
police force in the country at that date, so that any mob
could at any time secure easy possession of almost any
place and work its evil will. The calling out of the military was the only remedy for disorder—a remedy slow in

operation, imperfect in application, and deplorable in consequences. In the circumstances the passing of the " Five Acts " of 1817, and of the " Six Acts " of 1819, was a mild and necessary precaution. These laws suspended the Habeas Corpus Act once more; they prohibited the carrying of arms by civilians, and the military training of unauthorised persons; they strengthened the laws of libel, sedition, and blasphemy; they limited the licence of the press, and prohibited the holding of revolutionary assemblies. They were sound and necessary measures; but they were not enough. They ought to have been accompanied by sympathetic inquiries into the causes of the discontent that were producing the widespread riots and rebellions. And the conservatives were the very persons who ought to have conducted those inquiries. For, as taught by Burke and his living representative Coleridge, they held the organic theory of the state, and believed that the health of the body politic implied the well-being of all its members of every class. They, too, were the very persons who ought to have taken up the problem of parliamentary reform where Chatham and Pitt had left it; and to them the cause of catholic emancipation was peculiarly bequeathed by Burke and Windham. Alas, that in the day of their power they were not able to rise to the height of their opportunity. They did good service by maintaining indispensable law and order; but they failed in that they left the causes of necessary reform in the dangerous hands of radicals and revolutionaries.*

* Cf. Smith, F. E. [Lord Birkenhead], *Toryism* (1903), p. lxxx: " Moderate measures of reform in 1816 would have prevented the crisis of 1832, and would have given the party a new lease of life."

CHAPTER XII

CANNINGITES VERSUS REACTIONARIES AND
RADICALS
1822–1834

"Those who resist indiscriminately all improvements as innovations may find themselves compelled to submit to innovations although they are not improvements."—GEORGE CANNING.

"In philosophic grasp and expression of political ideas he [Canning] has been surpassed only by Burke."—H. W. V. TEMPERLEY.

"The Party! What is the meaning of a Party if they don't follow their leaders? Damn 'em; let 'em go."—DUKE OF WELLINGTON.

§ 49. GEORGE CANNING

IN England by the year 1822 the panic caused by the French Revolution had died down, although on the Continent it endured in an acute form for another thirty years, and even after 1852 never wholly passed away. But in England, in spite of the fact that Liverpool's long premiership lasted till 1827, in 1822 the character of his ministry subtly changed: until that date it had been dominantly reactionary; from that date it became conservatively reformative. The change was not due to any perceptible alteration in Lord Liverpool himself. He remained as before, only more so. Of all the line of British prime ministers he was, indeed, the one who displayed the fewest positive characteristics of any sort. His merit was his mediocrity. He did not impose his opinions or his determinations upon his colleagues in the cabinet; he took his tone from his company, and in his mild emulcent personality harmonised antagonisms, mollified antipathies, unified incompatibilities. No one but he could have kept together in one team men so diverse and dominating as Castlereagh and Canning, Wellington and Huskisson, Palmerston and Peel. The value of his achievement was

179

most fully realised and appreciated after his fatal illness
and resignation, when the oils and vinegars that he had
emulsified, the acids and alkalis that he had neutralised,
began to react upon one another with disintegrating consequences.   The quiet success of his fifteen years' incon-
spicuous governance of Britain was due to his generous
self-effacement, his transparent honesty, his imperturbable
good humour, his unfaltering bravery, his unquestioned
loyalty, his complete freedom from ambiguity, and his
remarkable business capacity.   These private virtues more
than atoned for an almost complete lack of ideas, a total
absence of imagination, and an entire incapacity for inspiring leadership.

For his cabinet was embarrassingly rich in men of commanding power.   Until 1822 Castlereagh was the outstanding figure; a statesman, indeed, of world-wide influence.
He as secretary for foreign affairs (1812-22) played an all-
important part in building up the coalitions that overthrew Napoleon; in determining the provisions of the
Vienna settlement; in establishing and maintaining the
concert of Europe; in formulating and enforcing the
British doctrine of non-intervention in the internal affairs
of other states.   At home he was the strong supporter of
order and authority, the proposer of the necessary although
unpopular Six Acts of 1819.   He was a man of the highest
personal courage, sublimely indifferent to both the
plaudits and the objurgations of the mob.

Castlereagh's death in 1822 opened the way for the
return to high office, and to supreme influence in the
cabinet, of George Canning.   He and Castlereagh had long
been antipathetic : they represented two different types of
character and two different orders of conservatism.   In
1809 their mutual animosities had involved them in a duel
(wherein Canning was wounded), and had caused the
collapse of Portland's ministry.   True, they had much in
common.   Both were Ulstermen of about the same age;
both had arrived at conservatism after a bout of rabid
radicalism; both were avowed disciples of Pitt; and both,
as secretaries for foreign affairs, pursued substantially the
same policy.   But Castlereagh was the proud, reserved,

titled aristocrat, trained in administration, sound in judgment but unimpressive in debate, scrupulously honourable and disinterested, a citizen of Europe. Canning, on the other hand, was a brilliant, conceited, ambitious, and pushful parvenu of the middle class, trained in school and college debating societies, erratic in judgment but a veritable Rupert of oratory, incurably addicted to intrigue, obviously self-seeking, awkward and difficult to get on with, insular in his interests and outlook; nevertheless a political genius, gifted with vision and insight, capable of inspiring immense enthusiasm and devotion in men who, like the young Disraeli, viewed him from afar. It fell to his lot, as Liverpool's foreign secretary (1822-27), to make vitally important decisions respecting the Concert of Europe, the independence of Latin America, and the revolt of the Greeks against the Turks. As a member of Liverpool's cabinet he favoured and supported the conservative reforms that distinguished the years 1822-27 from the preceding septennium of reaction—*e.g.*, the revision of the criminal code, the repeal of the settlement and anti-combination laws, the amendment of the navigation and mercantile acts, the reorganisation of the national finances. The conservative creed which he expounded and exemplified was a curiously composite one. From Bolingbroke he took his reverence for monarchy, his belief that the king should actively participate in politics, his intense dislike of the whig oligarchy; from Walpole he inherited his respect for the office of prime minister and his acceptance of the cabinet mode of administration; from Pitt he learned the principles of freedom of trade and devotion to the cause of catholic emancipation. But Burke was his great master. It was Burke who opened his eyes respecting the French Revolution, converted him from incipient jacobinism, and made him the principal parliamentary antagonist of the "regicide peace." As an avowed disciple of Burke he emphasised the religious basis of society and the organic nature of the state, opposed revolutionary change, but steadily advocated economic and social reform. Burke, too, combined with Bolingbroke and Pitt in impressing upon him

the necessity of religious toleration.   One unfortunate
prejudice, however, he acquired from Burke—namely, a
prejudice against parliamentary reform; that is to say,
against a democratic extension of the franchise, and
against a novel redistribution of seats.   Circumstances
had changed materially since Burke's day, and the old
parliamentary system needed readjustment to the new
conditions.   Canning was the very man who should have
undertaken the readjustment.   But he remained blind to
his great opportunity.   Probably if he had lived but a few
years longer he would have realised the necessities of the
occasion.   For in 1830 his followers, the " canningites "—
Melbourne, Palmerston, Huskisson, Dudley, and the rest—
took up the cause of parliamentary reform and helped to
carry the Act of 1832.   But in 1830 Canning himself had
been three years dead.   In April, 1827, he succeeded
Liverpool as prime minister.   But even then he was a
dying man, and in August of the same year he passed
away, at the age of but fifty-seven.   Had he lived, the
whole course of the subsequent history of conservatism
would have been different.   Whatever his attitude towards
parliamentary reform, he would never have made the
mistakes of Wellington, and he would certainly have called
the bluff of Grey and Brougham.   And as to the other
great issue of the day—namely, catholic emancipation—
he was one of the oldest, most consistent, and most enthusiastic advocates of that long-overdue concession.*

   * Cf. Alington, C., Twenty Years (1921), p. 96: " The year
1827 marks a turning-point in the history of English parties.
Had Canning lived and prospered, the tory party would have
learned to appreciate him as it learned later on to appreciate
Disraeli, and he would have found it as easy as his successor did
to achieve one of those restatements of tory principles which
good tories distrust and good whigs despise, but which arc
necessary for any party which is to be a living force in the
country." For a different opinion, however, see Cooke, G. W.,
History of Party (1836-37), vol. iii., p. 542.

§ 50. Catholic Emancipation

The policy and practice of religious persecution was, of course, the *damnosa hæreditas* taken over, together with many other undesirable antiquities, by protestantism from mediæval catholicism. It was not, however, original to Christianity in any of that religion's protean shapes or forms; for it was derived from that old tribal or political conception of religion—common alike to Greeks and Romans, Jews and Barbarians—which identified worship with citizenship, piety with loyalty, rudimentary church with incipient state. At the time of the Reformation, and for long after, there was no serious thought among men in authority of any sort of toleration : victorious catholicism burned out protestantism in enormous *autos-da-fé*; victorious protestantism suppressed catholicism by test acts, recusancy laws, and devastating fines. The two could not live together, any more than the subjects of two rival monarchs could peacefully occupy the same tract of territory. Thus in England and Scotland catholics were excluded from office and from parliament as adherents of an alien and hostile power; while in Ireland they were, after 1689, subjected to still more formidable disabilities because of their active and belligerent support of the Stuart and anti-British cause.

The eighteenth century, however, which prided itself on being an " age of reason," saw a marked diminution of religious enthusiasm. To decaying faith persecution appeared to be an irrational anachronism. The Act of Toleration (1689) itself, as we have observed, was a revolutionary recognition of the separation of church from state. Both catholic and protestant nonconformists, abstaining from treasonable correspondence, settled down loyally as innocuous sects. Hence very soon a movement commenced for the removal of their political disabilities. As to protestant nonconformists, from 1727 onward annual Acts of Indemnity relieved them from all practical inconveniences : they were exempted from the penalties imposed by the Corporation and Test Acts; so that the formal repeal of these Acts in 1828 made no difference to their actual status. As to the catholics, however, the case was different. They did not benefit from either the Toleration Act or the annual Indemnity Acts; for they were barred from office and from parliament not only by the Corporation and Test Acts, but also by the oaths of allegiance and supremacy exacted from all servants of the state. Dread of catholicism was slow to die down in Great Britain : the papacy to British minds was associated with Marian burnings, jesuit conspiracies, Spanish armadas, gunpowder plots, secret treaties, jacobite invasions, and countless other menaces to the peace and security of this island kingdom. Nevertheless, gradually, under the influence of whig indifference and radical secularity, relaxation of the recusancy laws began to be made. Conservatism, which naturally clung to the mediæval ideal of the *Respublica Christiana*, was brought to see the necessity of religious equality by the arguments of such "men of light and leading" as Bolingbroke and Burke. In 1778 Savile's Act, and in 1791 Mitford's Act, removed some of the more oppressive disabilities of catholics; while in Ireland catholics were admitted to the franchise in 1793. But both in Great Britain and in Ireland they continued to be excluded from office and from parliament. Nor, as we have noted, did the repeal of the Corporation and Test Acts in 1828 help them. For the oaths of allegiance and supremacy still remained as insuperable barriers.

But no sooner were these Acts repealed than a tremendous agitation began, especially in Ireland, for the complete removal of the remaining disabilities. During more than thirty years it had been impending; for so far back as 1795 Earl Fitzwilliam, the lord-lieutenant of Ireland, a convinced emancipationist, had committed himself to the granting of the catholic demand. Irish hopes had mounted high; but Fitzwilliam had failed to carry the cabinet, and he had had to retire. Pitt and Portland, the two men who counted, were both in favour of emancipation; but they did not think that it could safely be conceded to the Irish catholics apart from a union between Great Britain and Ireland which would lessen the probability of a catholic persecution of Irish protestants. Hence one of the inducements which led the Irish parliament to vote itself out of existence in 1800 was the expectation that union would be immediately followed by emancipation. Pitt's resignation when he failed to secure the king's consent to emancipation was a poor compensation for the intense disappointment which this breach of faith entailed. From this time onward the problem of catholic emancipation rent the conservative ranks in hopeless schism. Pitt, Grenville, Castlereagh, Canning, all were for it; Wellington, Sidmouth, Eldon, Peel, all were against it. In 1812 Lord Liverpool, that man of peace and compromise, proclaimed catholic emancipation to be an open question, and allowed the members of his cabinet to take any line upon it that they liked. In doing so he abdicated leadership, suspended cabinet government, and relegated the realisation of Irish hopes to the Greek Kalends. In 1827 Canning, on becoming prime minister, prepared to face the problem. Hence, *inter alios*, Wellington, Sidmouth, Eldon, and Peel all refused to serve under him, and he was compelled to form a coalition with the more moderate of the " new whigs "—*e.g.*, Lansdowne, Brougham, and Tierney. These, of course, were all emancipationists. There seemed, then, good hope of a settlement of the question. But once again the hope was dashed, this time by the early death of Canning (August, 1827). And hope was succeeded by blackest despair when Wellington took Canning's place as prime minister, bringing with him Sidmouth, Eldon, and Peel, and soon compelling all the canningites to resign. The schism in the conservative ranks now became open and irremediable. Stark reaction reigned, and the progressives were driven into exile.

In these circumstances of discouragement and exasperation the Irish catholics, under the resolute and able leadership of Daniel O'Connell, took decisive action. A parliamentary vacancy having occurred in County Clare, O'Connell got himself elected, although as a catholic he could not take the oaths. In vain the house of commons refused to receive him and ordered a new election. He was again returned, and the Irish prepared themselves to compel by force of arms his recognition as their representative.

Then Wellington and Peel, faced by the prospect of civil war, made the great surrender. They conceded to violence what they had refused to grant to argument. They brought in a Catholic Emancipation bill, and carried it against their former supporters by the aid of the radicals, the new whigs, and the canningites. They had, indeed, made a gross mess of the matter, and in doing so they had inflicted a grave injury upon the constitution. They disrupted their party; they engendered an incurable distrust of their own political integrity; they betrayed their followers; they were false to their own convictions; above all, by yielding to the threat of violence, they taught the revolutionaries in Ireland and the radicals in England a lesson which they were only too ready to learn—namely, that they could get anything they wanted if they were prepared to shed blood in order to procure it. Incidentally, they vindicated Canning and doomed themselves to everlasting execration for having deserted him in 1827.*

§ 51. PARLIAMENTARY REFORM

The duke of Wellington was a great soldier, but an execrable politician. He treated the members of his cabinet as though they were junior officers whose sole duty was to obey his commands; he regarded political controversies as mere campaigns the issue of which was to be determined by strategy and force; he looked upon principles merely as positions which were to be held or abandoned as circumstances might require. On one occasion, during the short period when he had canningites in his ministry, he complained to Lady Salisbury : " One man in

---

* For the speeches of Wellington and Peel in defence of their abdication of principle, see Smith, F. E., *Toryism* (1903), pp. 184-193. For an attempt to justify their conduct, see Ramsay, Miss A. A. W., *Sir Robert Peel* (1928), pp. 111-121. For a measured condemnation of their betrayal, see Clark, G. K., *Peel and the Conservative Party* (1929), pp. 4 and 39-40.

the cabinet wants one thing, and one another. They agree
to what I say in the morning, and then in the evening
they start with some crotchet that deranges the whole
plan. I have not been used to that in the earlier part of
my life. I have been accustomed to carry on things in
quite a different way. I assembled my officers and laid
down my plan, and it was carried into effect without any
more words." As to principles, he seemed unable to distinguish them except geographically : " We hear a great
deal," he said, " of whig principles, and tory principles,
and liberal principles, and Mr. Canning's principles; but I
confess that I have never seen a definition of any of them,
and I cannot make to myself a clear idea of what any of
them mean " ! It was an incalculable disaster that, at the
crisis of its fate in the first half of the nineteenth century,
the conservative cause should have been in the hands of
such a leader. For the great qualities of the duke, his
lofty and noble character, the splendid services that he
had rendered in his proper sphere, his unequalled reputation in the world, combining as they did to give him almost
dictatorial power, conduced to make his political failure
the more spectacular and deadly. He had made an appalling bungle of the catholic emancipation business : he had
conceded the Irish demands in circumstances that deprived
the concession of all reconciling value; his gift excited no
gratitude, for it had been extorted by violence; his surrender merely excited the insatiable rebels to plan further
successive attacks upon the established church and the
British constitution. Whilst the Irish were working up
their next agitation, against the payment of tithes and the
maintenance of the union, he was called upon to deal with
the other crucial question of the day—namely, parliamentary reform. Once again he made a colossal and disastrous muddle of the matter.

The problem of parliamentary reform had been before
the country for two generations, and it was a problem
with which the moderate conservatives were peculiarly
fitted to deal. For the essence of the problem was the imperative need to adapt the venerable and admirable institutions of the past to new conditions. The two kindred

necessities were, first, cautiously to extend the franchise so as to include such of the new commercial middle class and the new industrial artisan class as were fitted by character, position, and education to share in the government of Britain and the Empire; secondly, carefully to redistribute seats so as to lessen the representation of old and decayed boroughs and increase the representation of the new manufacturing centres. The task of the moderate conservatives was to steer a safe middle course between the reactionaries, who said that no change was called for, and the radicals, who were clamouring for manhood suffrage and equal electoral districts. On this question the gulf between the radicals and the conservatives was profound. The radicals regarded the franchise as an individual right which every man could claim on the principle of universal equality; the conservatives maintained that the exercise of the vote was a public responsibility, and that the grant of the franchise should be strictly limited to those who could and would use it for the general service of the community. The radicals were prepared to sweep away all the old constituencies as completely as the French revolutionists had swept away all the ancient provinces of France; the conservatives, on the contrary, wished to retain them, however they might be regrouped or revalued, realising that the very foundations of the English constitution were laid in the ancient personalities of borough and of shire.

It was conservative reformers who had first taken up the cause of parliamentary evolution. In 1766 and again in 1770 the great Lord Chatham had advocated an increase in the number of county members in order " to counter-balance the weight of corrupt and venal boroughs," and on the second occasion he had gone so far as to prophesy that " before the end of the century either the parliament will reform itself from within or be reformed with a vengeance from without." His son, the younger Pitt, during the four years 1782-85 inclusive, introduced into parliament no fewer than three bills to remove anomalies in the representative system. His third bill was remarkably comprehensive : it included an important extension of the county franchise and the transfer of one hundred members from the old "rotten boroughs" to the new industrial towns. The French Revolution, as we have noted, put a stop to this, as to the other of Pitt's progressive projects. And until the panic caused by the Revolution passed away the advocacy of parliamentary reform was left to the handful of "new whigs" and radicals in parliament and to irresponsible agitators throughout the country. In 1820, however, Lord John Russell, a waspish "new whig," venomous in his antagonism to the reactionaries of Liverpool's government, took up the cause with (as Chatham would have said) "a vengeance," and for ten years he in the house of commons, together with earl Grey in the house of lords, assisted by a growing band of followers, made the country ring with attacks on "rotten boroughs" and radical projects of general reform. The extreme violence and irrationality of Grey, Russell, and their associates probably accounts for the fact that all sections of the conservative party during the eight years 1820-28 replied to the swelling demands for reform by a simple *non possumus*. But, although explicable, it is nevertheless lamentable that the conservatives let the settlement of this vital constitutional question pass into the hands of their enemies; and particularly lamentable, as we have observed, that Canning, the avowed disciple of Pitt, should have failed to make the matter his own.

After the death of Canning the settlement could no longer be delayed. First, the great schism in the conservative party—the division into wellingtonians and canningites—destroyed the conservative power of resistance: the canningites actually became parliamentary reformers. Secondly, the surrender of Wellington and Peel on the catholic emancipation question in 1829 showed the English radicals how to use violence to attain their ends. Thirdly, the French and Belgian Revolutions of 1830 provided fresh examples of successful revolt against constituted authority. Finally, Wellington threw down the gage of battle when, in a speech in the house of lords on October 26, 1830, he said: "I am fully convinced that the

country possesses at this moment a legislature which
answers all the good purposes of legislation, and this to a
greater degree than any legislature ever has answered in
any country whatever"; and when he announced his intention to oppose all change of all sorts. Wellington's
challenge was immediately taken up, and as the result of
a two years conflict of unparalleled ferocity the duke and
his reactionary followers were driven from their defences
and were forced to allow the revolutionary Reform Bill of
1832 to become law.

§ 52. The Disintegration of Toryism

It has rightly been said that " the Act of 1832 was not
a reform of the old constitution, but the creation of a new
one," and that " it was an entire change of system; an
advance out of one zone of politics into another; a
political revolution not less pregnant or far-reaching than
the deposition of an ancient dynasty."* It, of course,
effected some of the changes rendered necessary by the
growth of population, by the migration of the working
class, by the spread of education, and by the extension of
political consciousness. It lessened the power of the
corrupt borough-mongers; it enfranchised a large new
electorate. But it carried through these needed reforms
with a deplorable disregard of prescriptive rights, venerable traditions, and the old-established balance of the
constitution. It ruthlessly destroyed the ancient constituencies which had had an organic existence from the
Middle Ages; it abolished the rich variety of electoral
units that had characterised the old régime, substituting
for it a monotonous uniformity of villadom; it recognised
one qualification only for the possession of political power,
and that the sordid one of the possession of property;
thus, while enfranchising the ten-pound householder, it
also disfranchised multitudes of old-time electors who had
voted in virtue of other qualifications; it ignored the
various interests and groups into which the population
was divided, and recognised only the isolated individual;

* Kebbel, T. E., *History of Toryism* (1886), pp. 206 and 224.

it conceded the vote to the individual, not as a public
function to be exercised for the good of the community,
but as a private right to be used for the attainment of his
own ends; and, most fatal of all, it resulted in the transfer
of sovereignty in the state from the aristocracy of the
realm—the old aristocracy of land and the new aristocracy
of commerce—to the *petit bourgeoisie,* the lower middle
class, the unconsolidated shopkeepers of the kingdom.   It
did little for the working man of the towns, and nothing
for the agricultural labourer in the country : these were
left to find vent for their disappointment, disillusionment,
and disgust in the great Chartist agitation of 1837-48, and
in the organisation of trade unions.

Until, thirty-five years later, Disraeli took up the question of parliamentary reform in the conservative spirit,
supreme political power was vested in that lower middle
class to which the Act of 1832 assigned it.   It must be
admitted that on the whole this novel sovereign used its
lordship and dominion well.   In the very first flush of its
ascendancy it abolished slavery throughout the empire;
made the first grant in aid of education ; passed a new and
effective factory act; and carried through a great and
necessary purgation of the poor law.   It was content for
some time to work through the agency of the old leaders,
such as the " new whig " Grey, the canningite Melbourne,
and the waspishly radical Russell.   They kept it from the
worst excesses of ignorance.   But it was wholly alien from
conservatism.   It had little respect for the church, being
much addicted to protestant dissent.   It had but slight
reverence for the constitution, save that pure and reformed
part of it that dated from 1832.   It regarded the crown as
an anachronism that would soon be removed to a museum
of historic antiquities.   It was devoid of the sense of the
living unity of society, being intensely individualistic and
laissez-faire.   It was incurably hostile to the landed
interest, devoting all its thought and care to the development of manufactures, the increase of commerce, the
making of money.   It was careless of the national honour
and prestige, feeling content if only new markets were
continually opened up.   It looked upon the army and the

navy as expensive luxuries, provocative to our foreign
customers; and the empire it positively hated as an
incubus and a constant source of trouble. For these thirty-
five years, as never before, Great Britain was indeed " a
nation of shopkeepers," viewing the whole world (not to
mention the other world) from the point of view of the
private salesman.

And during these same thirty-five years the conservative
forces of the country were disintegrated and dispersed.
Mr. Kitson Clark has given us a vivid picture of their
divisions and cross-divisions: "There were some who
wished to defend the right on the sheer edge of principle,
and others who believed in the relaxing doctrines of
moderation. Some remembered Canning as a leader, some
as a necessity, some as a sin. There were free-traders and
protectionists, gold-currency men and inflationists. There
were old high-churchmen and new low-churchmen;
generally moral and generally careless men; fierce Irish
protestants, erastians, and a few of the fashionable un-
godly. There were manufacturers, bankers, and agricul-
turists; independent country members, and men who till
1830 had been usually in office."* Such was the condition
to which had been reduced the great connection that, in
one form or another, had administered the kingdom and
the empire almost continuously for seventy years—that is
to say, ever since George III. got rid of the whig oligarchy
in 1762. And if we ask what was the cause of this chaos,
the answer is simple : it was because (thanks to Liverpool's
amiability and Canning's unamiability) the reactionaries
secured dominant power and blindly resisted reform instead of leading it and controlling it ; and because these
same reactionaries (and particularly Wellington and Peel),
when they found resistance no longer possible, scandal-
ously abandoned their principles, deserted their supporters,
and did the bidding of their enemies. No party could
possibly survive as an integer after it had come to realise
that its leaders regarded its fundamental principles as no
more than strategic positions in the line of retreat of a
beaten army. The action of Wellington and Peel in the

* Clark, G. K., *Peel and the Conservative Party* (1929), p. 6.

matter of catholic emancipation for ever destroyed the possibility of trust in their leadership. The great conservative coalition which had won the war, and had saved the country from revolution, was by 1834 broken up. Would it be feasible in any shape or form to restore it? Such was the problem which first Peel (unsuccessfully) and then Disraeli (successfully) tried to solve.

CHAPTER XIII

PEELITES VERSUS LIBERALS
1834–1846

" Those [*i.e.*, conservative] principles I for one consider to be perfectly compatible with cautious and well-digested reforms in every institution which really requires reforms, and with the redress of approved grievances."—SIR ROBERT PEEL.

" The property of the country desires a conservative and not an ultra-tory government—meaning by that [ultra-tory] a government deaf to all improvement."—HENRY GOULBURN (TO PEEL).

" Sir Robert's ultimate object was to build up a great middle-class barrier, combining popular progress with constitutional principles, against the radical revolution which seemed imminent. . . . He was the great minister of the middle class." —T. E. KEBBEL.

§ 53. SIR ROBERT PEEL

THE Duke of Wellington was, in a sense, not a party man. True, all his instincts, most of his opinions, and such of his actions as were voluntary, were ultra-tory. But that was a mere coincidence : the ultra-tories fortunately happened to agree with him. He regarded himself, in the old-fashioned way of the Elizabethans, as the direct and immediate servant of the crown. For the crown, even when it was worn by George IV. or William IV., he had a profound and almost superstitious veneration. Administration under the crown he considered to be the prime function of a place-holder. " The king's government must be carried on," was one of his favourite sayings—a saying especially frequent upon his lips when, from a sense of duty, he was about to do something which he felt to be wrong—*e.g.*, to support an emancipation bill, or admit a canningite to his cabinet. But political party he did not either understand or approve of. He considered it to be the duty of *every* member of parliament to support the

king's government. Those who did not do so he looked
upon, not as "his majesty's opposition," loyal if perverse,
but as his majesty's enemies, hardly to be distinguished
from traitors and rebels. Hence, when he spoke in the
king's name he expected obedience, even though he demanded from strong anti-catholics acquiescence in an
emancipation bill, or from strong anti-democrats withdrawal of opposition to a radical measure of parliamentary
reform. By his insistence on "patriotism" (in Bolingbroke's sense of the term) and by his disregard of principle he, during the four years 1828-32, broke up the tory
party which he led, far more effectively than George III.,
during the four years 1760-64, had broken up the whig
party which he had attacked.

Sir Robert Peel, who assisted him in effecting this process of disintegration, was not so completely superior to
party connections as was his chief. If Wellington regarded
politics from the military point of view, Peel's point of
view was the commercial. Peel himself was a first-rate
business man, and the governments that he formed were
emphatically business governments, with himself as a
highly competent but extremely autocratic managing
director. No prime minister—not even Walpole, or Pitt,
or Gladstone—more completely dominated his cabinets
than did Peel; and as to parliament, well, Disraeli, who
became one of the severest of his critics, declared that he
was "the greatest member of parliament who ever lived."
Nevertheless, although, as was further remarked, he played
upon parliament as a master-musician plays upon an old
violin, he failed to realise fully the nature and the importance of parliamentary party. He too much expected that
members who acknowledged his lead would display the
submissiveness of well-disciplined factory hands; nay,
according to Disraeli, even more than that, namely, the
abject subjection of West Indian slaves. Hence, although
he showed himself to be a splendid party organiser, and
although he devised for conservatism a new party programme excellently suited to the new conditions created
by the Reform Act, he nevertheless ended by involving
his party in a ruin from which it took Disraeli a quarter of

a century to effect any sort of stable reconstruction.
Three times he changed his mind, or at any rate his policy,
on matters of prime moment—namely, on resumption of
cash payments in 1819, on catholic emancipation in 1829,
and on the repeal of the corn laws in 1846. Three times he
called upon his followers in the house of commons to
swallow their prejudices, abandon their convictions, and
desert the causes to maintain which they had been elected.
It was a strain which no political party could possibly
stand. No doubt it is true that open-mindedness is in a
politician better, as well as rarer, than consistency; and
also that the interests of the nation are to be placed before
the interests of party. But it is equally true that a statesman ought to weigh the pros and cons of great arguments
before and not after he publicly proclaims his policy and
assumes the leadership of his host; and also that the
interests of the nation are very ill-served by the splitting
up of a great political party into wrangling groups; and,
further, that if a party leader comes to the conclusion that
on any primary question (such as emancipation or protection) he and his party have been wrong and his opponents
right, he should leave to his opponents the responsibility
and the honour of carrying their policy into operation. In
other words, Peel should have left the whigs and canningites to effect catholic emancipation; Cobden and Bright to
repeal the corn laws. Apologists for Peel make all sorts of
excuses for his tergiversations. They are worthless. No
benefits which he conferred upon the country can compen-
sate for the evil which he did when he thrice broke faith
with his followers and thereby shattered the party which
he had laboriously organised and led.

The great disservice, however, which Peel did to the
country when he shattered the conservative party in 1846,
and so inaugurated a quarter-century of parliamentary
chaos, must not blind us to the fact that Peel was a great
and good man, a remarkable parliamentarian, an administrator of outstanding ability, and a legislator who placed
upon the statute book a number of measures of the utmost
beneficence. As chief secretary for Ireland (1812-18) he
did valuable work in suppressing corruption, putting down

disorder, improving education, and reorganising the police
system. As home secretary (1821-27) he displayed a fine
and progressive activity in reforming the criminal code, in
abolishing the spy system, in repealing the settlement and
anti-combination laws, and in steering the country through
the financial crisis of 1825. The years 1827-34 were not
years of glory in his career, for it was in those years that,
in conjunction with the devoted but distracted duke, he
made the irreparable mistakes of deserting Canning, abandoning principle for expediency in the matter of catholic
emancipation, and resisting parliamentary reform.   In
1834, however, recovering from his excessive subservience
to the mighty duke, he hopefully and with splendid ability
undertook the task of reconstituting conservatism.

§ 54. The Tamworth Manifesto

Peel had steadily opposed catholic emancipation until
1829, and parliamentary reform until 1832. But in spite
of his resistance both measures had been carried—the first
of them, indeed, through his own improper instrumen-
tality. That being so, he recognised two things : one, that
the two measures together effected a complete revolution
in British politics—namely, the transfer of power from a
long-sovereign protestant aristocracy to a new sovereign
nondescript bourgeoisie ; the second, that these measures,
once passed, could never be repealed, and that consequently conservatism, if it were to survive, must make its
appeal to the new lords of the constitution, the mixed
middle class. He perceived, moreover, that this dominant
middle class, being prosperous and contented, was
naturally conservative in all matters that concerned itself.
He probably realised, indeed, what is, I think, a profound
general truth, that the contented are always conservative ;
so that if you want to make people conservative, all you
have to do is to make them happy. He therefore cast
about him to see how he could capture this natural if
rather sordid and selfish conservatism of the *petit-bour-
geoisie*, and use it for the maintenance and reconstruction
of the older and loftier conservatism that was concerned

primarily with the preservation of the church, the constitution, the crown, the landed interest, the nation, and the
empire. The first seductive bait that he threw out was the
so-called Tamworth Manifesto of December, 1834.

The circumstances in which the manifesto was issued
were unusual, and indeed unique. At the beginning of
November, 1834, the Melbourne ministry (canningite and
whig) seemed firmly established in office, on the basis of a
large parliamentary majority. On the tenth of that month,
however, the second Earl Spencer died, and his death
called up to the house of peers his son and heir, Lord
Althorp, chancellor of the exchequer and leader of the
house of commons. Melbourne nominated the waspish
Russell for the vacant positions. But William IV., who
detested Russell and distrusted Melbourne himself, seized
the occasion to refuse the one and dismiss the other, calling
upon the devoted Wellington to come to his help and see
him safe through the constitutional conflict, as Pitt had
triumphantly assisted George III. in 1783. Wellington,
however, disapproved of William's action, which was
indeed an exceedingly foolish and improper one. He had,
moreover, no desire whatever to take up again the office
of prime minister in which he had failed so conspicuously
only four years before. Hence, arguing that in the circumstances the prime minister ought to be a commoner, he
advised the king to send for Peel. Now Peel, blissfully
ignorant of the crisis, was away in Italy holiday-making,
and it took nearly a month to find him and bring him
back by coach across the wintry Alps. Meantime Wellington carried on the government for him, acting with
supreme self-abnegation as first lord of the treasury, home
secretary, foreign secretary, colonial secretary, and
secretary for war. If Peel had been at home in November
he would never have allowed the crisis to develop; he
would have advised the king to recall Melbourne. But
when he arrived in December the devoted Wellington,
operating as a cabinet sole, had complicated matters too
completely, and had exasperated the waspish Russell too
extremely, to permit of anything but an attempt to face
the task of governing. So Peel formed his cabinet, secured

from the king the dissolution of the hostile house of commons, and appealed to the nation to transfer to the new management its patronage and support. It was no small thing that he asked; for in the old house of commons his followers had numbered no more than 150 out of the total of over 600. To turn so small a minority into a majority required the winning of at least another 160 seats. The only hope of success lay in the capture of a large number of the urban constituencies, wherein whiggism and radicalism—now becoming collectively known as " liberalism "— were indigenous : the county constituencies were already dominantly conservative. Hence he drew up his Tamworth Manifesto—in the form of an address to the electors of his own constituency—the object of which was to go as far in allaying the alarms of urban liberals as was possible without raising the alarms of rural conservatives. The manifesto was approved, or at any rate accepted, by the new cabinet on December 17, 1834, and it was at once issued to the country. It became and it long remained the charter of the new conservatism—that is to say, of the Peelite attempt to reconstitute and reorganise the conservative party by the incorporation in it of a prosperous, contented, and largely nonconformist urban middle class.

The manifesto began (after the necessary compliments and apologies) with a frank and full acceptance of the Reform Act of 1832 : " With respect to the Reform Bill itself, I will repeat now the declaration which I made when I entered the house of commons as a member of the reformed parliament, that I consider the Reform Bill a final and irrevocable settlement of a great constitutional question—a settlement which no friend to the peace and welfare of this country would attempt to disturb either by direct or by insidious means." It then proceeded to intimate that Peel himself and his colleagues were prepared to take up the work of reform in a sound conservative way : " If the spirit of the Reform Bill implies merely a careful review of institutions, civil and ecclesiastical, undertaken in a friendly temper, combining with the firm maintenance of established rights the correction of proved abuses and the redress of real grievances—in that case I can for myself and colleagues undertake to act in such a spirit and with such intentions." Then, finally, it proceeded to specify a number of reforms which Peel and Company were prepared to undertake—municipal reform, abolition of church rates, licensing of dissenting chapels for marriages, opening of legal and medical education to non-conformists, commutation of tithes, and so on—reforms which hitherto had been regarded as peculiarly the province and function of the liberals. Of the mention of any specifically conservative principle there was a conspicuous absence. The whole tone of the manifesto was new-whig.

§ 55. THE NEW CONSERVATISM

The Tamworth Manifesto worked miracles in the constituencies. In the general election of January, 1835, the Peelites swept the counties and won such important urban seats as those of Bristol, Exeter, Hull, Leeds, Newcastle, and York. But the miracles were not quite numerous enough to place Peel in power. He came back with some 250 supporters; indeed, he actually commanded a majority of the English members. But the Celtic fringes—Scotland, Ireland, Wales—were against him, and the total " liberal " opposition—consisting of canningites, whigs, radicals, and Irish nationalists—numbered some 370. In these circumstances Peel's tenure of office was short and troubled. He was harassed almost to distraction, and irritated quite beyond endurance, by the waspish Russell, until finally, after three months of humiliation and misery, he was driven to resign (April 7, 1835).

The " liberal " coalition came back under Melbourne, and, thanks mainly to the demise of the unappreciative William IV. and the accession of the highly appreciative and extremely dependent Victoria, it managed to maintain itself in office for six full years (1835-41). During these six years Melbourne and his mixed collection of colleagues did a good deal of excellent middle-class work. They passed the Municipal Corporations Act (1835); commuted Irish tithes (1836); lowered stamp duties on newspapers (1836); instituted the penny post (1839); established the education department of the home office (1839); settled a serious agitation in Canada by a generous grant of self-government; and conducted foreign affairs, through the efficient Palmerston, with a masterly skill that immensely increased British power and prestige. Peel with complete complacency watched the policy of the Tamworth Manifesto being carried out by his opponents. He kept on the best of terms with Melbourne, and he even effected a *modus vivendi* with the waspish Russell. He rendered the government every assistance in the passage of measures of which he approved; he joined them in resistance to the cobdenites, in suppression of the chartists, and in coercion of the Irish rebels. He ostentatiously placed the interests of the nation before those of his party; he entirely repudiated the dogma that the prime duty of an opposition is to oppose; he gave a striking exhibition of the facility with which the lion can lie down with the lamb.

On the whole Peel's policy was both patriotic and prudent. For, on the one hand, it enabled many more beneficent measures to be passed than would otherwise have been possible, and, on the other hand, it showed that the Tamworth Manifesto had not been mere " eyewash "; that Peel really had the interests of the middle class at heart, and that he was already more than half a whig. Of course, the old tories, the dwindling group of the landed aristocracy and gentry, grumbled and growled; but the day of their ascendancy had passed. What was more remarkable, a new " Young England " group, the nucleus of a rising tory democracy, showed signs of disaffection and revolt. But Peel went on his steady way, and out of the solid and steady middle class constructed a new conservative party that placed him in office with almost dictatorial power in 1841. For Melbourne's government, with all its virtues, was extremely weak on its business side: it got the finances of the nation into an inextricable confusion. Hence Peel, his hour having come, was able to carry against it a direct vote of no confidence and compel it to resign. In the general election that followed the vote of no confidence and preceded the resignation, Peel achieved an overwhelming triumph. This suc-

cess was due in no small measure to the quiet but most
efficient work of party organisation which he had completed during the period of waiting. Until his time conservative party organisation had been almost wholly
wanting. On the one hand, conservatism had always
tended (as it still tends) towards local autonomy; on the
other hand, "the sublime instincts " of the ancient people
who had had the vote up to 1832 had in the main been so
safely and consistently conservative that there had been no
need to bother about organisation. After 1832, however,
things were different. Power had passed into the hands
of a new electorate, lacking experience in politics, and
liable to be misled by sophistries. There was need to
educate and to regiment the forces that tended to order,
stability,   and   authority.   Peel's   exceptionally   great
business capacities enabled him to do work of enduring
value for the conservative party. He helped to establish
a central organisation whose headquarters were the
recently constituted Carlton Club; he fostered the formation of local conservative associations, whose watchword
was " altar, throne, and cottage," and whose prime purpose was to secure the due registration and regimentation
of every qualified conservative voter. Another task which
he achieved with conspicuous success was the cultivation
of a sound conservative press, well informed on current
affairs, and qualified to correct radical misrepresentations.
The triumph of 1841 was to no small extent due to his
masterly managership.

Having secured office and power in 1841, he governed
with almost dictatorial authority for five years. He ruled
with immense energy and commanding ability : many of his
measures were undoubtedly sound and statesmanly. But
he ruled as a middle-class manufacturer for middle-class
manufacturers, and seemed scarcely able to envisage the
claims of classes to which he did not himself belong. Hence
he alienated the landed class—the " gentlemen of England," the tenant farmers, and the peasantry—who
realised that he did not understand their problems or care
for their interests. He also intensely exasperated the
radical ochlocracy of the towns, which found him loftily

indifferent to the hardships inflicted on the indigent by the new poor law of 1834, and hostile to the trade unions which were struggling into existence. His passion was for financial integrity and freedom of trade. His budgets of 1842 and 1845 were masterpieces of commercial genius : in the first he lowered the tariffs on some 750 articles, and made up for the entailed loss to the revenue by an income-tax of 7d. in the pound levied on incomes of £150 and over; in the second he made still further reductions on import duties, relieving in particular raw materials and articles of general consumption, such as sugar. Another of his notable achievements—and the one on which he always prided himself most—was the Bank Charter Act of 1844, the very basis of our present-day banking system. In short, under his capable managing directorship middle-class England grew wealthy and contented. The new conservatism seemed likely to take all the wind from the sails of Victorian liberalism.

§ 56. THE REPEAL OF THE CORN LAWS

Successful, however, as was Peel in his chosen sphere of commerce and finance, he had in other spheres to face difficulties which ultimately proved to be his undoing. First, the chartists gave him some trouble with their demands for manhood suffrage, equal electoral districts, vote by ballot, annual parliaments, payment of members, and abolition of property qualifications. But the worst phases of the chartist agitation (1838-40) were over before his time. After 1842 the ranks of the chartists were torn by dissensions between the advocates of moral suasion and the advocates of physical force. The increasing commercial prosperity of the country, moreover, turned many of the agitators to the more profitable task of making money. The great chartist demonstration of April 10, 1848, was but a belated and ineffective attempt to revive an almost extinct flame : its failure converted middle-class alarm to universal ridicule. A second, more serious, and more persistent source of anxiety was the chronic unrest of Ireland. No sooner was the tithe grievance removed

by the Commutation Act of 1838 than a new agitation
began, this time for the repeal of the union. The leadership of the movement passed from the hands of O'Connell,
who limited his violence to language, into the hands of a
" Young Ireland " group, who were prepared to go to any
lengths of criminality and rebellion. In vain did Peel try
to conciliate the catholic priesthood by the " Maynooth
Grant " of 1845 : he merely succeeded in alarming his
protestant supporters in the three kingdoms. Finally he
had to resort to coercion, and it was in trying to pass a
Coercion Bill in 1846 that he ultimately fell.

But the Irish Coercion Bill of 1846, although it was the
occasion, was not the real cause of his fall. He fell because
he had repealed the corn laws ; for in repealing the corn
laws he had shattered in irretrievable ruin the new conservative party which he had so laboriously constructed
and organised during the years 1834-41. Ever since his
accession to office the disintegration of the party had been
going on. For the " old tory " section, representing the
landed interest, disapproved of almost everything that he
did. It was not, however, until he declared against the
continuance of the corn laws, at the end of 1845, that
their discontent and disgust broke out into open rebellion
against his challenging autocracy. And, without doubt,
they had good cause for revolt. For Peel had come to
power in 1841 deeply pledged to maintain the corn laws ;
and his use of the power conferred upon him by protectionists for the destruction of the protective system was a
gross betrayal of a solemn trust. However necessary it
may have been to modify or abolish the corn laws, he, most
emphatically, was not the man to do it.

The regulation by statute of the export and import of
corn dated, of course, from the middle ages. But the
mediæval system had broken down in the eighteenth
century, mainly owing to the increase of population and
the constant recurrence of great wars, and the system in
vogue under Peel was instituted no earlier than 1815. In
that year, in order to prevent the falling out of cultivation
of large areas of inferior land which had been brought
under the plough during the perilous period of the

Napoleonic wars, an Act was passed which prohibited the import of colonial wheat until the home price reached 60s. a quarter, and of foreign wheat until a price of 80s. was attained. The purpose of the Act was to stabilise the price of wheat between the limits of 60s. and 80s. a quarter, and so to maintain the " landed interest "—that is to say, landlords, farmers, and agricultural labourers, the denizens of rural England—in prosperity. The Act did not work well, and in 1822 the 80s. limit was lowered to 70s. No improvement, however, followed, and in 1827 Canning proposed the substitution of a sliding scale which, in a modified form, was accepted and introduced by Wellington in 1828. The tendency of both the fixed duty and the sliding scale was, of course, to keep the price of wheat artificially high, and so to put ordinary bread almost out of the reach of the labouring poor. Hence in 1838—a time of bad harvests and scarcity, when the price of wheat was round about 80s.—an Anti-Corn-Law League was instituted by Cobden and others (mainly cotton manufacturers of Lancashire), whose purpose was the total abolition of all restrictions on the free import of corn. Peel, himself a cotton manufacturer, began to see the situation more and more from a cobdenite point of view, until by 1845 he had become a convert to cobdenism. The consciousness of this conversion caused him, Wellington tells us, agonies of conflict; for he intensely disliked Cobden and his associates, and felt it desirable at all costs to keep them from office and power. The occurrence of the Irish potato famine in the autumn of 1845, which gave rise to intense sympathy and large practical beneficence throughout the United Kingdom, seemed to him to provide the appropriate emotional environment for a general declaration against food taxes. It was really a totally irrelevant circumstance; for the Irish did not want wheat; had got plenty of wheat; were actually exporting wheat during the whole course of the famine; and in any case could not get wheat cheaper under the provisions of the Repeal Act until long after the time when the famine would be over. The Irish potato famine was, indeed, a palpable pretext by means of which Peel hoped to camouflage to the country and to his party the radical change of principle and policy to which he had been constrained by his enemies to come.

He could not carry it off with his cabinet or with his party. Lord Stanley (later earl of Derby) resigned his office of colonial secretary and led a formidable band of rebels in the house of lords, while Benjamin Disraeli and Lord George Bentinck organised a powerful conservative opposition in the house of commons. The duke of Wellington—true to his fatal policy of supporting the Queen's government whatever it did, and keeping out the radicals whatever they said—while professing the strongest detestation of cobdenite dogma and procedure, secured the passage of the cobdenite measure through the house of lords by unprincipled appeals to expediency and tactics. In the house of commons the repeal of the corn laws was carried, against the majority of the conservatives, by a coalition of peelites, russellites, and cobdenites. But the protectionist conservatives had their immediate revenge on the minister who had deserted and betrayed them. They not only defeated him on the matter of the Irish Coercion Bill (June 25, 1846) and compelled him to resign, but they organised themselves under other leaders in a manner that made his return to office for ever impossible. He lived only four years more, a lonely, impotent, reprobated figure. He had shattered the party that he had so laboriously constructed, and in doing so had inflicted an enduring injury upon the politics of the nation that he had hoped to serve.

CHAPTER XIV

TORY DEMOCRATS VERSUS BOURGEOIS INDIVIDUALISTS

1846–1880

" I am a conservative to preserve all that is good in our constitution, a radical to remove all that is bad. I seek to preserve property and to respect order. . . . I detest alike the despotism of an oligarchy and the pre-eminence of a mob."—BENJAMIN DISRAELI.

" I shall withhold my support from every ministry which will not originate some great measure to ameliorate the condition of the lower orders."—BENJAMIN DISRAELI.

" To turn from Peel's papers to Disraeli's political writings or his greater speeches is to turn from a limited outlook of a year or a generation, of a single party or people, to that of all political time and all political existence."—JOHN BAILEY.

§ 57. BENJAMIN DISRAELI

THE effective leader of the rural revolt within the conservative party against Sir Robert Peel's urban dictatorship was Benjamin Disraeli. Stanley in the house of lords made brilliant and rupert-like charges upon the Anti-Corn-Law League; but he lacked the energy for a sustained campaign. Bentinck in the house of commons acted as an impressive mascot for the outraged but inarticulate squirearchy; but he was deficient both in intellect and in organising skill. Disraeli, then at the very height of his unparalleled powers, supplied all that was needed of sustained energy, intellectual ability, and business capacity. It was he individually who brought Peel down, as clearly and certainly as it was David who brought down Goliath. And the one event was hardly less spectacular and sensational than the other.

Born 1804, the scion of an ancient and well-to-do Jewish family domiciled in England since 1748, Benjamin Disraeli had at the age of thirteen been baptised into the anglican

church. This formal membership of the establishment
opened up to him the pathway of politics, and that pathway—after hesitating for a time before the avenue of
literature—he determined to follow. He found some difficulty at first in selecting his party. For in 1832, when he
decided to stand for parliament, the tories were disintegrated by the emancipation schism, and were hopelessly
committed to reaction by Wellington's uncompromising
resistance to parliamentary reform. As to whiggism, Disraeli always detested it as irreligious, anti-monarchic,
materialistic, utilitarian, urban, and middle class.
"Toryism is worn out," he said, "and I cannot con-
descend to be a whig." He therefore stood as an independent reformer with a programme all his own : it included the ideals of a national church, a balanced constitution, a resuscitated monarchy, an active and beneficent
aristocracy, a prosperous and contented peasantry, a rural
England protected from spoliation and desecration. It
was an attractive programme, and it excited much interest.
But it failed, on three successive occasions, to secure him
election at High Wycombe, and his failure taught him the
important lesson that membership of a political party is
the indispensable condition of effectiveness in a parliamentary system of government. Fortunately, at the very
time when he came to this conclusion, the issue of Peel's
Tamworth Manifesto (December, 1834) seemed to indicate
that toryism was dissociating itself from reaction, and was
becoming progressive once more. He therefore enlisted
under Peel's banner, and, after suffering defeat at Taunton
in 1835, secured election for Maidstone in 1837. For six
years he faithfully, hopefully, and charitably followed
Peel, although now and again he showed a significant
independence—e.g., in his sympathy with the chartists
and in his criticism of the poor law of 1834. In 1843-44 his
alienation from Peel became evident : he resented and resisted Peel's growing inclination towards whiggism,
benthamism, and cobdenism, and his excessive cultivation
of the mercantile middle class. He attached himself to
the "Young England" group that looked to Bolingbroke
as its ideal guide—a group that sought to re-emphasise

the religious basis of the state, the sacred authority of the monarchy, the feudal obligations of the nobility, the rights and privileges of the peasantry. Thoroughly disillusioned, he roundly denounced the pseudo-conservatism of the Tamworth Manifesto as " organised hypocrisy." In 1844 he was formally expelled by Peel from the pseudo-conservative party. Hence he was free in 1845, when Peel perpetrated his final desertion and betrayal of the cause of rural England, to attack the traitor with unmitigated ferocity.

Never since the days when Bolingbroke assailed Walpole with winged and barbed invective had so devastating and destructive an assault been delivered against a great minister as that which Disraeli launched against Peel in respect of his abandonment of the corn laws. He was not primarily concerned to defend the corn laws on economic grounds. As a matter of fact, they had not worked well; they had been several times modified, and they were in admitted need of further revision. Cobden had, indeed, made out a strong case for their total repeal. That was not his point. The gravamen of his accusation of Peel was twofold: he charged him, on the one hand, with a gross betrayal of a party which had implicitly trusted him, and with a scandalous abandonment of principles which he had long publicly professed; and, on the other hand, with a total failure to appreciate the non-economic grounds for the continuance of the protection of rural England against the encroaching towns. He pointed out, on the one side, that he had been placed in power in 1841 as the professed champion of the landed interest; that his speeches in defence of the corn laws had been among the most eloquent and impressive that he had ever delivered; that he had given no indication during the four years of his ministry of any change of opinion; and that then suddenly in 1845, without warning, without explanation, without apology, and on grounds obviously irrelevant and inadequate, he had called upon his followers by his arbitrary authority, as though they had been slaves or sheep, to obey his command and vote for a measure which they and he together had hitherto agreed would be fatal

to the prosperity of the country. With damnatory
cogency Disraeli compared Peel to the Turkish admiral
who, only five years before, had betrayed the fleet that
he commanded into the hands of the enemy that it had
been commissioned to attack. Then, on the other side,
he argued that even if the corn laws did add slightly to
the cost of living, there were other considerations to be
taken into account beside that of mere cheapness. There
were political, social, and moral aspects of the problem.
Politically, it was essential that Britain should have a food
supply not liable to be instantly cut off in time of war;
socially, it was imperative that the fine and vigorous manhood of the healthy countryside should not perish and be
supplanted by the puny and degenerate denizens of factories and slums; morally, it was not less necessary that
the sturdy and self-reliant character of the great class of
yeomen-farmers should not be subdued to the sycophantic
socialism of the urban artisan. Rarely had such effective
and decisive speeches been heard in parliament. It has,
indeed, been plausibly maintained that Disraeli's crowning oration of January 22, 1846, actually turned the course
of politics. Peel, though mad with fury, was impotent in
reply. Of course he carried his measure: some 120 conservatives, headed by W. E. Gladstone, voted with him in
the house of commons, and these added to the solid
phalanx of the liberals sufficed to overwhelm the protectionist remnant. In the house of lords Aberdeen alone
among the ministers advocated repeal; but, as we have
seen, Wellington, for tactical reasons and against his convictions, supported the prime minister. So the corn laws
disappeared, and with them the laboriously constructed
peelite coalition of rural protectionists and urban free-
traders.

§ 58. THE PERIOD OF PERDITION, 1846-74

The peelite free-traders, severed from the main body of
the conservatives, maintained a precarious and purgatorial
existence as a separate group for about a quarter of a
century. After the death of Peel in 1850, they found

successive leaders in the worthy but woolly Aberdeen and
the word-chopping and wood-chopping Gladstone. But
their numbers steadily diminished. The election of 1847
reduced them from 120 to 60. This remnant became torn
by internal dissensions : in 1852 no fewer than four sub-
sections were discernible.* In December of that year,
when they helped to constitute, with the liberals, Aberdeen's coalition government that drifted ineptly into the
Crimean War, they numbered but 30. Impotent themselves, and a source of perpetual irritation and embarrassment to both the great parties in the state, they ultimately disintegrated, the major fragment led by Gladstone joining, and taking command of, the liberals, the
minor reverting to conservatism. The date of Palmerston's
death, 1865, may perhaps be taken to mark the time of
their final absorption.

The severance of the peelites from the main body of the
conservatives gave to the liberals twenty-eight years of
power, and left to the leaders of the deserted conservative
remnant a gigantic task of reorganisation and reconstruction. Who were these leaders ? In the house of lords
Stanley (who in 1851 became the fourteenth earl of Derby)
had no rival. He was a man who to high rank added great
wealth, quick intelligence, brilliant scholarship, and a wide
variety of interests. His exceptional pungency in debate
had given him a foremost place in politics ; but he did not
take his politics seriously, and his incurable frivolity made
him more of a burden than a blessing to any cause he
professed to support. He had been an advanced whig
until 1834, ardently advocating both catholic emancipation and parliamentary reform. Then, revolting against
Grey on the Irish church question (1841), he had supported
Peel until Peel abandoned the corn laws. From 1846 to
1868 he remained the nominal chief of the anti-peelite
conservatives, and during that period for three brief
intervals he held the position of prime minister in transient
and impotent minority governments.† He was emphatic-

* Cf. Morley, J., Life of Gladstone (1903), i., 419.

† February to December, 1852; February, 1858, to May, 1859;
June, 1866, to February, 1868.

ally not the man for the occasion; he was not prepared to do the hard thinking and the laborious work required to restore his shattered party. The main result of his long continuance in public life was to block the path of his great lieutenant, Benjamin Disraeli, to independent power.

For in the house of commons Disraeli, who had thrown all his genius and his tireless energies into politics, rapidly rose to indisputable pre-eminence. He had to win his way by slow degrees, and in his ascent to surmount almost insuperable obstacles. As a leader of the gentlemen of England he came from the wrong race, had the wrong education, had risen to influence by the wrong path. He was suspected both of religious heterodoxy and of political independence. Derby distrusted him and frequently treated him with intolerable insolence; the peelites, led by Gladstone, perpetually assailed him with merciless ferocity, and his own people often failed to rally to his aid; the queen and the prince consort, both of whom were friends and admirers of Peel, for a long time looked upon him askance. Nevertheless, in spite of all, by 1849 he had by sheer ability and determination established an unquestionable ascendancy and had begun his great task of reconstructing and educating the conservative party.

The story of that remarkable quarter-century 1849-74 is, in the biography of Disraeli, the record of how with infinite patience, long-suffering, loyalty, and fidelity he won the confidence of the distrustful Derby; how with incomparable tact, skill, and grace he conciliated the court and secured the cordial friendship of the queen and her consort; how by strong will, imperturbable good humour, untiring labour, and masterly management he reduced his insubordinate followers to admiring obedience; and how by means of superb courage and commanding ability he beat off the assaults of his embittered opponents—peelites, whigs, and radicals—and prepared the way for the great triumph of 1874.

Perhaps the most difficult and certainly the most permanently important of his tasks was the education of his party. It was a task not unlike that which had faced

Bolingbroke a century earlier. For just as Bolingbroke had had to educate the tories of his day out of jacobitism and into religious toleration, so now, in the middle of the nineteenth century, Disraeli had to educate the conservatives out of protection and into parliamentary reform. As to protection (*i.e.*, the corn laws), the educative task was not so difficult as—in view of the fact that the very cause of the peelite schism was the question of their repeal —might have been expected. Disraeli himself was not committed to the corn laws as such, but merely in general to the protection of the landed interest; to the defence of the farm against the encroaching factory; the safeguarding of the menaced village against the spreading slum; the maintenance of rural England with its incomparable beauties and sterling virtues against the horrors of the industrial revolution. He realised with respect to the corn laws, as Peel had realised in regard to parliamentary reform twelve years before, that when once a decisive step of that sort had been taken there could be no early return to the old way. He therefore educated his followers to seek the great end of the corn laws—namely, the prosperity of agriculture—by means of individual enterprise and resource, assisted by such governmental aids as reduction of taxes, adjustment of rates, repeal of malt duties, and so on. And, fortunately, circumstances favoured him. For Britain entered at that very time upon a thirty-year cycle of unprecedented prosperity. She became the manufacturer and the carrier of the world, and for the nonce agriculture, even without the protective corn laws, shared the general felicity. That felicity, as we are now painfully aware, was ephemeral and illusory: all too soon it was destined to give place to depression and adversity. But the men who experienced it regarded it as eternal, and ordered their lives accordingly. So Disraeli found no difficulty, apart from the taunts of his opponents, in dropping the corn laws.

The task of winning conservatism to parliamentary reforms was a more laborious one. For the advocacy of further " reforms "—that is, of a new advance toward democracy—was regarded as a speciality of the radicals,

and it caused grave apprehensions in the minds of most of
those conservatives who realised the defects of the Act of
1832 and perceived its consequences. But the subject was
congenial to both Derby and Disraeli. For both of them
had been on the side of reform in 1832, and Disraeli at
any rate had made the question the subject of continuous
study ever since. Between 1848 and 1866 the matter came
before the house of commons no fewer than twenty-six
times, and on each occasion Disraeli spoke at length, displaying a consummate mastery of the theme. The printed
collection of his speeches, indeed, with the preface by Mr.
Montagu Corry (afterwards Lord Rowton), provides an
almost perfect manual of progressive conservative policy
on this great constitutional problem. Disraeli pointed out
again and again how the Act of 1832—based on the false
principle that the franchise is a right to be claimed by the
individual and not a privilege to be conferred on behalf of
the community—had destroyed the balance of the constitution; had disfranchised large and important classes; had
conferred sovereignty upon one solitary social order—
namely, the *petit bourgeoisie*; had rejected all qualifications for the vote except the single one of property; had
ignored numerous and great " interests," and particularly
the growing interest of labour; had made unnecessary and
wanton havoc of the old and venerable constituencies; and
in countless other ways, owing to the neglect of conservative principles, had inflicted grievous wrongs upon the
body politic. He was fertile in criticisms of the proposals
of Joseph Hume, Locke King, Edward Barnes, and Lord
John Russell for the further prostitution of the franchise.
The great agitation, however, which accompanied Russell's
abortive Bill of 1866 convinced both himself and Lord
Derby that the time had come when the matter must be
dealt with decisively and cleared out of the way. The
queen, too, implored them, when in June, 1866, they came
in for a short spell of office, to take the problem up and
settle it on safe lines. Accordingly, in March, 1867, Disraeli introduced in the house of commons a Reform Bill
which in the following August became law. But in its
process through parliament it became changed almost

beyond recognition. The principles on which it was originally framed were explained with admirable lucidity by Disraeli in a great speech which he delivered in Edinburgh soon after the close of the session (August, 1867). They notably included the recognition of a number of other qualifications for the vote beside mere property— "fancy franchises" the doctrinaire radicals viciously dubbed them. They were also intended to extend political power to the responsible artisan class and so break down the middle-class monopoly. Disraeli had a profound trust in the British working man. He was the great "tory democrat" of his day. "I have no apprehension," he had said in 1859, "that if you had manhood suffrage to-morrow the honest, brave, and good-natured people of England would resort to pillage, incendiarism, and massacre." The actual result of the Reform Act of 1867— which established household suffrage in towns, supplemented by a £10 lodger qualification—was to enfranchise the artisan class. But all Disraeli's "fancy franchises" were swept away by the opposition, who had a majority in the house of commons, and it was only by a miracle of parliamentary management that Disraeli got his bill through at all. The reckless rage of Gladstone and his radical allies, who shrank from no excess of violence in their endeavours to destroy both the measure and the ministry, had the result that the Act of 1867 was much more sweeping and democratic in its results than Disraeli had intended, or than even Russell and Gladstone desired. But, at any rate, as a consequence of its passing, the middle class received notice to quit.

§ 59. THE GREAT RECOVERY, 1874-80

That Disraeli achieved an immense personal triumph in his successful carriage of the second Reform Bill in 1867 is unquestionable. It is further true that in securing so large an extension of the franchise he pacified an agitation that, although artificial in its origin, had been worked up by the gladstonians into a dangerous state of inflammation. But it is also true that under pressure of the glad-

stonian majority in the house of commons he had been
compelled, in order to save the bill from destruction, to
make concessions and to withdraw safeguards that entirely
altered its character. It did not, as he had intended,
redress the inequalities of the Act of 1832; and it did
administer to the country a far larger dose of democracy
than it was at that time fitted to bear. Even now elementary education has barely succeeded in neutralising
the danger of the possession of irresponsible power by ill-
informed, easily misguided, and impecunious multitudes.
But Disraeli felt that the undoubted danger had to be
faced, and he faced it with courage and faith, professing a
confidence, not shared by all his followers, in the fundamental good sense and noble intentions of the new
electorate.

Soon after the achievement of the great parliamentary
triumph of the Reform Act, Lord Derby, the prime
minister, delighted at ending his public career by " dish-
ing the whigs," resigned, and Disraeli succeeded him
(February, 1868). But, confronted as he was by a
furiously angry gladstonian majority, his tenure of office
was brief and unpleasant. In November, 1868, Gladstone,
who had taken up Irish disestablishment as an effective
anti-conservative bludgeon, defeated him and drove him
once more into opposition. He was already sixty-four
years of age; but he had to wait still another six years
before, as a result of his long labours, he attained both to
office and to power. During those six years (1868-74)
Gladstone, for the first time prime minister, carried a
number of measures pleasing to the nonconformist middle
class on whom his power was based : he disestablished the
Irish Church (1869); he set up undenominational board
schools (1870); he threw open the universities and their
emoluments to dissenters (1871); he placed upon the
statute book a Ballot Act (1872) which embodied the
radical principle that to vote is a personal right rather
than a public function; he remodelled the law courts
(1873). But he did nothing for the working man, the new
sharer of sovereignty with the *petit bourgeoisie*. And in
the spheres of imperial and foreign affairs he and his back-

boneless colleagues went from one humiliation to another. In 1872 it was evident that the tide of popular indignation was rising against them.   Disraeli received tremendous ovations when he addressed two great mass meetings, the one in the Free Trade Hall, Manchester (April), and the other in the Crystal Palace (June).   The speeches which he delivered on those occasions are magnificent expositions of conservative principles and policy : in the one he dealt with the constitution and the administration of the United Kingdom ; in the other he formulated the immediate conservative programme as consisting of, first, the maintenance of the institutions of the country ; secondly, the development of the empire ; and, thirdly, the improvement of the condition of the people.

Early in 1873 Gladstone realised that the days of his administration were numbered.   He then tried to resign ; but Disraeli refused to take office a second time in face of a hostile house.   Hence Gladstone had to struggle on for nine more months of ineptitude and humiliation.   In January, 1874, he appealed to the country, and, when the returns came in, found himself in a minority of fifty.   For the first time since 1841 the conservatives had a majority in the house of commons.   Disraeli's great educative and reconstructive work was rewarded.

The conservative ministry under its brilliant and popular chief accomplished much, particularly in three important spheres.   First, in the sphere of social legislation, which the middle-class and laissez-faire liberals had flagrantly neglected, it passed a remarkable series of Acts relating to artisans' dwellings, friendly societies, trade unions, agricultural tenancies, merchant vessels, public health, factories, enclosures, river pollution, and so on.   *Sanitas sanitatum omnia sanitas* was the guiding principle of Disraeli's domestic legislation.   Well said Mr. Alexander Macdonald, one of the first two labour members ever sent to parliament, in 1879 : " The conservative party have done more for the working classes in five years than the liberals have in fifty."   Secondly, it paid great attention to the development of the empire, towards which the gladstonians had displayed a strange indifference.   Specially

noteworthy were Disraeli's sensational purchase of the
Khedive's share in the Suez Canal in 1875; his organisation of the prince of Wales's visit to India the same year;
and his proclamation of the assumption of the title
" Empress of India " by the queen. Probably no British
statesman ever realised so fully as did Disraeli, with his
oriental imagination, the splendour and importance of the
British dominion in the East Indies. Thirdly, it completely restored Britain's shattered prestige in the Concert
of Europe. To Disraeli personally, through the agency
of Queen Victoria and the Tsar Alexander, was largely
due the frustration of the deadly Prussian plot for the
final elimination of France in 1875. Again, to Disraeli
himself, more than to any other single European statesman, was attributable the settlement of the Eastern
Question in 1878. " Der alte Jude, das ist der Mann," said
Bismarck in undisguised admiration. The return of Disraeli—who in 1876 had become earl of Beaconsfield—from
Berlin, bringing " peace with honour," registered the high-
water mark of his influence and renown. All, and more
than all, that *Vivian Grey and Contarini Fleming* had
aspired to do half a century earlier he had achieved.

    After 1878, however, things began to go awry. The
government became involved, against its will, through the
action of local officials, in needless and inglorious wars in
Afghanistan and Zululand; commercial depression set in;
the long-postponed agricultural decline, predicted in 1846,
began; Mr. Gladstone, emerging from premature retirement, deluged the unhappy electorate with turgid oratory.
Hence in 1880 the great conservative ministry came to an
end. On April 19 Lord Beaconsfield resigned, and precisely one year later died at the age of seventy-six.

§ 60. THE PRINCIPLES OF TORY DEMOCRACY

    The principles of Disraeli were those of tory democracy.
So far back as the 'forties, when he was at the very
summit of his extraordinary powers, he had joined himself
to the " Young England " group, one of whose main concerns had been to remedy the deplorable condition of the

labouring poor doomed to a life of wretchedness and disease in the factories and slums of the new industrial
towns. His deep sympathy with their sufferings, and his
profound detestation of the middle-class mercantilism
wherein he saw the cause of their woes, inspired the burning pages of that greatest of his novels, *Sybil: or the Two
Nations* (1845). He and his " Young England " allies—
Smythe, Manners, Baillie-Cochrane, and the rest—preferred to call themselves " tories " rather than " conservatives " because the name " conservative " (only recently
made current by J. W. Croker and the *Quarterly Review*)
unfortunately at the moment stank from its association
with the " organised hypocrisy " of Peel's camouflaged
whiggism. Peel's pseudo-conservatism, in fact, became
increasingly manifest as middle-class liberalism. After
1846 Peel, at the head of his dwindling band of seceders,
steadily supported the government of Lord John Russell,
and he hobnobbed with Cobden and Bright. If Peel had
lived longer he would undoubtedly have accompanied his
chief disciple, Gladstone, into the ranks of conservatism's
chief enemies. Both Peel and Gladstone were essentially
middle-class mercantilists, believers in laissez-faire, indi-
vidualists, free-traders, utilitarians, political economists,
everything that Disraeli and his friends most cordially
detested and distrusted. The term " tory," however inappropriate it might be on historic grounds, at any rate
was free from association with the horrors of the industrial
revolution. The " Young England " tories, indeed, with
their curious affection for an idealised feudalism and
chivalry, had much in common with the chartists and
other proletarian reformers of the early Victorian days.
With them they deplored and resented the operation of
the new poor law of 1834; they opposed the principles of
laissez-faire; they hated the new machinery and the
hideous mills in which it was housed; they protested
against the repeal of the usury laws and the corn laws;
they distrusted the new stock-jobbers and the joint-stock
bankers. Only from one group of professed reformers did
they hold steadily aloof. They could have nothing to do
with Karl Marx and the other bourgeois ideologues who

formulated the *Communist Manifesto* in 1848.   For the
communistic revolt against religion; its attack on the constitution and the crown; its false and subversive egali-
tarianism; above all, its promulgation of the dogma of the
class-war—the very negation of the conservative doctrine of
the solidarity of the nation and the organic nature of the
state—filled them with inexpressible abhorrence and alarm.
An interesting study in contrasts could, indeed, be made
between the two most potent Jews of the nineteenth
century—namely, Karl Marx (1818-83), the would-be
destroyer of Christian civilisation, and Benjamin Disraeli
(1804-81), its devoted conservator.

If we ask what were the principles of Disraeli and of the
tory democracy of which he was the pioneer, the answer,
I think, is that they were principles which, in the circumstances of the nineteenth century, flowed naturally from
the main stream of conservative tradition.   Disraeli was
the legitimate successor of Bolingbroke and Burke.   From
the brilliant tory-conservative of the early Hanoverian
period he inherited his spirit of patriotism, his profound
devotion to England, his sensitiveness to the national
honour and prestige, his reverence for the monarchy, his
dislike of the whig oligarchy, and his contempt for the
mercantile middle class.   From the great whig-conserva-
tive of the revolutionary age he derived his passionate
belief in the religious basis of society and the sanctity of
the state, his profound reverence for tradition and precedent, his zeal for cautious reform, and his recognition of
the value and necessity of political party and party
organisation.

But the teachings of Bolingbroke and Burke, his
eighteenth-century masters, were reinforced for him by
those of a number of contemporary thinkers, to whose
writings he undoubtedly owed much.   Prominent among
these were Coleridge, the sublime mystic, to whom faith
in divine providence was the very vital breath of politics;
Carlyle, the vociferous idealist, who denounced mammon
and mercantilism with a stentorian insistence that
drowned even the reverberations of the new machinery;
Cobbett, the rural rider, who depicted in prose of match-

less nervousness and vigour the deplorable condition of the peasantry of England; Newman, the implacable foe of liberalism of all sorts; Maurice, the pioneer of a " Christian socialism " which was Christian just so far as it was not socialistic, and socialistic only so far as it was not Christian; Wordsworth, Southey, Scott, Byron, Shelley, and other of the poetic crowd, whose verses, amid all their variety, were eloquent of a passionate interest in the welfare of the people.

Disraeli's principles—the deep, underlying conceptions which were the foundations of his policy and the motives of his actions—can, it seems to me, be grouped under four main heads, as follows :

(1) *The Religious Basis of Society.* Disraeli was a profoundly religious man, as witness his two remarkable novels, *Alroy* (1833) and *Tancred* (1847). His religion, no doubt, was unusual : it was, indeed, probably (like the religion of Milton and of most other original geniuses) peculiar to himself. Such as it was, however, it was centred in Jerusalem, rather than in Rome or even Canterbury. Christianity he regarded as completed Judaism, and Christ as the flower and perfection of the Jewish race. The organised hierarchical church he defined curiously—in words that would apply equally accurately to the theosophical society—as " a sacred corporation for the promotion and maintenance in Europe of certain Asian principles." The anglican establishment, of which he had been admitted a member in 1817, he regarded as a localised branch of this sacred corporation, adapted to the English climate and regulated by Act of Parliament. It was essentially a national institution; a formal communal recognition of the supreme authority of God, and a constant reminder of the divine ordering of human affairs. Perhaps, indeed, the strongest of all Disraeli's religious convictions was his belief in the overruling of the will of man by the divine providence.

(2) *The Organic Nature of the State.* Next to the will of God, the most potent factor in determining the course of human affairs is the will of man in community as expressed by means of the state, government, and law.

Disraeli was thoroughly imbued with the organic conception of the body politic. He realised keenly the peril to the national life involved in breach of continuity, departure from tradition, violation of instinct, repudiation of custom, destruction of order, disobedience to law. But at the same time he clearly perceived that in a swiftly progressive age—an age marked by revolutionary scientific discovery, miraculous invention, profound intellectual change—to stagnate in mere stability is to die. No man was more vividly aware than he that if the body politic were to escape debility and death it would be necessary constantly to adapt its institutions to the changing conditions of the moving world. He knew that the very essence of sound conservatism is cautious reform.

(3) *Solidarity of the Community.* But he was painfully conscious that much of the so-called reform advocated with insane enthusiasm by doctrinaire radicals was vitiated by the fact that it was change advocated in the interests of sections of the population only, regardless of the fact that it would be ruinous to other sections. Nothing was more alien from his large and catholic spirit than the diabolical wickedness and folly of the class-war. He realised, of course, as every believer in the social organism must realise, that no class can suffer without injury and loss to the community as a whole. He wished, then, to maintain the prosperity of the menaced landed interest and to raise the low estate of the industrial labourers, without in any way diminishing the well-being of the enterprising merchants and manufacturers who by their energy and initiative were making wealth for themselves and for their country. He was singularly free from that vile spirit of envy, hatred, malice, and uncharitableness which is the distinguishing characteristic of the Marxian obsession. His passionate desire for the welfare of the nation as a whole, and for every one of its constituent classes, is the secret of his support of protection for agriculture, factory laws for the workers in industry, health legislation, housing schemes, and social reform generally.

(4) *Balance of Powers and Interests.* Like Montesquieu and Burke (not to mention Aristotle and Plutarch) before

him, he was convinced that the health of the body politic would be best secured if there were a carefully adjusted and consistently maintained balance among the various constituent members of the state. He wished to see a balance of classes in the nation—aristocracy, bourgeoisie, and proletariat co-operating for the good of all; a balance of interests—agricultural, industrial, commercial, financial —in the sphere of economic activity; a balance of estates in the constitution—king, lords, and commons, each and all performing their proper functions; a balance of orders in the electorate—neither middle class nor artisans, neither propertied people nor merely educated people preponder- ating; a balance between local and central government; between mother-country and colonies; between the empire and the other states of the world. Rarely have views so sane and moderate been advocated with zeal so constant or abilities of so high a quality.

The practical policy which followed from the pursuit of these fundamental principles may be summarised in the four words, conservatism, solidarity, patriotism, imperial- ism. He was a conservative in that he strove to preserve the constitution of church and state; a collectivist, in the sound non-socialistic sense of the term, in that he sought to use the strength and resources of the state in the interest of every class of citizen, whether prosperous or otherwise; a patriot, in that he was nobly jealous of Britain's honour and prestige in the world; an imperialist, in that he was one of the first to perceive the splendid possibilities that lay before the widespread dominions of the queen.

That Disraeli was the outstanding British statesman of the nineteenth century there can be little question. He was a man of high ambition with a calm consciousness of power; he was endowed with a superb courage, confidence, and capacity for command; he displayed, moreover, an extraordinary patience, forbearance, fortitude, equanimity, and freedom from petty malice; he showed, too, a mar- vellous tact in his dealings with his fellows, a charming conciliatoriness, a singular power of winning affection. Well said J. A. Froude in the first biography of him that made any pretence of a sympathetic estimate of his character : " In public or private he had never done a dishonourable action. He had disarmed hatred, and had never lost a friend."

His high moral qualities, however, would not by themselves have given him rank as the major prophet of modern conservatism. He had supreme abilities as well : an intellect eminent for its range and power ; a will strong as adamant in its persistence of purpose ; an emotion sensitive to the hopes and fears of a wide humanity. No wonder that his achievements were great. In respect of conservatism, with which alone we are now concerned, we may say that he reconstructed the conservative party after the disruption of 1846, that he educated it, that he nationalised it, and that he democratised it. The influence of most prime ministers is ephemeral : it ceases to be felt soon after they pass from office. But Disraeli's influence is enduring and increasing. The celebrations that mark each " Primrose Day " (April 19) and the unceasing activities of the " Primrose League " witness to his possession of a power that transcended the limits of death. For the ideals of tory democracy stand as a perpetual memorial to his name.

CHAPTER XV

UNIONISTS VERSUS HOME RULERS

1800–1901

" The conservative party will never exercise power until it has gained the confidence of the working classes; and the working classes are quite determined to govern themselves."—LORD RANDOLPH CHURCHILL.

" If I were asked to define conservative policy, I should say that it was the upholding of confidence."—LORD SALISBURY.

" The tory creed, so far as it implies maintenance of historical continuity, and calculated, practical, well-meditated reform without unnecessary risk to precious institutions, is a respectable and healthy faith."—LORD ROSEBERY.

§ 61. LORD RANDOLPH CHURCHILL

THE torch of tory democracy held aloft by Disraeli was taken up after his death by the hand of the lively but unbalanced Lord Randolph Churchill. This fearless and unconventional young aristocrat was thirty-two years old at the date of Disraeli's demise. He had frequently, when a sportive and illiterate undergraduate at Oxford (1867-70), come into contact with his great leader, who was a constant visitor at the Churchill mansion of Blenheim. Disraeli, who loved the unusual and bizarre, was attracted by the irresponsible gaiety and sparkling audacity of the young man, and soon perceived that beneath the turbulent surface of his uncultivated mind were powers of uncommon promise. Randolph recalled, in fact, to Disraeli his own erratic and belligerent youth. There was, indeed, in him something of the same daring originality, the same independence of judgment, the same love of adventure, the same capacity for leadership, the same supreme self-confidence, as had characterised Disraeli forty years before. Above all, there was the same profound concern for the " condition of the people," and the same firm belief in the essential sanity and conservatism of the working man. He had a convinced faith, as he said later on in his career, in "the ascertained and much-tried common sense which is the peculiarity of the English people." His motto was, like Disraeli's, "Trust the people," and with as much boldness as ever Disraeli had displayed even in 1867, he cried : "If you want to gain the confidence of the working classes, let them have a share and a large share—a real share and not a sham share—in your party councils and your party government."*

He entered parliament, as member for the family borough of Woodstock, in 1874, the year that saw the inauguration of Disraeli's great ministry. So long as things went well with the government—that is, down to 1878—he said and did little. His attendances at the house of commons were irregular, and the average annual output of his parliamentary oratory was no more than fifteen minutes. But in 1878 his volcanic powers began to be eruptive. We have observed how in that year the fortunes of the country and of the conservative party declined : troubles in Egypt, Afghanistan, Zululand; depression in both agriculture and industry; difficulties with Russia and with France; these and other causes sapped the strength of the government in parliament, and its popularity in the constituencies. Disraeli, harassed by gout and asthma, feeling himself unequal to the task of leading the house of commons, had already retired to the house of lords as Earl of Beaconsfield (1876). He had been encouraged to make this exchange of toil and power for leisure and impotence by the ostentatious withdrawal of Mr. Gladstone from public life in 1874. In the circumstances, and in view of the large conservative majority in both the houses, he had felt it safe to leave the leadership of the commons in the hands of the mild and benevolent Sir Stafford Northcote. But the return of Gladstone with rejuvenated fury to politics at the time of the "Bulgarian atrocities" had altered the whole position of things. Northcote had at one time been Gladstone's private secretary, and he had never shaken off his awe of the Grand Old Man : he had not the spirit, and he had not the ability,

* Churchill, W. S., *Lord Randolph Churchill* (second edition, 1907), pp. 239 and 251.

to stand up to him. The conservative bump of veneration was too strongly developed in him. For the sake of
the life of peace and piety he allowed too many gauntlets
to lie untouched on the ground.

Here was Lord Randolph's opportunity and the occasion of his call to activity. During the closing two years
of Beaconsfield's ministry (1878-80) he gave several displays of effective pugnacity which equalled the best performances of Cranborne in the 'sixties or Disraeli himself
in the 'forties. Indeed, he manifested an even superior
insolence, and an even greater pungency of epithet. And
he directed his assaults at least as often upon the silly
sheep on his own side of the house as upon the obnoxious
goats on the other side. It was not, however, until the
fall of the Beaconsfield government, and the installation
of Mr. Gladstone as prime minister in April, 1880, that the
full measure of his reckless ability was revealed. He was
roused to almost equal fury by the policy of the gladstonian government, and by the feebleness of the opposition offered to it by Northcote, Smith, and Cross. Hence
he gathered round himself a small company of like-minded
men—Wolff, Gorst, and Balfour being the inner circle—
who, taking as their motto the slogan, " The duty of an
opposition is to oppose," raised the standard of incessant
war against both democrats who were not tories, and tories
who were not democrats.

This so-called " fourth party " (the Irish nationalists
being the third) held together for four years, 1880-84, and
during that period it made itself, and particularly its
leader, a power in parliament and in the land. But its
interventions—e.g., in the debates on the Employers'
Liability Bill, the Game Preservation Bill, and the Burials
Bill—all tended not to defeat radical measures, but to make
them more radical still. The official conservative leaders,
not unnaturally, protested; but Disraeli, during the one
year that he lived after his fall, gave his blessing to the
vivacious little band: " I wholly sympathise with you
all," he said, " because I never was respectable myself."*
Perhaps if Disraeli had lived he could have kept the " tory

* Churchill, W. S., op. cit., p. 127.

democracy " of Lord Randolph Churchill within the limits of conservatism; but it is doubtful. Certainly the " old gang "—Northcote, Smith, and Cross—who succeeded Disraeli in the house of commons could not do so; and though Lord Salisbury, to whom the volatile Randolph temporarily transferred his allegiance, by means of infinite patience and forbearance managed for a time to hold him in leash, even he ultimately had to let him go. Lord Randolph, after straining the cohesion of the "fourth party " by his attitude towards free-trade, the Boers, Irish coercion, the parliamentary closure, Egypt, and other matters (1881-83), finally disrupted the party in 1884 by his support of Gladstone's Reform Bill. But he still claimed to be Disraeli's heir, and he played an important part in the founding of the " Primrose League " (1883) instituted to perpetuate Disraeli's memory and to continue his work. He loudly preached to vast and enthralled audiences Disraeli's creed. " To rally the people round the throne, to unite the throne with the people, that," he cried, " is our policy; that is our faith." So powerful an influence did he become in the big towns, and in the National Union of Conservative Associations, that he began to have dreams of the speedy attainment of a position similar to that which Disraeli himself had reached after a half-century of patient effort. He was put in charge of the India Office during Salisbury's brief ministry of 1885-86, and when for a second time (August, 1886) Salisbury became prime minister, he made Lord Randolph his chancellor of the exchequer and the leader of the house of commons.

Better for him if his rise had not been so rapid, his ascent so easy. The son of a duke, he had found society open to him and the way into politics smooth. An ample allowance at school and college had rendered it unnecessary for him to work, and, in spite of a final cram for his degree, he remained an ignoramus. Numerous interests and distractions had prevented him from making that serious and profound study of political problems which had been the hidden source of Disraeli's strength. He had not the capacity, and he lacked the patience, to make himself master of the subjects that he fluently discussed. Above all, he belonged to " the governing class," regarded rule as his right, and so was intolerant of opposition, arrogant and insolent, incapable of conciliating antagonists or placating enemies. The discovery that he possessed the gift of effective oratory unduly exalted him; he was carried away by the crowds that cheered his audacities and roared with laughter at the pugnacities that poured from his curiously canine countenance. He became increasingly reckless in his appeals to the popular fancy, until in his notorious Dartford speech (October, 1886) he formulated a programme of " tory democracy " that was indistinguishable from the radicalism of Chamberlain and Bright.* It was, indeed, incompatible with any form of conservatism. And it was promulgated by the person who happened at the moment to be chancellor of the exchequer and conservative leader of the house of commons. The position was an impossible one. And it was complicated by the fact that, at the time, the speaker was at loggerheads with the majority of the cabinet on matters of foreign policy, local government policy, naval and military policy. He was, in fact, with inadequate resources of knowledge and power, aping the rôle of dictator. On December 20, 1886, he rashly put his fate to the test by sending in his resignation to Lord Salisbury. To his amazement it was accepted, and to his disgust the world did not come to an end. He had, indeed, ruined himself by his impetuosity, and, what is worse, he had for a time thoroughly discredited " tory democracy " by formulating under its name a policy that was essentially anti-conservative. As Lord Rosebery well says, the so-called " tory democracy " of Randolph Churchill was merely " the wolf of radicalism in the sheepskin of toryism."†

* For the Dartford speech, see Churchill, W. S., *op. cit.*, pp. 558-562, and compare Rosebery, *Lord Randolph Churchill* (1906), pp. 48, 97, 109, 137.

† Rosebery, *op. cit.*, p. 136. *Cf.* Gladstone's view of " tory democracy " as expounded by Churchill, contained in a letter to Lord Acton, quoted in Morley's *Life of Gladstone* (1903), iii., p. 173.

§ 62. The Home Rule Issue

To the camouflaged radicalism of Lord Randolph
Churchill, however, there was one exception—an exception
which, curiously enough, it had in common with the nude,
rude, and crude radicalism of Joseph Chamberlain and
John Bright. It was invincibly opposed to the grant of
" home rule " to Ireland. Ireland, as it happened, was
the one subject within the sphere of politics concerning
which Lord Randolph really knew something. In 1876
his father, the seventh Duke of Marlborough, had been appointed lord-lieutenant of the country. Randolph had
accompanied the duke to Dublin, had established himself
in the " Little Lodge " of Phœnix Park, and for the next
four years had spent most of the time not absorbed by his
parliamentary duties, in the Emerald Island, taking part
in its sports, gaining familiarity with all classes of its
people, and investigating its problems. He had acquired
a warm affection for the beautiful land and its fascinating
folk; but he had come quite definitely to the conclusion
that the union of Ireland with Great Britain should be
strenuously maintained. Home rule, which Isaac Butt
had begun politely to ask for in 1870, and Charles Stewart
Parnell ferociously to fight for in 1877, would, he felt, be
fatal both to the country that conceded it and to the
country that received it. It would mean, he was convinced, the beginning of the disruption of the British
Empire; chaos and bloodshed in Ireland; the spoliation
of Ulster; the persecution of protestantism; the establishment of a tyranny of priests. Chamberlain and Bright
concurred.

Until 1885, however, the " home rule " issue was little
more than academic in interest. For no responsible leader
on either side of the house of commons had given it his
countenance and support. Nevertheless, the violent antics
of Parnell and his nationalist followers in parliament, and
the remorseless ferocity of the parnellite faction in Ireland,
forced Irish problems into the forefront of practical
politics. In the house of commons the Irish nationalists,
some eighty in number, developed the art of mere obstruc-

tion to so high a pitch of perfection that a whole new procedure of " closure " had to be introduced in order to enable anything at all to be done.   In Ireland a " Land League " (instituted 1879), together with various subsidiary secret organisations, by means of a campaign of deliberate terrorism—boycott, looting, arson, cattle-maiming, and murder—reduced the unhappy country to a condition of barbarism and savagery.   In dealing with this dreadful menace to civilisation the gladstonian government (1880-85) showed most culpable feebleness.   It tried to pacify the parnellite tiger by means of small saucerfuls of liberal milk.   It sent " messages of peace " ; it instituted " land courts " whereby the " land hunger of the peasants " could be satisfied ; it appointed commissioners to assist emigration ; it advanced money to enable tenants to purchase their holdings ; and so on.   But the boycotts and the burnings and the murders went steadily on.   Then it entered into negotiations with the criminal instigators of the outrages and made a compact with them—the Kilmainham Treaty of April, 1882—whereby they found themselves once more free to resume their careers of violence. The immediate sequel was the assassination of Lord Frederick Cavendish (chief secretary) and Mr. Burke (under-secretary) in Phœnix Park on May 6, 1882.   This crowning atrocity stirred even the bewitched gladstonian cabinet to action, a long overdue *Prevention of Crimes Bill* was passed, and a stronger and more equitable administration established under Mr. Trevelyan.   The elementary duties of a civilised government—namely, the protection of life, liberty, and property—once more began to be performed.   But the parnellite agitation for " home rule " still continued, and even increased, although it was now restrained within constitutional channels.

The gladstonian government ended its inglorious and disastrous career in June, 1885.   Thoroughly discredited by humiliations abroad and disorders at home, it fell to a defeat on its budget proposals.   Lord Salisbury became prime minister.   The sequel showed that he made a mistake in thus, by accepting office, relieving his rival of the obloquy which he had justly incurred.   For when at the end of the year (December, 1885) he appealed to the country, he secured only 249 seats as against 335 gained by the liberals. But, besides the conservatives and the liberals, there were returned 86 Irish nationalists. Hence it was at once clear that these held the fate of the parties and of the government in their hands. For whom would they declare ? Parnell detested equally both of the English parties : his alliances were determined solely by what he judged to be his interests at the moment. During the election his instructions to the Irish voters in English constituencies had been to vote conservative. If he should continue to lean to the conservative side, the life of a liberal ministry would be short and troubled. Rumours soon began to spread that the conservatives were about to secure the Irish alliance by conceding the demand for " home rule." The rumours, as we now know, were baseless ; but they served their immediate purpose. They brought Gladstone to heel. The venerable dupe, having drugged his conscience with sophisms, saw Parnell and made the great surrender. He had his reward on January 26, 1886, when a combination of liberals and Irish nationalists drove the Salisbury government from office.

Then Gladstone, restored to a precarious power as Parnell's deputy, was called upon to fulfil his part of the pact. Accordingly he brought in his first *Home Rule Bill* in April, 1886. He had anticipated an easy passage, for his followers together with those of Parnell numbered 421, as against 249 conservatives. But he had reckoned without his host. He had made precisely the same mistake as his autocratic predecessor, Peel, had made respecting his conservative supporters forty years earlier. As Peel wrecked the conservative party over the corn laws in 1846, so did Gladstone wreck the liberal party in 1886. Lord Hartington and Mr. Joseph Chamberlain re-enacted the parts played in the previous melodrama by Lord George Bentinck and Mr. Benjamin Disraeli. They were joined, to Gladstone's immense surprise and intense disgust, by Mr. John Bright, who denounced in no measured terms his leader's desertion of the Ulster protestants, and his surrender to the parnellite rebels and traitors. The adherents of Hartington, Chamberlain, and Bright—to whom Lord Randolph Churchill gave the appropriate name of " liberal unionists "—were reinforced in debate by the full force of conservative oratory; in particular by the massive statesmanship of Salisbury, and by the incomparable badinage of Churchill, who poured corrosive ridicule on the political antics of " the old man in a hurry." The consequence was that when on June 8, 1886, the fate of the *Home Rule Bill* came to be decided in the house of commons, it was rejected by 343 votes to 313— the largest vote ever recorded in the annals of parliament. The majority included 93 " liberal unionists."

§ 63. Robert Cecil, Marquis of Salisbury

The defeat of the *Home Rule Bill* was speedily followed by the dissolution of parliament, the resignation of Mr. Gladstone, and the re-establishment of Lord Salisbury in office (August, 1886). The country emphatically declared itself against " home rule," returning 316 conservatives and 78 " liberal unionists " as against 191 Gladstonian liberals and 85 Irish nationalists. The shattering of the liberal party by Mr. Gladstone in 1886, which was followed in 1890 by the violent schism of the Irish nationalists over the Parnell-O'Shea scandal, gave the unionists a twenty years ascendancy in parliament, scarcely interrupted by a brief interlude (1892-95) during which the liberals impotently and ineffectually held office under Mr. Gladstone and Lord Rosebery successively. Throughout the major portion of these twenty years the great outstanding conservative figure was that of Robert Cecil, third Marquis of Salisbury. At the beginning of the period he was, indeed, but one of a triumvirate, his possible peers being Lord Randolph Churchill, the pseudo-tory democrat, and Sir Stafford Northcote (created Earl of Iddesleigh in 1885), the semi-liberal peelite. But the rash resignation of Lord Randolph in December, 1886, followed within a month by the tragic death of Lord Iddesleigh, left him wholly without a rival. He stood for an older type of conservatism than the democratic toryism of Disraeli or the middle-

class mercantilism of Peel. He was aristocratic to his
finger-tips; the great county magnate, lord of broad acres,
splendid representative of rural England; the faithful son
and generous patron of the church; the sustainer of the
constitution, both central and local; the devoted servant
of the crown; the inheritor and the perpetuator of the
glorious Elizabethan tradition. In many ways he recalled,
and almost seemed to reincarnate, his noble ancestor
William Cecil, Lord Burleigh. Both were lords of Hatfield; both sat in the house of commons as members for
the same borough of Stamford; both rose to the position
of chief minister and most trusted adviser of a great queen;
both were men of superb ability, untarnished honour, and
exemplary loyalty; both lived to render almost half a century of faithful service.* Robert Cecil in his early years
had given but little hint of the greatness that he was later
destined to display. He was the third son of his father,
so that his succession to the marquisate had seemed re-
mote: it was not, in fact, until he was thirty-five years old
that he had become heir-apparent as Lord Cranborne.
As a child he had been delicate and backward, at school
unhappy and undistinguished; and he had come down
from Oxford in December, 1849, with an "honorary
fourth-class" degree. Two years of travel (1851-53) had
vastly improved his health and had awakened his dormant
intelligence. Diligent reading and much solitary meditation (the supreme source of his strength) had developed
his naturally powerful mind. But writing and speaking
had been necessary for the full realisation of his capacities.
And fortunately circumstances had provided him with
opportunities for both. He had secured without a contest
a seat in parliament for the family borough of Stamford
(1853), and in the house of commons had soon made a
name for himself as a critic, fearless and independent, both
of the "happy family" that governed the country under
Aberdeen, and of the distracted opposition under Derby
and Disraeli that vainly tried to disturb the coalition's
complacent felicity. He had been an Ishmael whom both

* William Cecil, Lord Burleigh, was born 1520 and died 1598;
Robert Cecil, Lord Salisbury, was born 1830 and died 1903.

Palmerston and Disraeli had agreed in regarding as
" malignant." As to writing : domestic circumstances had
compelled him in 1857 to earn a living, and he had become
a notable contributor, on political themes, to the *Quarterly*
and other reviews.   He had developed a literary style of
unsurpassed pungency and precision, and had made a
great name for himself as an exponent of the conservatism
of Pitt and Castlereagh.   He had denounced the concessions which Wellington had made to catholics in 1829 ;
which Peel had made to the anti-corn-law league in 1846 ;
and which Disraeli had made to the parliamentary reformers in 1867.   Disraeli, recognising his high abilities
and sterling character, had done his best to win him over,
and by 1878 he had completely succeeded in doing so.   As
minister for foreign affairs at the time of the Congress of
Berlin he had played a part only second to that of the
prime minister himself in securing " peace with honour."
After Disraeli's retirement and death he had, as we have
noted, rapidly risen to the supreme place in conservatism.
    Salisbury's ascendancy, which after the fall of Bismarck
in 1890 was European as well as insular, was due purely
to character and intellect.   He remained as a man, what
he had been as a boy, solitary, aloof, unapproachable,
independent, self-sufficient, cold.   He was not a society
man or a committee man.   He had no skill in party
management or in the marshalling of mobs.   He was an
ingrained individualist, resenting interference himself, and
instinctively refraining from interfering with others.   His
cabinets were congeries of uncoördinated atoms.   But so
great was the trust that he inspired, so firm the faith in
his honour and loyalty, so strong the belief in his wisdom,
so secure the confidence in the sanity of his judgment, that
few of his colleagues dreamed of abusing the large liberty
that he left them.   He himself, in marked contrast to Mr.
Gladstone, believed in administration rather than in legislation ; in deeds rather than in verbiage.   He did not think
that the course of the world's affairs could be materially
modified by all the winds of eloquence ; nor, indeed, did
he suppose that even the art of skilled political navigators
could do anything to alter the trend of the great currents

that determined the destinies of nations. In his opinion the function of the statesman was to steer the ship of which he had charge clear of the obvious shoals and rocks that threatened to wreck it. He lived in days that filled him with alarm: in particular he dreaded the rising tide of democracy and the swelling menace of socialism. He had not that faith in the essential conservatism of the British working man that made Churchill so buoyant and Disraeli so serene. All he could do was to hope for the best, and try to avoid the worst.

The sphere, of course, which he chose as his own was that of foreign affairs, and in this sphere he rendered service to the nation of incomparable value. His policy was the maintenance of peace, the increase of international goodwill, the removal of causes of friction. His method was usually that which he called " graceful concession," and there were some who thought that he gave up too much to Russia in the Middle East, to the United States in South America, to France in Madagascar, and to Germany in Africa and Heligoland. Yet when occasion arose he could be rigid as steel: respecting Major Marchand's seizure of Fashoda in 1898, for instance, there was no inkling of surrender. The real interests of Britain were safe in his strong keeping. The persistent unfriendliness of France and Russia during the closing decade of the nineteenth century threw him on to the side of the Triple Alliance, and both Bismarck and William II. sought to lure him, or to force him, into an overt union. But he resisted the lure and repelled the force, and kept Britain free from foreign entanglements. Less skilful hands could hardly have avoided a catastrophe in the dark days of the Boer War.

§ 64. The Unionist Coalition

Three times was Lord Salisbury prime minister. His first ministry was but brief: it lasted only from June, 1885, to January, 1886. It was, moreover, a ministry on sufferance, a " cabinet of caretakers "; for it was in a hopeless minority in the house of commons, and it was precluded from appealing to the country for six months, because not until then would the parliamentary reforms of 1884-85 come into operation. Salisbury undoubtedly made a mistake in taking office in the circumstances, and he made a still greater mistake in appointing his friend Lord Carnarvon to the lord-lieutenancy of Ireland. For Carnarvon had a leaning towards "home rule," and, being deficient in worldly wisdom, he got himself entangled in some highly compromising negotiations with the utterly unscrupulous and infinitely crafty Parnell. These two mistakes of Salisbury were the proximate causes of the unsatisfactory issue of the election of December, 1885, and of Gladstone's precipitate conversion to "home rule."

We have already noted how Gladstone's attempt in 1886 to rush his party into an Irish policy which he and they had hitherto repudiated resulted not in the tactical triumph that he had anticipated, but in the disruption of the party and his own expulsion from power. The conservative whigs led by Hartington, the protestants led by Bright, the imperialists led by Chamberlain, combined to resist the Gladstonian autocracy; to oppose the proposed "march through rapine to the dismemberment of the empire"; to denounce their leader's unprincipled surrender to violence and outrage; to defend the abandoned interests of the Ulster protestants and the Southern loyalists; to prevent the disintegration of the queen's dominions, and the dangerous cession of the Emerald Island to Britain's avowed and malignant enemies. Hence speedily—as the result of the defeat of the *Home Rule Bill* in June and the decisive general election in July— Salisbury came back to office, and this time to power also. The "liberal unionists" and conservatives together gave him the comfortable majority of 120 in the new house of commons.

At first the "liberal unionists" held aloof from the ministry. Lord Salisbury much wanted to include them; he even went so far as to urge Lord Hartington to become prime minister, offering to serve under him. But they were liberals as well as unionists, and except on matters of Ireland and the Empire they differed considerably from the conservatives in their outlook. Even Hartington, the most conservative of whigs and the most conspicuously level-headed of all modern English politicians, differed from Salisbury in his attitude to the church, the constitution, the crown, the land, and education. Still more radical were the divergencies of Bright and Chamberlain. It was only, indeed, the imperative need of keeping an unbroken front in face of the ferocious and incessant assaults of the combined gladstonians and nationalists that maintained the unionist coalition in being. In particular Chamberlain, who seemed disposed to make a close alliance with Lord Randolph Churchill, caused much embarrassment in conservative circles by his advocacy of measures quite emphatically radical. He was a unitarian advocating secular education and disposed to disestablishment; he was a constitutional innovator, hostile to the house of lords and inclined to such novelties as the payment of members; he was believed to be, or to have been, a republican with scant reverence for the crown; he was an agitator for drastic changes in the land laws—and so on *ad infinitum.* His watchword of " free church, free land, free schools, free labour " was about as far removed as could well be imagined from any watchword acceptable to Lord Salisbury. So during the six years of Salisbury's second ministry (1886-92) the conservatives had to be content with an uneasy and narrowly restricted alliance with the "liberal unionists." The alliance was undoubtedly cemented and made more intimate when Mr. Goschen (January, 1887) consented to succeed Lord Randolph Churchill as chancellor of the exchequer; but still no fusion took place. Nevertheless, the influence of liberal unionism upon conservative policy was pervasive and profound. In particular, the *Allotments Act* (1887), the *County Council Act* (1888), the *Oaths Act* (1888), the *Local Taxation Act* (1890), and the *Free Education Act* (1891) are eloquent of liberal initiative.

In 1892 a slight swing of the electoral pendulum brought Mr. Gladstone back to office : England, it is true, still declared herself strongly unionist; but the " Celtic fringe " —Wales and Scotland—gave the home rulers a majority. Mr. Gladstone at once brought in his second *Home Rule*

Bill, which differed materially from the first. It, of course, passed the house of commons, but was rejected in the house of lords by 419 votes to 41. The consequence was naturally a raging and tearing campaign against the house of lords, with which was associated a vehement advocacy of such radical measures as Welsh disestablishment, manhood suffrage, payment of members, and local veto. It was evident that unless the English constitution were to be submerged by Irish, Welsh, and Scottish particularists, it would be necessary to convert the unionist alliance into a permanent coalition and fusion.

Hence when in 1895 Lord Salisbury came back to power for the third and last time, he took the momentous step of including the " liberal unionist " leaders—in particular Lord Hartington (who in 1891 had become the eighth Duke of Devonshire) and Mr. Chamberlain—in his cabinet. The Duke of Devonshire, entirely in his element, settled down easily and somnolently as lord president of the council. Mr. Chamberlain, with restless energy and consuming zeal, as head of the colonial office, inaugurated a new era of imperialism. His avowed purpose was (1) to tighten the bonds which united the different parts of the empire to one another; (2) to develop the resources of the crown colonies; and (3) to increase the commerce both of the mother-country and of the dominions. For eight years (1895-1903) he laboured at his great task with conspicuous success. He caused the important colonial conference to be summoned in 1897, and he laid before it countless proposals for cementing the unity of the empire and for increasing its security. He played a prominent part in establishing the School of Tropical Medicine. He did much to revive the failing prosperity of the West Indian Islands by his measures for assisting their sugar industry and their shipping. He secured large additions to the British dominions in West Africa. He took a leading place in the negotiations that resulted in the formation of the Commonwealth of Australia. But his most laborious efforts had to be devoted to the affairs of South Africa. He was determined to maintain the supremacy of the British Crown over both English and Dutch settlers and this determination brought him into conflict with the dominant majority in the Transvaal and the Orange Free State. The culmination of this conflict was the Boer War (1899-1902), which was still unconcluded when Queen Victoria died (January 22, 1901). The death of the great queen marked the end of an epoch, and Lord Salisbury, who belonged to the vanished Victorian age, and whose health was rapidly failing, would fain have retired at once. Duty, however, compelled him to remain in office until the Boer War was ended (May, 1902) and the arrangements made for King Edward's Coronation. Then, full of years and laden with honours, he resigned, and sought his well-earned retirement and repose (July, 1902).*

* Lord Salisbury died at Hatfield on August 22, 1903.

CHAPTER XVI

IMPERIALISTS VERSUS LITTLE ENGLANDERS
1901–1914

"I am more or less happy when being praised; not very uncomfortable when being abused; but I have moments of uneasiness when being explained."—LORD BALFOUR.

"It is because the conservative party has known how to discipline its own enthusiasms and to adapt itself to new conditions that it has retained its strength. And that it has been able to do so is largely the work of Balfour."—"SCRUTATOR," in *Sunday Times*, March 23, 1930.

"Great and lasting reforms are impossible unless they be based upon the old tradition of the conduct of public affairs and the working of national institutions."—F. E. SMITH [LORD BIRKENHEAD].

§ 65. ARTHUR JAMES BALFOUR

LORD SALISBURY'S successor in the headship of the conservative party was his nephew, Mr. A. J. Balfour. Ever since 1891, when he had been appointed first lord of the treasury and leader of the house of commons, he had been the inevitable man. This is all the more remarkable because up to 1887, although he had been over twelve years in parliament, and had held two minor offices, so far from being regarded as inevitable, he would hardly have been looked upon as possible.

Born 1848—the son of Lord Salisbury's sister and her husband, the lord of Whittingehame—he had sauntered comfortably and innocently through school, college, and society until in 1874 he had found himself in parliament. Indolence, indifference, lack of interest, absence of energy, were the negatives that impressed most of those who made his acquaintance. But those who knew him more intimately, and in particular Sidgwick the philosopher and Salisbury the politician, realised that beneath the dilettante surface of his character there lay an intellect of exceptional acuteness, a judgment of unusual sanity, a courage of superb imperturbability, and a will of inflexible

strength. During the 'seventies, although he accompanied
his uncle to Berlin in 1878, his interests were rather in
philosophy than in politics. The publication of his first
book, entitled *A Defence of Philosophic Doubt*, in 1879,
showed the world at large that a thinker of uncommon
ambiguity had arisen. Only the elect could form any conception of what he was driving at. His very title seemed
to have been carefully chosen so as to obscure the purport
of his work. For what he was really defending was not
philosophic doubt, but instinctive faith. He was attacking
alike the naturalistic materialism of Mill and the nebulous
idealism of Hegel, and was arguing, after the manner of
Coleridge, that the understanding is more than reason,
and that the highest truths are hidden from the wise and
prudent, but are revealed to babes. This was precisely
the same doctrine that he preached fifteen years later under
the very different title *The Foundations of Belief*. And
this very same reliance upon instinct, which was the basis
of his life-long religion, was also the groundwork of his
politics. His whole being was conservative. He had a
profound trust in inherited wisdom, in institutions tested
by long experience, in traditions handed down from times
immemorial, in customs sanctified by incessant use. And
he had an ineradicable " philosophic doubt " of abstract
theories, such as those that formed the stock in trade of
the early Victorian radicals or the late Victorian socialists.
Few have shown greater skill than he in pricking the
bubbles of pretentious sophistry.

His first efforts as a pricker of sophistical bubbles, however, had not enhanced his reputation. Perhaps they had
been misunderstood. He had joined himself to Lord
Randolph Churchill, and as the fourth member of the
" fourth party " he had amused himself for four years
(1880-84) by exposing, with irreverent levity, the fallacies
of Mr. Gladstone and the corresponding futilities of Sir
Stafford Northcote. But in 1884 he had dissociated himself from Lord Randolph and had sobered down. In 1885
his uncle had placed him over the local government board,
and next year had made him secretary for Scotland. It
was, however, in 1887 that his great occasion had come.

The Irish secretariate had unexpectedly fallen vacant, and to this he had been transferred. The appointment had caused amazement everywhere, and among the unruly Irish intense hilarity also. The parnellites, those pucks of contemporary politics, had promised themselves a gay and festive time. They had mistaken their man. Painted to look like a lath, his substance had been revealed to be the most finely tempered steel. He had found the nefarious " plan of campaign " in full operation—refusal of rent, resistance to law, boycotting, maiming, arson, murder, the whole repertory of devilry. In four years by fearless and impartial enforcement of justice he had entirely stamped it out. In the face of constant peril of assassination he had calmly and courageously done his duty. And with infinite resource and skill, as well as with baffling good humour, he had met and defeated the raving nationalists in the house of commons. At the same time he had given close and careful attention to the means for improving the material condition of the Irish people : he had set up the congested districts board; had organised the department of agriculture; had facilitated land purchase; had framed schemes for the reform of local government. When in 1891 he had laid down his secretariate in order to take up the leadership of the house of commons, he had left an Ireland more peaceful and prosperous than it had been for several generations. His position both as a great parliamentarian and a great administrator had been firmly established. The silly bogey of " home rule " had been effectively laid, and it need never have been revived again but for the exigencies of the rival politicians.

Mr. Gladstone, however, had got " home rule " on the brain, and in 1892 he had secured a Celtic majority pledged to support him. Mr. Balfour, with his inimitable dialectic, as leader of the opposition, had played a part even superior to that of the Duke of Devonshire, Mr. Chamberlain, and Lord Randolph Churchill in securing the rejection of the second *Home Rule Bill* (1893). With Mr. Gladstone's final retirement in 1894 the " home rule " question again had passed, for some fifteen years, out of the sphere of practical politics.

In Lord Salisbury's third ministry (1895-1902) Mr. Balfour's rôle had become increasingly important. The great prime minister's failing health had caused ever-growing responsibilities to devolve upon his nephew's shoulders. In particular, it had fallen to his lot to have much to do with the delicate negotiations that centred round Russia's occupation of Port Arthur in 1898. He, too, had been intimately concerned with the discussions that culminated in the Anglo-Japanese Alliance of 1902. Hence the retirement of Lord Salisbury in the middle of that year had almost automatically left him in command.

§ 66. The Conservative Debacle of 1906

That Mr. Balfour made a good prime minister cannot, I think, be maintained. The unprecedented conservative debacle of 1906 was, indeed, to no small extent due to the defects of his leadership. He was, in the supreme office, too slack and easy-going; too much inclined to let things slide; too indifferent to public opinion; too negligent of opposition; too contemptuous of criticism; too inaccessible to his followers; too coldly aloof; too ambiguous and un-intelligible in his utterances. As prime minister he did little to inspire and much to depress his supporters; much to irritate and little to alarm his opponents. The academic philosopher in him prevailed increasingly and excessively over the practical politician.

Circumstances, moreover, were against him. On the one hand, he had an awkward team to drive. Mr. Joseph Chamberlain, the ubiquitously energetic and masterful colonial secretary, with his own ideas and policy, and with his own organisation behind him, was a virtually independent potentate. The "liberal unionists" as a body, too, were still merely allies, and not members, of the conservative party; so they too had to be conciliated rather than commanded. And their ideas on several matters, such as religious education and protective tariffs, were by no means those of the majority of their colleagues. On the other hand, a subtle but portentous change had come over the constituencies. The new electorates, urban and rural, enfranchised respectively by Disraeli in 1867 and by Gladstone in 1884, had at last become conscious of themselves and of their powers, and had begun to organise themselves in trade unions and in labour representation committees for independent action in politics. They had begun, too, to formulate demands that lay outside the programmes of both the old parties. "Labour" was not much interested in home rule, or disestablishment, or religious education, or any other of the political and ecclesiastical questions that divided gladstonians from unionists. But it was intensely concerned with questions relating to wages, hours of work, conditions of employment, pensions, poor law, industrial insurance, and countless other matters of a similar kind connected with social and economic well-being. Unhappily, too, "labour" had become infected with socialism, and in addition to its objects of sane and legitimate pursuit, it was being persuaded by misguided intellectuals to clamour disastrously and iniquitously for such undesirable things as the nationalisation of the land, the socialisation of capital, the suppression of private enterprise, and the abolition of individual freedom. It was natural and indeed inevitable—as Salisbury (then Lord Cranborne), Lowe, and Carlyle had pointed out in 1867—that a new and ignorant electorate, devoid of political experience and unrestrained by any sense of responsibility, should, in the process of its education, and under the misguidance of mischievous demagogues, make appalling mistakes and advance irrational demands. But now that the day of its dictatorship was at hand, the position of a prime minister, whether conservative or liberal, was one of crucial difficulty.

A Disraeli or a Randolph Churchill might have been alive to the significance of the new movements, and might have been skilful enough to demonstrate to the working classes that their true and permanent interests lay not in attempting to wreck the capitalist system, but in taking advantage of its immense undeveloped possibilities; not in shattering the ancient constitution of church and state, but in enjoying the large liberties which they provided and protected; not in pursuing wild schemes of imaginary

utopias, but in building on the sure foundations of prosperity already laid; in short, not in socialism, but in conservatism. To some extent the gladstonian leaders, and
in particular Mr. Lloyd George, whose left ear was always
on the ground, were cognisant of the transformation that
was taking place. And they were quick to lure the new
electorate by promises of the relaxation of trade union
laws, offers of non-contributory pensions, schemes of insurance whereby the artisan could secure "ninepence for
fourpence," and revision of taxation which would mean
cheaper and stronger beer. Mr. Balfour, however, stood
serenely aloof, raised by both character and intellect far
above the muddy plain on which socialists and radicals
strove to outbid one another in promises of reckless prodigality for the votes of the newly awakened proletariat.
He seemed to be sublimely unaware that the Victorian
age had for ever passed away, and that a new world that
recked nothing of either Lord Salisbury or Mr. Gladstone
had come into existence. So he let things drift. He and
his cabinet, it is true, did some good work on the old
lines. They passed a useful *Education Act* (1902), which,
however, needlessly offended the nonconformist conscience.
They effected an invaluable *entente cordiale* with France
in 1904. They instituted a new army council and an all-
important committee of imperial defence. But they did
not accede to the growing demand for social and economic
reform.

One man, however, there was in the cabinet who was by
no means out of touch with the world of business and
finance. That man, of course, was Mr. Joseph Chamberlain, the successful and prosperous Birmingham manufacturer. His function in the government was, as we have
remarked, the management of the colonies. But this
management involved not only the conduct of the Boer
War and the settlement of the peace of 1902, but also the
supervision of a vast stream of commerce. Early in the
century he began to note with anxiety the relative decline
of trade between the mother-country and the dominions,
and the steady increase of imports from foreign countries.
In particular, after the conclusion of the Boer War he paid

a visit to South Africa which had a lasting effect on his policy. He pressed upon South African statesmen various schemes for the consolidation of the empire, and they in turn told him that an indispensable means to the end he desired was a tariff union in which all the constituent members of the empire should give preference to one another's commodities over those of foreigners. He, accordingly, came back to England in 1903 filled with newly generated enthusiasm for tariff reform, and in the course of that year he inaugurated the great campaign by means of which he hoped to conquer the country. He failed to carry the cabinet with him, and in the course of his vehement efforts to do so broke it up, Mr. Balfour vainly struggling to hold it together by adopting an attitude of neutrality, procrastination, studied ambiguity, protracted mystification, persistent refusal to be drawn.* It was an attitude that bewildered everyone and pleased no one. In September, 1903, the leading free-traders in the cabinet resigned—namely, Lord George Hamilton, Mr. Ritchie, Lord Balfour of Burleigh, and Mr. Arthur Elliot—and they were followed early in October by the decisive Duke of Devonshire. Mr. Chamberlain himself also resigned in order that, without forcing Mr. Balfour off the fence to which he had nailed his colours, he might conduct what his unsympathetic brother described as a " raging, tearing propaganda."

His propaganda, however, was at the time unsuccessful. Mr. Chamberlain, in fact, made the same mistake in respect of tariff reform as Mr. Gladstone had made in respect of home rule. He was too autocratic and too much in a hurry. He made other mistakes also, of which the chief was in departing from his original simple and defensible idea of advocating a revision of tariffs for imperial purposes, and going on to argue that the same tariffs that would serve to bind the mother-country to the dominions would also in some gratifying way serve further

* One of the most unintelligible and exasperating economic pamphlets ever written is Balfour's dissertation on *Insular Free Trade*, prepared originally for the cabinet, but published on September 16, 1903.

to stimulate home industries, to increase employment, to broaden the basis of taxation, to provide old age pensions, and to enable the government to retaliate upon foreigners who themselves enjoyed tariffs. He promised too much, and he got himself involved in controversies in which he was hopelessly outclassed by his free-trade opponents, both liberal and conservative. The working-class electorate was scared by the spectre of dearer food, and long before the election of January, 1906, the cause of tariff reform was for the time completely crushed.

Other causes, moreover, besides the ambiguity of Mr. Balfour and the precipitancy of Mr. Chamberlain, tended to produce the disastrous debacle. The nonconformists in general, and the "passive resisters" in particular, had never forgotten or forgiven the Education Act of 1902; the country as a whole resented the long continuance of war taxation in time of peace; a great outcry was raised at the introduction of Chinese labour into South Africa; the trade unions were restless and rebellious at the non-reversal by legislation of the Taff Vale judgment of 1901; there was an almost universal feeling of irritation and disgust, and a passionate desire at all costs to get rid of Mr. Balfour.

The immediate cause of Mr. Balfour's retirement was the issue of an ultimatum by Mr. Chamberlain on November 21, 1905 : he insisted on the ending of ambiguity and the full acceptance of his programme. To evade the necessity of lucidity Mr. Balfour resigned on December 4, and Sir Henry Campbell-Bannerman was called upon to form a ministry. He at once dissolved parliament, and by the election of January, 1906, was placed in a position of power unparalleled since the triumph of Pitt in 1784. Supported by 374 liberals, 84 nationalists, and 54 labour members (a total of 512), he faced a unionist opposition of but 158 (131 conservatives and 27 liberals). Mr. Balfour himself was defeated at East Manchester.*

* A seat was shortly afterwards found for him in the City of London. He remained leader of the conservative party until November, 1911, and then retired, being succeeded by Mr. A. Bonar Law.

§ 67. THE DELUGE

Those moderate liberal electors who in irritation and disgust gave their votes in 1906 to swell the huge majority of the Campbell-Bannerman ministry soon had cause to regret the temerity which had substituted King Stork for King Log. Mr. Balfour may have done too little; his hyphenated successor was soon compelled to do too much. He was not himself King Stork, but merely King Stork's bewildered and rather reluctant agent. The trade unions were King Stork, and within them the effective governing power was the socialist oligarchy which since 1890 had gradually captured and possessed them. Between 1906 and 1914 the country was destined to learn what socialist tyranny, exercised by means of trade unions, would mean. The gigantic liberal majority of 1906 had bound itself hand and foot by pledges to the exigent trade unions : it was to all intents and purposes a socialist-labour majority.

The unionist minority, hopelessly outnumbered, were, of course, impotent to check the deluge of socialist and radical legislation. But they did much by means of effective parliamentary debate and extensive platform oratory to expose the peril of the new despotism and to rouse the country to a consciousness of its danger. Mr. Balfour was as usual superb in destructive criticism ; but in pungency and popular appeal even he was surpassed by the brilliant and volatile F. E. Smith (later Lord Birkenhead), who for thirteen years (1906-19) represented the Walton Division of Liverpool. A sound scholar, a learned historian, a political philosopher of no mean order, few have excelled him in knowledge of tory history or in grasp of conservative principle. He was, moreover, a great lawyer, a pleader of immense power, and he became in time a lord chancellor of exceptional competence. It is one of the tragedies of modern politics that, after thirteen years in the house of commons, he should have drifted more and more away from the inner circle of conservative leadership and should have died prematurely in 1930.*

* F. E. Smith's *Toryism* (1903) and *Unionist Policy* (1913) should be studied by all interested in conservative history and ideas.

The educative work of A. J. Balfour, F. E. Smith, and their colleagues in parliament and throughout the country had, of course, little effect upon the trade-union controllers of the course of events during the years of the deluge, 1906-14.* It was only slowly that iterated warnings, reinforced by the painful demonstrations of bitter experience, taught the immature democracy that their real and permanent interests did not consist in the mulcting of the prosperous by means of predatory taxation; in the distribution of indiscriminate doles; in the piling up of pensions; in the conversion of poorhouses into palaces; and of prisons into places of entertainment. Indeed, even at the present moment this all-important truth is but very imperfectly realised. During the eight years that preceded the war, sloppy sentiment, rampant socialism, trade-union tyranny, were in full and raging flood. The evil that they wrought is incalculable and in part irremediable.

The socialist dictators of the trade unions and controllers of the government had two modes of operation. They proudly compared them to the two legs of the giant who advances to destroy his enemy, first one then the other carrying the monster forward. The first was the indirect or legislative method, made effective through the subservience of the pseudo-liberal majority in the house of commons; the second was the direct or militant method, made effective through strikes—strikes increasingly frequent, increasingly big, increasingly violent, and increasingly unreasonable and outrageous. The chief legislative triumphs of the new dictators during these disastrous years were (1) the iniquitous Trades Disputes Act of 1906—the Magna Carta of syndicalism and anarchy—which gave the trade unions permission to break contracts and commit torts with impunity; (2) the Old Age Pensions Act of 1908; (3) the predatory Finance Act of 1909-10; (4) the fatal Parliament Act of 1911, by means of which a virtual single-chamber government was set up in this country; an

* Mr. Joseph Chamberlain, unhappily, had a serious breakdown in health in July, 1906. He never recovered sufficiently to take a leading part in public life again, and he died on July 2, 1914.

Act destructive of the old English constitution; (5) the *National Insurance Act* of 1911, the burdens of which have proved to be incomparably in excess of the benefits; (6) the *Trade Union Act* of 1913 legalising the political activities of the unions, and making the position of all except socialist members extremely difficult and uncomfortable; and (7) the *Plural Voting Act* of 1913, whereby, in the name of democratic equality, second votes were taken away from various classes not likely to support socialist candidates. Rarely has so complete a legislative revolution been effected in so short a time. But even worse was to follow. For the *Parliament Act* of 1911, which deprived the house of lords of its right of veto, opened the way to the passage of subversive measures from which hitherto the country and the constitution had been secure. The Celtic fringe could now get its way irrespective of the wishes of England. Hence in 1912 a *Home Rule Bill* for Ireland and a *Disestablishment Bill* for Wales were brought in, with a knowledge that by 1914 they could be forced on to the statute book in spite of anything that the house of lords could say or do. It was a horrible situation, and it made abundantly clear the fact that the first duty of conservatism, whenever the nation should become sufficiently sane to return it to power, would be to amend the Parliament Act, so as to restore the lords' right of control, and to reform the upper house so as to make it an effective and defensible chamber of revision.

Meantime, while, as the result of the *Parliament Act*, a legislative revolution was being accomplished, as the result of the *Trades Disputes Act*, social anarchy was being precipitated. Strikes, which no longer involved anyone connected with them in any legal responsibility, increased with progressive frequency. In 1905 there had been 358; in 1906 there were 486; in 1907 there were 601; by 1913 the number had risen to 1,497; while in 1914, during the seven months preceding the outbreak of the war, there were 836, and the country was on the eve of a gigantic and general industrial conflict that threatened to assume the dimensions of a civil war.

§ 68. The Intervention of the Great War

Never within living memory had the United Kingdom
been reduced to so deplorable and alarming a condition
of disorder and distress as, owing to eight years of revolutionary misgovernment, prevailed in the summer of 1914.
Side by side with the threatened general strike, headed
by the newly organised " triple alliance " of miners, railwaymen, and transport workers, an armed conflict in Ireland seemed to be inevitable, owing to the determination of
the government to compel Ulster, against her will, to sever
her connection with Great Britain and submit herself to
the mercy of her mortal enemies, the Southern nationalists.
From imminent chaos the kingdom was saved by the sudden
precipitation of the great war (August, 1914). The outbreak of the war and the approach of civil disturbance
were probably not quite so devoid of inter-connection as
at the moment they appeared to be. We now know that
the Germans, before they declared war, made a very careful study of the conditions of all the powers likely to be
their opponents, and that they came to the conclusion
that Great Britain would in the autumn of 1914 be so fully
involved in an Irish civil war and a British general strike,
tending to a social revolution, that she would be quite
unable to intervene in any European conflict that might
be going on.

But, apart from the question whether or not Great
Britain would be in a position to go to war, in the autumn
of 1914 Germany had come to the definite conclusion that
the realisation of her destiny demanded another great
conflict. Only by force could she complete the work that
had been begun in 1864, continued in 1866, and temporarily ended in 1871. She had by violence snatched
Schleswig-Holstein from Denmark; extruded Austria from
Germany; and overthrown France, depriving her of Alsace
and Lorraine. It remained for her now, by means of her
incomparable army and her newly developed navy, to
complete the destruction of France, to remove the menace
of Russia, to secure dominance in the Balkan peninsula,
to deprive Britain of the command of the sea and shatter

her sea-linked empire, and finally to challenge the " Monroe doctrine " of United States diplomacy and assert Germany's claim to dominate and develop South America.

For a quarter of a century Germany had been preparing for " der Tag "—the day that was to give her an enduring world dominion.   The fall of Bismarck in 1890 had opened the way.   The great chancellor, it is true, had laid the foundations of German ascendancy : he had, with masterly skill and perfect ruthlessness, engineered and precipitated the three wars that resulted in the creation of the German Empire.   But after 1871 Bismarck had been cautious, unadventurous, almost pacific.   He realised that the newly fashioned and half-baked empire that he had set up needed a long period of tranquillity in which to set and harden. Hence he frowned upon colonial aggression, discountenanced naval expansion, kept free from Balkan entanglements, maintained good relations with Russia, made alliances with Austria and Italy, and carefully isolated intransigent France.   Only once, in 1875, had he for a moment leaned to the militarist view that the time had come to crush France entirely out of existence.   But, with Bismarck out of the way, an entirely new set of actors had entered.   The young Kaiser and his warlike associates did not hesitate to alienate Russia, cultivate Turkey, challenge France in Morocco, Britain in South Africa, and America in Brazil.   On every hand Germany became aggressive and provocative.   Britain realised her deep-seated hostility when the Kaiser, with the approval of his council, sent his telegram of congratulations to Kruger, and when, during the South African War, he tried to form an anti-British coalition.   Still more alarming to Britain was the challenge of the great navy which from 1898 the Kaiser began to construct : it was obviously intended to challenge the British command of the sea as well as the United States command of the American continent.

At the end of Queen Victoria's reign the British Empire was dangerously lonely in an unfriendly world.   Lord Salisbury has sometimes been blamed for pursuing a policy of " splendid isolation."   The isolation was deplorable and not splendid ; and the blame for it was not Salisbury's.

Lady Gwendoline Cecil in her fine biography of her father
has shown how much he disliked and dreaded Britain's
diplomatic solitude, and how strenuously he strove to
remove the misunderstandings that caused it. As a matter
of fact, it was his cautious and conciliatory policy that
paved the way for the alliances and ententes that happily
characterised the early years of the twentieth century. He
had virtually concluded the Anglo-Japanese alliance before
he retired in 1902; he had made possible those friendly
conversations which resulted in the *entente cordiale* with
France in 1904; and these again made smooth the path
for the more difficult negotiations that ended long friction
with Russia in 1907.

Germany intensely resented the drawing away of
Britain from the circle of the Triple Alliance and the formation of what she chose to regard as a hostile Triple
Entente. And she did her best to shatter the Entente in
the early stages of its development. She challenged France
at Tangier in 1905; she challenged Russia respecting Serbia
in 1908; she challenged Britain at Agadir in 1911. In 1911,
indeed, when Britain was internally involved in one of her
worst coal and railway strikes, the outbreak of an Anglo-
German war seemed imminent.

In 1911, however, Germany's hour had not yet struck.
Her army was not yet at its full strength; the big krupp
guns were not all ready; the navy was still incomplete;
the widening of the Kiel Canal was not fully accomplished;
subversive intrigue had not yet achieved its underground
work in the Entente countries; nor had diplomacy finished
its task of deluding the world into submission. Hence
with ill-suppressed fury the challenging warship was recalled from Agadir, and mild pacifists among the minor
British ministers—meek young men who seemed incapable
of wrath until the name of Lord Roberts was mentioned—
went about proclaiming that (January 15, 1914) " we live
at peace and goodwill with the great empire across the
North Sea " and that (May 19, 1914) Britain's " relations
with Germany were never more cordial than they are
to-day."

When these last soothing and soporific words were

uttered the " day " of Germany had all but dawned; her
" hour " was on the point of striking. The Balkan wars
of 1912-13 had profoundly disturbed her, weakening the
Triple Alliance, injuring her protégé Turkey, humiliating
the friendly Bulgaria, and exalting the Russophile Serbia.
So much perturbed and annoyed had she been by the
course of Near Eastern events that, as we now know, she
had sounded her allies in August, 1913, as to their willingness to embark on war at once. Italy, however, had refused to join the two empires in an unprovoked attack
upon Serbia, and so a new occasion had to be sought. It
was provided by the assassination of the Austrian Arch-
duke, Franz Ferdinand, at Serajevo on June 28, 1914.

CHAPTER XVII

PATRIOTS VERSUS THE OTHERS

1914–1922

" Why not admit what is and must be the truth—namely, that between Vienna and Berlin everything was fully prepared? We should be mere slaves, unworthy of the men who achieved predominance in Germany, if fifty years after Königgrätz things could be otherwise. . . . Cease the pitiful attempts to excuse Germany's action. Not as weak-minded blunderers have we undertaken the fearful risk of this war. We wanted it."— MAXIMILIAN HARDEN.

" Germany alone made this war. Germany herself, constituted, organised, and governed as she is, is the cause of the war."—J. W. ALLEN.

" We are fighting for our national existence, for everything which nations have always held most dear. But we are fighting for something more. We are fighting for the moral forces of humanity. We are fighting for the respect for public law and for the right of public justice, which are the foundations of civilisation."—ANDREW BONAR LAW.

" Human memory recalls no parallel to that uprising of the spirit which led five million Britons to fight as volunteers for the honour of their country and the liberty of other lands."—A. F. POLLARD.

§ 69. THE INFLUENCE OF THE WAR ON POLITICS

THE outbreak of the great war in August, 1914, and still more its unexpected protraction during four tragic and tremendous years, had a profound and permanent effect upon British politics and parties. First, the mere incidence of the war acted as an acid test, dividing all that was sound and rational in the nation from all that was visionary and out of touch with reality. The immense majority of the members of all parties of the state and all classes in society speedily recognised the fact that never before had the British Empire, the European state system, and even Christian civilisation itself, been faced by so

256

frightful a menace as that involved in this great outburst
of German militarism, this Teutonic bid for world
dominion. The conservatives, always sensitive to everything that concerns the national safety and honour, perceived instinctively and at once that, if Great Britain
should stand aside in neutrality and allow France and
Russia to be crushed, she would rightly be regarded with
execration by the whole world, and that when her turn
should come to be attacked—as it assuredly would come
within a very brief period—she would perish unaided and
unregretted. The mere instinct of self-preservation indicated to them the imperative necessity of immediate and
decisive action. On August 2—the day on which the
German onslaught commenced—Mr. Bonar Law wrote a
notable letter to Mr. Asquith (who in 1908 had succeeded
Sir Henry Campbell-Bannerman as liberal prime minister)
in which, on behalf of the responsible leaders of the conservative party, he expressed the opinion that " it would
be fatal to the honour and security of the United Kingdom to hesitate in supporting France and Russia at the
present juncture." As to the liberals, they did hesitate
and in the end divide into two sections. It required the
wanton and wicked German invasion of Belgium, with its
accompanying barbarities and atrocities, to rouse the
majority of them to a sense of the magnitude of the
German menace. Not until August 4—after a delay of
two days that in the circumstances might have been fatal
—did this majority perceive that the decisive day of
Britain's destiny had arrived. If Germany had pursued
any other plan of campaign than this supremely diabolical,
and therefore superlatively idiotic, devastation of Belgium (whose neutrality and security she had guaranteed),
British intervention would have been delayed until it
would have been too late to be of any avail. Paris would
have fallen ; Petrograd would have been forced to make a
peace of subjugation and servitude, and then the way
would have been clear for the long-anticipated demolition
of the British Empire. Even the labour party, dominated
as it was by socialistic " mugwumps," was shaken in its
cosmopolitanism and pacificism. Many of the more sober

and patriotic leaders, together with the masses of the right-minded rank and file, joined the conservatives and the majority of the liberals in whole-hearted support of the government. Mr. Asquith, although later he displayed a lamentable slowness and hesitancy in action, gave a magnificent oratorical lead to the nation in the autumn of 1914. " We shall never sheathe the sword, which we have not lightly drawn," he said, "until Belgium recovers in full measure all and more than all that she has sacrificed; until France is adequately secured against the menace of aggression; until the rights of the smaller nationalities of Europe are placed upon an unassailable foundation; and until the military domination of Prussia is wholly and finally destroyed." The informal union of majority liberals and non-socialist labour with the whole body of the conservatives in the patriotic defence of religion, country, empire, and honour, left in opposition only a miserable and discredited remnant of communists, conscientious objectors, cosmopolitans, and cranks. They were sufficiently numerous, however, when organised in such nefarious societies as the misnamed Union of Democratic Control, to do immeasurable mischief—hypnotising Mr. Asquith, encouraging the enemy, impeding recruiting, resisting conscription, prolonging the war, and in countless other ways helping the Germans towards victory. Some of them were good men, although deluded and enraged— that is, good men in the worst sense of the term. But they were all the more dangerous and pernicious because of their goodness. For just as the path to hell is paved with good intentions, so the most potent allies of the devil are pious sentimentalists. If the war was all but lost, and if it was ultimately won only at an appalling cost of wealth and life, they were primarily to blame.

The first effect of the war upon British politics was, then, the reshuffling of parties, and the re-grouping of the peoples of the United Kingdom into the two categories of patriots and pacificists. One supreme issue—the issue of life or death—subordinated all other questions. A second and happy consequence of the war was the postponement of the operation of the Welsh Disestablishment and Irish Home Rule Acts, which, under the new regulations of 1911, had become law in 1914, in spite of the sustained opposition of the house of lords. They were held over during the continuance of the war—a postponement which in the case of the iniquitous Home Rule Act was equivalent to repeal. Thus Ulster escaped the horror of civil war, and Great Britain the indelible disgrace of a great betrayal.

A third effect was the cancellation of the great general strike which the triple alliance of miners, railwaymen, and transport workers had prepared for the autumn of 1914. This was all to the good. But, unfortunately, the strike fever which since the passing of the deplorable Trades Disputes Act of 1906 had possessed organised labour could not be wholly exorcised. The socialist and syndicalist camarilla that had captured the trade union executives took advantage of the nation's extremity of peril not only to extort monstrous concessions and privileges, but also to foment strikes in key-industries that inflicted incalculable injuries upon the community as a whole. The South Wales miners' strike of August, 1915, the Clyde munition workers' strike of March, 1916, the engineers' strike of May, 1917, were but three of the worst of a series that reflected infinite disgrace upon those who organised them. The actions of these strike fomenters were treasonable, and the government showed culpable weakness in condoning crimes that in earlier days would have been deemed worthy of death.

Even as it was, before many months had passed, and when the true nature of the great conflict had revealed itself, it became clear that the liberal cabinet—weakened by pacificist secessions and lacking in energy and initiative—needed reinforcing and recasting. Hence in May, 1915, a coalition government was instituted, in which eight leading conservatives occupied important offices.

§ 70. ANDREW BONAR LAW

In May, 1915, the conservative party had been led for nearly four years by Mr. Bonar Law. He had succeeded

Mr. Balfour in November, 1911, when that old leader, after twenty-one years' continuous service, had felt it desirable to retire, because of the intense dissatisfaction expressed in certain " die-hard " quarters at the ineffectiveness of his resistance to the predatory budget of 1909; his failure to carry the country at the two crucial elections of 1910; and his refusal to advocate the rejection of the Parliament Bill by the lords in 1911.   Mr. Balfour had retired to philosophy, science, tennis, and golf, emerging, however, from time to time to make important pronouncements on political issues.   He had remained cordially loyal to his successor all through the period, never making himself a nuisance, as had the retired Mr. Gladstone to Lord Hartington in the 'seventies.   In 1915, although sixty-seven years of age, he loyally and devotedly joined the coalition cabinet as first lord of the admiralty, and in one capacity or another he continued to serve his country with consummate ability and efficiency until a few months before his death in 1930.   The successes of his early service for Ireland were repeated, and in the noble triumphs of conciliation that he achieved at Versailles, Washington, and elsewhere in the years following the war, the disasters of his days of leadership were forgotten.   He was at his best when he was second in command.   He had shown that he was not *capax imperii.*

Mr. Bonar Law, on the other hand, whom few had suspected of prime-ministerial powers, had displayed, when called upon unexpectedly to succeed Mr. Balfour in 1911, surprising administrative abilities and capacity for command.   Born in 1858 in Canada, he had been forty-two years of age when, after a prosperous business career in Glasgow, he had entered parliament for the first time.   At that age Pitt had already been prime minister for eighteen years, and in 1900 there were veteran unionists in both houses whose claims to the conservative leadership were incontestably strong.   Mr. Law, however, had between 1900 and 1911 made rapid headway in virtue of his modesty, his integrity, his high business ability, his admirable lucidity and directness as a speaker, his extraordinary effectiveness and readiness as a debater, his

enthusiasm for tariff reform, his devoted attachment to
Mr. Chamberlain, and his loyal defence of Mr. Balfour
against his critics during the critical years 1909-11. Nevertheless, when in 1911 the conservative leadership had
fallen vacant Mr. Law had never held any office more
elevated than that of parliamentary secretary to the board
of trade (1902-5), and his election as successor to Mr.
Balfour had been due to the graceful withdrawal of
superior claims by Mr. Austen Chamberlain and Mr.
Walter Long.   As leader of the opposition during the
troublous biennium 1912-14 he had distinguished himself
by his resistance to the government's Home Rule Bill,
and by the support that he had given to Ulster's determination not to surrender herself to her remorseless and
merciless enemies.

In May, 1915, Mr. Bonar Law became colonial secretary in the first coalition government.   The presence of
himself and his seven conservative colleagues in the
ministry immensely strengthened the executive, and that
at a time when every available source of strength was
needed.   For what with the defeat of Russia, the subjugation of Serbia, the entry of Turkey on the German side,
the shortage of munitions, the treachery of the Southern
Irish, and the recrudescence of treasonable strikes throughout the kingdom, the prospects of Britain were dark
indeed.   The conservatives more than any others instinctively realised the gravity of the situation, and rightly
estimated the issues at stake.   They perceived that everything which they held dear was in danger of destruction—
church, constitution, crown, landed interest, sea-power,
empire, and all the liberties of the people.   In particular,
since public duty rather than private right is the keynote
to their creed, they were free from that doctrinaire and
anti-social resistance to conscription which characterised
the liberal and labour parties.   The first great benefit that
Mr. Bonar Law was able to confer upon the cabinet and
the country was the skilful conduct through the house of
commons of the Military Service Bill of January, 1916.   A
second task, hardly less important, then awaited him, also
a task for which his colonial antecedents and his known

political principles well fitted him. He attended, as chief
British representative, the important economic conference
held in Paris in June, 1916, and he was largely instru-
mental in securing the acceptance of the protective and
co-operative proposals there formulated. He and his colleagues, however, were increasingly dissatisfied with the
course of domestic politics, and with the conduct of the
war. The year 1916 saw the failure of the Gallipoli ex-
pedition; the crushing of Rumania; the monstrous Irish
rebellion; the doubtful naval engagement off Jutland; and
the frightful carnage of the three months' battle of the
Somme. It was evident to Mr. Bonar Law and his friends
that more vigour, more sacrifice, more determination, were
needed in high places. With this view Mr. Lloyd George
—who at this stage of his chameleon-like career was virtually a conservative—entirely concurred. Hence in
December, 1916, Mr. Lloyd George presented an ultimatum
to Mr. Asquith which led to the latter's resignation. In
the course of the protracted crisis that ensued, Mr. Bonar
Law was invited to become prime minister. He modestly
and patriotically, however, declined the invitation, recognising that Mr. Lloyd George was the man the country
called for. He was content to support him as his chancellor of the exechequer and leader of the house of
commons.

§ 71. THE WINNING OF THE WAR

The second coalition government (December, 1916, to
October, 1922) was a dominantly conservative body. Besides Mr. Bonar Law, it included Mr. Balfour (foreign
affairs), Lord Derby (war), Mr. Long (colonies), Mr.
Austen Chamberlain (India), Sir G. Cave (home), Sir E.
Carson (admiralty), Lord Curzon (president of the council), Lord Finlay (lord chancellor), Sir F. E. Smith
(attorney-general), and Lord Crawford (privy seal). During its continuance, of course, it underwent many changes,
but its dominantly conservative character was thereby increased rather than diminished. So prominent, indeed,
was the conservative element in the coalition that Mr.
Bonar Law was less a subordinate to Mr. Lloyd George

than an ally on equal terms. His modesty, however, his loyalty, his devoted patriotism, enabled him to work comfortably in conditions that others would have found intolerable. For Mr. Lloyd George possessed a dictatorial and encroaching personality that tended to interference and monopoly. At the back of 10, Downing Street he planted a " garden suburb " wherein he located a secretariate of his own—a secretariate ultimately numbering 114 persons—into whose hands he seemed disposed to transfer the whole administration of the empire. There had been nothing quite like it since the days of the encroaching Wardrobe of Edward II.

The times, however, were such as precluded the careful consideration of constitutional niceties. The destiny of the world remained long in the balance; and more than once during the terrible two years 1916-18 the immeasurable disaster of a German victory seemed imminent. In 1917 the Anglo-French attack on the western front failed; the Italians were routed at Caporetto, and, worst of all, the Russians, owing to a succession of deplorable revolutions, were withdrawn from the war, thus freeing great German armies for concentration in France and Belgium. To counter-balance these disasters, the one hopeful event was the entry of America into the war on the side of the allies (April, 1917). But, of course, it was evident that at least a year would elapse before the arrival of American troops in Europe could begin to redress the scale. Hence in the spring of 1918 Germany made her last and her supreme effort to smash the allied line in the west, capture Amiens and Paris, drive the British into the sea, and dictate terms of peace. So tremendous was the force of her attack, and so prodigal was Germany in her expenditure of human life, that she came within an ace of success. Nevertheless, she failed; and as the result of her failure she broke and collapsed. On July 18 the final victorious advance of the allies began under the unified command of Marshal Foch, and in a few months the war was over. Bulgaria was compelled to cry for mercy in September; Turkey had to follow suit in October; early in November Austria had to admit that she could fight no more. Then

Germany, left alone in face of an outraged world, and on the eve of a military disaster unprecedented in history, was forced to ask for an armistice and to accept it on terms dictated by the allies (November 11, 1918).

The cessation of hostilities was accompanied by the abdication and flight of the arrogant and guilty kaiser; by the deposition of all the petty kings and princes of the empire, and by the setting up of a German republic. The French revenge for 1870 was dramatic and complete.

Whilst the soldiers, aided by the seamen—who, in spite of Germany's ruthless submarine warfare, succeeded in establishing a strangling blockade of Central Europe—were effecting the destruction of the German war machine, the statesmen of the coalition government were facing tasks of unprecedented administrative difficulty. First, the conduct of the war, to the immense increase of promptitude and efficiency, was placed in the hands of a " war cabinet " of seven, consisting of one liberal (Mr. Lloyd George), one labour member (Mr. Henderson), four conservatives (Mr. Bonar Law, Lord Milner, Lord Curzon, and Sir E. Carson), and General Smuts.   Secondly, the whole civilian life of the nation was reorganised by means of new government departments—shipping, food control, pensions, national service, transport, and so on; labour was " diluted " by means of old men and young women, so as to release men of military age; conscription was extended to include all men under fifty-one; an attempt was made to apply compulsion to Ireland (which till 1918 was most inequitably exempted), but the result was negative, for troops much needed abroad had to be sent to quell the riots caused by the rooted Irish objection to fight any people except the English.   Thirdly, the food supply of the nation had to be maintained in face of the frightful destruction of shipping and of heroic seamen caused by the intensive German submarine campaign; a strict system of rationing had to be devised and applied; prices, too, had to be rigidly controlled so as to prevent unequal distribution and undue profiteering.   In all this difficult and novel work the business genius of Lord Rhondda rendered memorable and invaluable service.   Fourthly, the supply of munitions, which were demanded by the new armies on a scale never so much as conceived of before, had to be maintained and constantly increased. Here the great scientific knowledge and administrative ability of Lord Moulton were utilised. On his appointment, says his son, "the output of high explosives was about a ton a day. Lord Moulton raised it before the end of the war to over a thousand tons a day." Fifthly, enormous sums of money had to be raised, for apart from loans which had to be provided in order to keep the exhausted allies going, the cost of the war to the United Kingdom alone amounted in 1917 to nearly £8,000,000 a day. All previous nightmares of expenditure were immeasurably surpassed by the grim reality of this inevitable squandermania. Mr. Bonar Law, as chancellor of the exchequer, showed amazing skill and ingenuity in tapping new sources of revenue, and in floating illimitable loans. All thoughts of economy had to be (or at any rate were) abandoned, and posterity had to be (or at any rate was) saddled with a debt of £7,000,000,000 as a charge for the privilege of a continued existence free from German control.

So the war was won. But, beside the prodigious cost in wealth, it is estimated that the cost in men to Britain and the devoted Dominions who so loyally came to her aid was 885,743 killed and 2,047,211 wounded. *Tantæ molis erat Romanam condere gentem.*

§ 72. The Losing of the Peace

When the war was over the coalition had completed its appointed task. Well would it have been both for conservatism and for the country if then and there it had been dissolved, and if normal party government had resumed its sway. For coalitions, although in times of national extremity they may be proper and even necessary, have two grave disadvantages. First, they involve abandonment of principle and blurring of policy: each of the constituent members has to consent to the dropping of projects and programmes which it regards as essential to the national prosperity; all are deflected from their natural and straight line of movement. Secondly, coalitions wipe out of existence that wholesome and necessary body known as " his majesty's opposition," without which democratic government inevitably degenerates and decays. No doubt it is pleasant to ministers to be virtually uncriticised and unrestrained; to be free from all immediate fear of supersession : but it is not good either for them or for the country. For, attractive as a "national"—*i.e.*, coalition—government may appear to be both to its constituent members and to political idealists, it has this fatal disadvantage, that the only alternative to it is an " anti-national " government. Gratifying as it may have been to Mr. Lloyd George, Mr. Bonar Law, and Mr. Henderson, or his successor Mr. Barnes, to fraternise and cooperate, instead of debating and dividing; and pleasing as it unquestionably was to the denizens of the New Jerusalem to behold the lion lying down with the two lambs; it was not satisfactory that the only opposition should consist of the deplorable company of cosmopolitans, communists, conscientious objectors, anti-conscriptionists, and cranks, who for four years had " done their damnedest " to make the allies lose the war. And however good a government may be, it cannot last for ever; however excellent its work, it inevitably rouses antagonisms; however efficient it may remain, people get tired of it, become dissatisfied with its achievements, wish to try something— anything—else. Mere lapse of time saps its strength; unavoidable mistakes weaken it; necessary severities lessen its popularity; in the end it falls. And then, if it is a "national" coalition, the "anti-national" rout comes in, and with it comes chaos. The continuance of the war coalition after 1918 was the direct cause of the lamentable tragi-comedy of 1924—that is to say, the direct cause of the increase of the socialist vote from $2\frac{1}{4}$ millions to $4\frac{1}{3}$ millions, and of socialist members from 57 to 191. Under the banner of socialism gathered together all that was disgruntled, disillusioned, decadent, and desperate in the kingdom.

We can readily realise, as we survey the historic scene from the vantage ground of distance, what were the causes

that led the conservative leaders to remain under Mr.
Lloyd George's command for the disastrous four years
1918-22. On the one hand Mr. Lloyd George appeared to
have become a new creature since his wild pre-war Lime-
house days. But little seemed to be wanting to convert
him into a good conservative. At any rate, he was on
the worst of terms with most of his former liberal cronies.
Moreover, he had undoubtedly done magnificent work
during the later phases of the war. His fiery tempera-
ment, his buoyancy, his energy, his courage, his irre-
pressible optimism, his superb confidence, his oratorical
agility, had been prime factors in that stimulation both
of the British and of their allies that had carried the war
to its successful conclusion. In 1918 he was unquestionably the dominant personality in European politics. His
shallowness, his untrustworthiness, his lack of political
principle, his "great but concealed incompetence," had
not as yet been made manifest. On the other hand, the
war had left so awful a mess to be cleared up—peace
treaties to be framed, a league of nations to be instituted,
armies to be demolished, navies to be disbanded, industries to be re-established, commerce to be reorganised, and
so on indefinitely—that it seemed natural and proper that
the war government should be perpetuated, in order to
deal with this portentous aftermath. At any rate, perpetuated it was, and when in December, 1918, it appealed
to the country, the country responded by returning 484
"couponed" members pledged to support it, as against
222 opponents, of whom 73 were Irish Sinn Feiners.

The consequence of the coalition was the corruption of
conservatism. It lost sight of its fundamental principles. It became involved in the meshes of compromise
and concession. It found itself engaged in enterprises that
would have filled its great old leaders with amazement
and horror. It all but lost its soul. The circumstances,
of course, were those of unprecedented perplexity. The
war had swept out of existence both the institutions and
the ideas of the pre-war world. It was difficult indeed to
decide where the old should be restored and where the new
should take its place, where necessary reform ended and

where deadly revolution began. I think, however, that it may safely be said that no conservative government true to its principles and conscious of its power would have done some of the things that were perpetrated by the coalition administration (in which conservatives predominated) during the six years of its existence, 1916-22.

First, it would not have extended the franchise with the reckless prodigality of the Act of 1918, which increased the electorate from eight to eighteen millions. In particular, it would not have removed the pauper disqualification for voters in local elections. Any recognition of the conservative principle that the franchise is a public function rather than a private right would have prevented the transference of so much political power to ignorance and irresponsibility. Secondly, it would not have sanctioned the reckless extravagance in public expenditure—expenditure which, however desirable, was beyond the capacity of the exhausted taxpayer to stand—which marked these madcap years: expenditure on pensions, doles, agriculture, education, housing, road-making, trade guarantees, and countless other things good, bad, and indifferent. Thirdly, it would not have made the fatal mistake in Indian policy involved in the " self-governing " proclamation of 1917, and immensely aggravated by the Montagu-Chelmsford Report of 1918, and by the Government of India Act of 1920. Already the fruits of this disastrous aberration—this attempt to confer self-government upon a continent unready to receive it—have been sufficiently displayed in widespread ruin and bloodshed. And the end is not yet. Fourthly, and finally, it would not have made the great betrayal of Irish loyalists involved in the Government of Ireland Act of 1920 and the " treaty " of 1921. It would have realised that to concede to violence what has been denied to argument is the very abdication of civilised authority.

CHAPTER XVIII

FRIENDS OF FREEDOM VERSUS SOCIALISTS
1922-1931

" We are spending the savings of the past; we are stopping the possibility of saving in the present; we are mortgaging the savings of the future."—SIR ERNEST BENN.

" If I had the power, as I have the will, I would arraign the labour party before the national conscience and ask it to show cause why it should not be condemned for corrupting the citizenship of the working man."—SIR HENRY JONES.

" When a conservative government acquiesced in the Parliament Act and in political levies by trade unions, cold-shouldered the reform of the House of Lords, maintained state control of rents and prices, proposed to hew a way through city slums, bestowed old age pensions on an unexampled scale, and lavished subsidies on coal and protection on efficient industries, it was difficult to discern a basic principle of differentiation between the parties."—A. F. POLLARD.

§ 73. THE CONSERVATIVE RECOVERY, 1922-23

So numerous and grave had been the departures of the coalition government—that is to say, of Mr. Lloyd George and his satellites—from conservative principle that in the autumn of 1922 it at last became evident to clear-sighted conservatives that, if the coalition were to continue to exist much longer under Mr. Lloyd George's command, the conservative party would be wrecked and the conservative cause would perish. Indeed, so far back as June of that year a large group of conservative peers and commoners had publicly declared that " to drift further with ever-changing policies must quickly produce chaos, disaster, and ruin." Not, however, until October did the actual conservative revolt take place. It was precipitated by Mr. Lloyd George's persistent interference in foreign affairs, and in particular by his Near Eastern bungling which alienated France and Italy, lured Greece to destruction, and all but involved Britain in a single-handed war with Turkey. On October 19, 1922, a great conservative meeting was held at the Carlton Club, and at that meeting Mr. Stanley Baldwin took the lead in denouncing the coalition and demanding the emancipation of conservatism from the fetters of Mr. Lloyd George's dictatorship. He was supported by Mr. Bonar Law, who unfortunately had been compelled by ill-health for many months to withdraw from active political work. And these two carried the meeting, in spite of a vigorous defence of the coalition made by its conservative members. The recovery of freedom was voted by 187 to 87. The coalition was at an end, and Mr. Lloyd George had nothing to do but to resign. He did so with a fury that knew no bounds, and with a vindictive hatred of Mr. Baldwin, whom he has since pursued in an undying vendetta marked by an ingenious malignity devoid of all mercy and all scruple.

Mr. Baldwin had not until that critical and decisive day occupied a very prominent place in politics. He was but president of the board of trade, and he had been a minor cabinet minister for rather less than two years. But he was favourably known in the house of commons as a man of scholarship and cultivated taste, a successful and wealthy ironmaster, humane and sympathetic, careful of his workpeople, and on the best of terms with them. In politics his dominant notes were his patriotism, his hatred of profiteering, and his profound belief in the necessity of protection for British industries. His high integrity, his freedom from personal ambition, his kindliness and genial humour, his keen sense of honour, his burning zeal for the welfare of the nation as a whole and of the poor in particular, gave him a great and growing hold on the confidence and admiration of his colleagues and his countrymen. He was an avowed disciple of Disraeli, and more fully and deliberately than anyone since that great leader's death did he seek to realise the ideals of the genuine " tory democracy."

On October 19, 1922, he took his fate in his hands when he declared against the continuance of the coalition. He had against him all the chief conservative leaders except Mr. Bonar Law and Lord Curzon. If he had wrongly

judged the temper of the great conservative congregation,
he would have faded away instantly and finally into the
oblivion that engulfs unsuccessful rebels. His appeal, however, to character and principle prevailed. He convinced
the assembly that the continuance of the coalition under
Mr. Lloyd George's discredited control would mean that the
demoralisation and disintegration of conservatism, already
begun, would " go on inevitably until the old conservative
party was smashed to atoms and lost in ruins." When
Mr. Bonar Law, who had long hesitated between loyalty
to Mr. Lloyd George and his growing dissent from all
Mr. Lloyd George's doings, declared himself on Mr. Baldwin's side, the battle of independence was won.

This striking triumph of character and conviction, of
course, at once raised Mr. Baldwin to the front rank of
conservative statesmen. So that when Mr. Bonar Law
(stricken as he was with mortal disease) heroically
accepted the office of prime minister, it was natural that
he should make Mr. Baldwin his chancellor of the exchequer. The general election of November, 1922, confirmed the bold action of Mr. Baldwin and his chief. The
conservatives secured 347 seats as against 142 labour and
118 liberal, a clear majority of 87.

Mr. Bonar Law's premiership lasted but little more than
two hundred days. Illness compelled him to resign on
May 20, 1923, and five months later he died. During his
brief tenure of office his policy was " tranquillity and
stability." There was urgent need of both. Unrest and
insecurity were paralysing all beneficent human activity.
Everywhere abroad racial and national conflicts abounded ;
at home Irish civil war and a series of revolutionary strikes
in Great Britain kept the country in a turmoil. Industry
and commerce languished ; currencies collapsed ; unemployment increased ; costly projects of " social reform "
failed to fulfil the promises of their projecters ; unproduc-
tive taxation sapped the sources of the nation's solvency.
Mr. Bonar Law, before he retired, was able to make one
supremely important contribution to the world's recovery.
Through the able agency of Mr. Baldwin, he came to terms
with America concerning the mode and rate of the repay-

ment of the enormous debt of £963,000,000 which Great
Britain, on her own behalf and that of her allies, had
incurred during the course of the war. The terms exacted
by the Americans were hard; but their acceptance immensely increased British prestige in the world, and at
the same time gave Britain a financial stability that served
as a basis for a general European resettlement.

When Mr. Baldwin became prime minister in succession to Mr. Bonar Law at the end of May 1923, faced as
he was by the problem of languishing industry and swelling unemployment, he soon arrived at the conclusion that
the only effective remedy for the economic distress would
be a more or less general tariff. The conservative party,
however, was bound by old pledges not to introduce such
a tariff without a special appeal to the electorate for a
mandate. Accordingly, in November, 1923, Mr. Baldwin
advised the dissolution of the parliament in which he still
had a secure majority of 85, and went to the country on
the issue of tariff reform. His anticipations of electoral
support were disappointed. The election of December 6,
1923, resulted in the return of 258 conservatives (as against
346 at the dissolution), while labour secured 191 seats
(*vice* 144), and the liberals 158 (*vice* 117). Mr. Baldwin,
at the head of what was still the largest of the three
parties, faced the new parliament in January, 1924; but
a direct vote of no confidence, supported by combined
liberals and socialists, at once compelled him to resign.
It might have been said of him as was said by Sheridan of
Grenville when he raised the catholic emancipation question in 1807 : "I have known many men knock their heads
against a wall; but I never [or only once] before heard of
a man collecting bricks and building a wall for the express
purpose of knocking out his own brains against it." The
dissolution of the 1922 parliament in 1923, with four years
of life yet to run, was a disastrous tactical mistake.

§ 74. A SOCIALIST INTERLUDE, 1924

The defeat of Mr. Baldwin in December, 1923, was due,
first, to a widely diffused conviction that a general tariff,

particularly if it should include food taxes, would increase the cost of living more than it would raise wages or extend employment; secondly, to the extreme hostility of the liberals towards the breaker of the coalition, and also to the lavish expenditure of money from that mysterious and nefarious fund which Mr. Lloyd George had accumulated by what was commonly called "the sale of honours"; and, thirdly, to the antagonism of certain great newspaper magnates, controllers of a large proportion of the nation's press, who resented the fact that Mr. Baldwin had shown himself far less amenable to their influence, and far less free in taking them into his confidence, than had Mr. Lloyd George.

The enforced resignation of Mr. Baldwin in January, 1924, was, however, merely the beginning, and not the end, of a complicated and difficult political crisis. The evils of a three-party system had never been more apparent than they were then. The conservatives under Mr. Baldwin were still by far the largest party in the house of commons; the socialists came an easy second; but the decision who should be prime minister and what should be the policy of his government rested with the minute liberal rump, which consisted of 158 members in a house of 607. The liberals decided to put the socialists in, hoping that they might continue to control them and keep their socialism within the limits of "progressive liberalism." So Mr. Ramsay Macdonald became prime minister (and also secretary for foreign affairs), and for ten dreadful months, the mere memory of which is a nightmare, the country had to behold the spectacle of an inexperienced, unskilled, and internally divided minority ministry, torn between a desire to placate its own red supporters and the necessity of keeping the favour of its yellow patrons. The government had responsibility without power; the liberal caucus had power without responsibility. Rarely have British politics been in a more unhealthy condition. The disillusioned electorate was made to realise that unless it wished to stultify itself, reduce democratic control to a mockery, and hand over sovereignty permanently to an unrepresentative cabal, it must eliminate the third party and return to the normal two-party system which alone is satisfactorily workable in a house with only two division lobbies, Aye and No.

In one important department it must be admitted that the socialist government with its liberal allies did well. And credit for this is specially due to Mr. Macdonald personally. In friendly conversations with M. Herriot he was able to ease Anglo-French tension and to come to an agreement, too long delayed, concerning the evacuation of the occupied German territory and the payment of the overdue German reparations. But almost everywhere else was humiliation, failure, and disgrace. The diplomatic recognition of the criminal Soviet régime in Russia, forced upon the government by its communistic left wing, was followed, as was to have been expected, by an orgy of subversive propaganda, treachery, and intrigue. All the forces in the country, already too numerous and powerful, that were antagonistic to religion, constitutional government, individual freedom, financial stability, economic sanity, and christian civilisation, were deplorably encouraged and stimulated. They began to anticipate the early approach of " the day " on which the " social revolution " should be realised. For example, in September, 1924, Mr. Wheatley, minister of health, prophesied that "within ten years, probably within five, capitalist society in Britain will fall about our ears." Meantime, however, Mr. Wheatley's feeble and misguided efforts to solve the housing problem, in spite of lavish expenditure of public money, were spectacular failures. Such small successes as they achieved were secured by the aid of capitalists and the employment of capitalist methods. The socialist government as a whole, indeed, was prosperous just in proportion as it abandoned socialism ; and it failed conspicuously and disastrously wherever it attempted to put its theories into practice.

Most lamentable of all was its failure to solve the pressing problem of unemployment, concerning which it had loudly boasted that it, and it alone, had the secret of solution. After ten months of futile fumbling, devoid of principle and wholly unoriginal, it left the numbers of

unemployed much what they had been at the beginning—
namely, over twelve hundred thousand.

The conservatives, led by Mr. Baldwin, were much
kinder to the struggling and rather pathetic socialistic
administration than were the liberals.   While the liberals
showed intense resentment at any signs of socialistic independence, the conservatives manifested a readiness to let
the ministers have a fair run in their anomalous and difficult course; to assist them in such good works as the improvement of Anglo-French relations; and to guide them
when their errors were due merely to ignorance and in-
experience.   They had, however, strenuously to oppose
them when they betrayed the empire and threatened the
British command of the sea by the abandonment of the
Singapore naval base; and when they threatened to desert
the cause of the loyalists in Ireland.   In respect, however,
of both Singapore and Ireland they had the support of the
liberals, and so survived.

Towards the autumn, however, two causes emerged
which strained the consciences of the liberals too far, with
the result that a sufficient number of them reverted to the
conservative side to bring down this unhappy and rickety
ministry, which but for supreme liberal folly and perversity would never have been set up at all.   The first of
the two was a proposal to conclude a treaty with the Soviet
government, accompanied by an enormous loan of British
money—a treaty negotiated behind the prime minister's
back by a group of unofficial " reds " who had increasingly usurped control of socialist policy; a treaty to be
concluded with a power which had established itself by
means of rapine and murder, accompanied by a general
confiscation of British property in Russia and by a complete repudiation of public debts.   This was too much for
even liberal complacency.   Still worse was the Campbell
scandal—the inexcusable withdrawal, apparently at the
same " red " dictation, of a governmental prosecution (for
seditious libel of an aggravated nature) directed against
the acting editor of the communistic *Workers' Weekly.*
Liberals and conservatives combined in demanding the
appointment of a select committee to inquire into this

judicial scandal, and they carried their demand by 364 votes to the government's 198.   Mr. Macdonald, not wholly sorry to be relieved of the troubles he had got himself into, and above all happy to be freed from the tyranny of his own " red " supporters, treated this defeat as a vote of censure, and procured the dissolution of the parliament (October, 1924).

§ 75. THE CONSERVATIVE OPPORTUNITY, 1924-29

The alarm and disgust of the country due to the monstrous iniquities of the Russian loan and the Campbell scandal—iniquities which revealed the persistent opera-tion of subterranean forces utterly subversive of both the honour and the interests of Britain—were raised to the height of intense indignation by the discovery and publi-cation of the now notorious Zinovieff letter, in which the president of the communist international secretly incited the communists of Britain to violence and revolution.   The result was that in the general election of October 29, 1924, the socialists lost 40 seats, the liberals 118, leaving the conservatives with a clear majority of 222.*   The electors by almost extinguishing the liberal party showed that they realised two things : first, that the liberals were really responsible for the setting up of the socialist government in January, 1924, and for its subsequent misdeeds; secondly, that a three-party system, with its divorce of responsibility from power, is fatal to the working of any sort of democratic administration.

The conservatives, then, in October, 1924, received their mandate and got their opportunity.   Mr. Baldwin secured his second innings as prime minister, and he was joined by most of the coalitionist conservatives (such as Mr. Austen Chamberlain and Lord Birkenhead) who had been excluded from his 1922 cabinet.   A clear course of five years lay before the fortunate ministers.   What did they do during its process ?

In the spring of the year the conservative leaders, in the

* The returns were : conservatives, 413; socialists, 151; liberals,

early days of their relegation to the rank of the parliamentary opposition, having surveyed the scene of their recent electoral catastrophe, had issued a statement of their principles and their policy, under the title *Looking Ahead.* It was a mild and emollient document, considered by enthusiasts of the junior imperial league to be somewhat deficient in what they called "vim" and "pep," but eminently well calculated to allay the tremors of agitated liberals and to win the approval of semi-christian socialists. It contained nothing alarmingly, and little distinctively, conservative. Its aim was obviously to generate that atmosphere of tranquillity and that sense of stability which seemed to be so needful in a world distracted by strife and haunted by the demon of insecurity. It dealt first with the empire, advocating unity, cooperation, federation, and progressive self-government; secondly, with foreign affairs, ingeminating peace, speaking hopefully of the league of nations, but stressing the danger of inadequate defence; and thirdly, with domestic concerns, approving of the extension of the franchise, mentioning the need of other reforms—*e.g.*, of the house of lords—but stressing the primary urgency of social and economic problems. It deplored unemployment and suggested palliatives, deprecated strikes and advocated industrial partnerships, disapproved of socialism and recommended a mild form of conservatism as an alternative. There was little in it that might not appropriately have been broadcast as a sermon from St. Martin-in-the-Fields.

The policy of conciliation and peace adumbrated by the amiable authors of *Looking Ahead* was that adopted by the conservative government when it assumed office in November, 1924. It, of course, allowed the disgraceful and humiliating treaties with the Soviets to lapse, and it formally condemned the interference of political conspirators with the course of criminal justice. It further ordered the renewal of the work on the Singapore naval base, imperatively necessary for the security of our Pacific dominions. But apart from these inevitable reversals of socialist impolicy, it followed the soft and comfortable path of concession and compromise, anxious to avoid sub-

jects of controversy and to generate a feeling of contentment. Hence, like any socialist government, it avoided
any painful insistence on economy; it lowered the qualification for old age pensions from 70 to 65; it extended the
pension scheme to widowed mothers; it subsidised the
building of 150,000 necessary but uneconomic houses.
Beyond this, it took a long step towards the re-establishment of financial stability by the restoration of the gold
standard; but this heroic and honourable procedure had
the regrettable results of depressing prices and increasing
the burden of our already prodigious war debts. The
estimated expenditure of the government during its first
year of office exceeded the appalling total of £800,000,000.
Never had economy been more obviously necessary, and
never, without a radical change of programme, had it
appeared more difficult to achieve.

In the midst, too, of the struggle to balance the budget,
a new menace to " tranquillity and stability " displayed
itself. The socialist left wing, furious at the exposure and
frustration of its conspiracies in the autumn of 1924, was
determined—abandoning all pretence of constitutional
procedure—to use industrial unrest to precipitate a social
revolution by means of " direct action "—that is to say,
by means of a general strike. The coal industry, with the
socialist-ridden miners' federation, was unfortunately
ready as an instrument to work their will. Ruined by a
long succession of previous strikes, harassed and fettered
by masses of injudicious government regulations, grossly
over-manned as the result of a gigantic influx of conscientious objectors during the war, the coal industry,
once a prime source of Britain's wealth, now bankrupt and
semi-derelict, was kept going only by heavy government
subsidies. The government very properly announced that
these subsidies must cease and that the industry must
reorganise itself so as to pay its own way. This reorganisation necessarily involved *inter alia* closing of exhausted
pits, dismissal of superfluous men, increase of hours of
work, and reduction of wages. The miners' federation—
dominated by violent revolutionaries, and eager for war
rather than for peace—refused all concessions and called

upon the general council of the trade-union congress to bring out the whole industrial community in a gigantic general strike. The general council, which was also in an intransigent mood, and confident in its prodigious power for mischief, responded by proclaiming the general strike at midnight on May 3, 1926.

Never before within the memory of any living person had there been in England so direct and deadly a challenge to constitutional government. Well said Lord Balfour: " It is what I have called it—an attempted revolution. Were it to succeed, the community would thenceforth be ruled not by parliament, not by the parliamentary labour party, not by the rank and file of the trades unions, not by the moderate members of the trades union council, but by a relatively small body of extremists who regard trade unions not as the machinery for collective bargaining within our industrial system, but as a political instrument by which the industrial system itself may be utterly destroyed." Fortunately, Mr. Baldwin and his colleagues rose to the height of the great crisis, and happily the community as a whole (including the immense majority of the loyal and patriotic rank and file of the trade unions) recognised instinctively the magnitude of the revolutionary menace. The result was that in nine days the strike was broken, the crisis ended, the constitution and the country saved. But at what a cost! First, the great trade unions were reduced to bankruptcy and impotence, having squandered in a reckless attack upon the community the funds painfully accumulated during many years.* Secondly, industry and commerce, the prime sources of the nation's wealth, barely beginning to recover from the disorganisation due to the war, received injuries from which they have not yet recovered; in particular the coal industry threw away markets which probably it will never win back. Thirdly, the state, already labouring under excessive financial burdens, was compelled to spend fresh millions of money in the fulfilment of its primary duty of safeguarding the nation's existence and

* The National Union of Railwaymen alone spent over £1,000,000 on this suicidal civil war.

crushing abominable rebellion. But one good thing resulted from the strike and its defeat.

§ 76. The Gadarene Descent, 1929-31

The defeat of the revolutionary general strike in 1926 incalculably cleared the political atmosphere. In the region of domestic affairs it did what the overthrow of Germany had done eight years earlier in the realm of international relations. Ever since the iniquitous Trades Disputes Act of 1906 had legalised anarchy, calling it " the restoration of trade-union conditions," the community had been menaced by a constant succession of conspiracies on the part of the now irresponsible socialist oligarchy which had secured control of the executives of the great trade unions and of the trade-union congress. This misguided oligarchy had now done its worst, and, gravely as it had injured the community, it had injured itself still more severely. One is reminded of the story of the mad dog who attacked a man :

> " The man recovered of the bite;
> The dog it was that died."

For a long time to come, if not permanently, the extreme peril of " direct action " was removed. The government was free, although with diminished resources and sadly disorganised services, to resume its interrupted task of restoring national prosperity. It went gently to work, cautiously " safeguarding " industries threatened by unfair foreign competition; relieving local burdens by a masterly scheme of " derating "; endeavouring to open foreign and colonial markets; seeking to soothe the numerous agitations of international politics. Only two big controversial problems did it touch. On the one side, under strong pressure from its working-men supporters, it modified the oppressive regulations of the Trade Unions Act of 1913, under which all members of a union who did not expressly " contract out " were compelled to pay the union's political levy—that is, to finance socialist candidates and support socialist propaganda (1927). On the other side, in the hope of finally settling the franchise question, and so terminating the struggles of a hundred

years, it equalised male and female suffrage, thus giving
the vote to women between the ages of twenty-one and
thirty. The arguments generally employed to justify this
final " leap in the dark " would have come more appropriately from radical than from conservative lips. They were
either merely opportunist or they treated the franchise
as a private right rather than a public function (1928).

When in 1929 the five years of conservative administration due to the electoral victory of 1924 drew to a close,
there was a widespread feeling that—even allowing for the
difficulties of the time and for the wanton disturbance
caused by the general strike—the government had not
made the best use of its opportunities. It seemed to have
lived too much from hand to mouth ; it appeared to have
lacked both ideas and courage. Its failings were both
positive and negative. On the positive side, its lavish
increase of pensions, and its prodigious extension of the
franchise, were more consonant with socialism and radicalism than with conservatism. On the negative side, it had
failed to enforce the economies urgently required by the
country's financial situation ; it had failed to modify the
dangerous Parliament Act of 1911 by reforming the house
of lords and restoring it to its proper place in the constitution ; it had failed to revise the Trades Disputes Act of
1906 by taking away from trade unions the iniquitous
permission to break contracts and commit torts thereby
conferred upon them ; it had failed to secure justice for
the persecuted and despoiled loyalists of Southern Ireland ;
above all, it had failed to solve the dreadful problem of
unemployment, the numbers of those without work remaining steadily at over the million figure. The country
was disappointed, wearied, and rather bored. It wanted
a change. Hence when in May, 1929, the time came for a
general appeal to the people, the electorate (swelled to the
prodigious number of 28 millions by the extension of the
franchise in 1928) returned 287 socialists as against 260
conservatives and 59 liberals. The prime determinant of
the socialist victory was unquestionably the loudly trum-
peted boast of the socialist leaders that they could and
would within a very brief period of time solve the problem

of unemployment. This boast, iterated all over the country by the socialist rank and file, made a stronger appeal to the newly enfranchised young women, as well as to the sad army of the deluded workless, than the conservative slogan of " safety first."

The two years of socialist government (June, 1929, to August, 1931) were a period of deplorable disappointment and disillusionment to the distressed proletariat. The bewildered and resourceless ministers complained that circumstances were against them : they might have been expected to take this possibility into account before they made their profuse boasts and unconditional promises. As we have already observed, the numbers of unemployed, so far from being diminished, rose from 1,112,000 in 1929 to the appalling total of 2,714,000 in 1931. The rules for the administration of relief were relaxed until pauperism became one of the most profitable of professions; the character of the people was rotted by indiscriminate doles, and the nation was saddled with a burden amounting to £135,000,000 a year. The public expenditure of the government rose from £691,000,000 in 1929 to £751,000,000 in 1931, and this gigantic total had to be supplemented by ever-increasing borrowings. In 1931 first £50,000,000, then another £80,000,000, had to be sought from abroad in order to meet current expenses. Meantime our commerce declined : returns from coal, textiles, shipping, interest on foreign investments, all fell off : our exports as a whole were diminished by 45 per cent.

But, in spite of all, the government recklessly piled up its commitments. It steadily increased the already bloated bureaucracy ; it extended the pensions of widows, orphans, and the aged ; it framed an education bill calculated to add £9,000,000 a year to the annual cost of the schools ; it passed a Coal Mines Act which, by reducing the hours of labour and setting up a national wages board, enhanced the price of coal and so still further depressed all subsidiary industries ; and so on *ad infinitum*.

The end of this Gadarene descent came suddenly and dramatically in August, 1931, when the herd reached the verge of the bottomless sea of insolvency.

PART III

POLITICAL

CHAPTER XIX

THE PRESENT SITUATION

" We alone among the nations of Europe persist in thinking ourselves better off than before the war; have forgotten the meaning of economy and settled down to the enjoyment of the 'fruits of victory.' We are interested in our wages rather than our work, in the price rather than the products, are obsessed with the spirit of grab, and decline to give value for value."—SIR ERNEST BENN.

" Partnership in empire, peace with foreign nations, union of all classes at home, liberty, opportunity for every individual subject of the king—these are the ideals that inspire the unionist party."—" LOOKING AHEAD."

§ 77. THE VERGE OF THE ABYSS, 1931

THE swift descent of the nation towards bankruptcy had long been alarmingly evident to calm and impartial observers both in Britain and abroad. On the one hand, foreign financiers had become increasingly unwilling to lend their clients' money to bolster the credit of irresponsible ministers who could no longer balance their budgets. On the other hand, British economists had initiated an impressive campaign against the swelling extravagance of the state. In 1930, for instance, had appeared Sir Ernest Benn's masterly and conclusive *Account Rendered*, in which the talented and patriotic author, with admirable pungency and precision, had revealed to the insensate public the enormity of the burdens which they were recklessly transmitting to posterity. In December of the same year Sir John Davidson had brought the matter before the house of commons in a powerful speech : the current charges on the national debt, he had said, amounted to £350,000,000; the cost of pensions was £120,000,000; payment to the unemployed, £105,000,000; poor relief, £44,000,000. He had argued that there was urgent need of drastic economy, and he had suggested, first, the reduction of the bureaucracy; secondly, the conversion of the 5 per cent. loan; and, thirdly, the stoppage of the abuses of the dole. Of course, nothing had been done. Hence two months later (February 12, 1931) Sir Laming Worthington-Evans, with all the weight of his high official position, had returned to the charge, and the gravity of his warning had been recognised and reinforced by the chancellor of the exchequer himself, Mr. Philip Snowden. But so entirely oblivious to the obvious had been the socialist rank and file that the trade-union congress at its meetings in April, 1931, had actually propounded new schemes of so-called " social reform " calculated to add another £115,000,000 to the annual expenses of the government! *Quos deus vult perdere prius dementat.*

But next month the rude awakening to reality had come. The continental bankers, alarmed at the patent incapacity of the government to check extravagance or balance its budgets, began to withdraw their menaced deposits from the Bank of England. The directors, hoping that the run was merely a temporary one, tried to strengthen their reserves by borrowing from France and the United States. But French and American financiers soon indicated that the limits of their accommodation had been reached. The situation was one of profound humiliation for a power that had during the war been the banker of the world—the giver, not the begger, of loans. Ample justification, however, of the caution of the French and American financiers was provided by the report of a special Economy Committee, presided over by Sir George May, issued on July 31, 1931. This report announced that the deficit on the budget for the year 1931-32 would be at least £120,000,000, and it stressed the urgent and immediate necessity for (1) the levying of £30,000,000 by new taxation; (2) the reduction of expenditure, mainly on doles and on educational paraphernalia, by £90,000,000. The cabinet prepared plans to meet the painful but pressing needs of the situation. They felt it necessary, however, before communicating them to parliament, to submit them to the approval of the national executive of the labour party and the general council of the trade-union congress! Such was the condition of the constitution in the summer of 1931! These august oligarchies signified their refusal to endorse the suggested economies, and consequently those members of the cabinet who regarded themselves as the delegates of the trade unions rather than the representatives of the nation resigned, and the socialist government was at an end (August 24, 1931).

Mr. Ramsay Macdonald, Mr. Philip Snowden, Mr. J. H. Thomas, and Lord Sankey patriotically and courageously remained to form the nucleus of a national government—a coalition of the sound members of all the three parties—instituted for the purpose of carrying through the imperative but unpopular tasks of effecting drastic economies, and of extorting more millions of money from taxpayers already impoverished by excessive demands. The conservatives who entered the composite cabinet included Mr. Baldwin, Sir Philip Cunliffe-Lister, Lord Peel, Sir Samuel Hoare, and Mr. Neville Chamberlain. The liberals supplied, among others, Sir Herbert Samuel, Lord Reading, the Marquis of Crewe, Sir Donald Maclean, and Sir Archibald Sinclair.

Probably none of those who entered this national coalition really liked doing so. For if a fusion of two parties entails inevitably some abandonment of principle, a fusion of three parties means the dropping of all the distinctive policies of all of them. So the prime minister was no doubt expressing the views of all his novel colleagues—so recently his opponents—when he said that, as soon as the immediate task of the government had been performed, the old party system would be revived. He wished to carry on with the old parliament, in which the coalition had a majority of about 60 over the opposition: he did not want the national government as such to appeal to the country.

Circumstances, however, proved to be too strong for him. The crisis was much graver and more protracted than had been anticipated. The drain on the bank's reserves continued, and on September 21 it became necessary to abandon the gold standard to which a return had

been made six years before.   Moreover, when the complex
business of the restoration of the country's trade balance
came to be considered it was evident that many months
of labour would be required before stability would be
achieved.   Hence early in October, 1931, Mr. Macdonald
sought the king's assent to a dissolution of parliament.
The elections to the new parliament were held on
October 27.   The results exceeded all expectations.   The
unfaithful socialist ministers who had deserted Mr. Macdonald and their country's cause in the crisis of August,
and had bowed to the dictation of the trade-union caucus,
were defeated almost to a man.   The socialist rank and
file also were almost swept out of existence : they lost 213
out of 265 seats held at the dissolution.   The national
government came back 554 strong (conservative supporters
numbering 471), the opposition being reduced to a leader-
less and almost inarticulate remnant of 56.

§ 78. The National Government

It is not a healthy condition of things to have a composite and heterogeneous " national " government with 554
variegated supporters in the house of commons, faced by
an " anti-national " opposition consisting of 56 exasperated
and dangerous, if temporarily impotent, extremists.   For,
on the one hand, the extremists, being the only centre of
resistance to a government that is bound to do a number
of painful and unpopular things, must inevitably increase
in numbers, in power, and in ferocity as the months pass.
On the other hand, the coalition, being composed of
elements widely diverse and incongruous, must infallibly
disintegrate and decay.   The " national government,"
indeed, is a political trinity in which the persons are dangerously and even damnably confounded.   Most desirable,
therefore, is it, especially from the point of view of the vast
conservative majority, that it should complete its appointed
task at the earliest possible moment, and should allow the
wholesome party system once more to prevail.   But let us
hope for the country's sake, and for the sake of rational
majority rule, that when the parties re-emerge there may

be only two of them, by whatever titles they may be
called—namely, the party of order, the essential conservative party, and the party of progress, the essential
radical party.   The present liberal party has been by the
recent crisis sharply and logically dichotomised into
"national" and "anti-national."   It is natural and
proper that the small "anti-national" section should
coalesce with the socialists, from whom they are divided
by no fundamental principle, their individualism long having lapsed into collectivism.   It is equally natural and
proper that the "national" majority should join the conservatives, for the question of free-trade or protection,
which alone keeps them apart (although not so far apart
as it did a generation ago), is not a fundamental of either
conservatism or liberalism.   It is merely a question concerning means to an end that both have in common—
namely, the well-being and prosperity of the nation.   All
the great eighteenth-century conservatives—Bolingbroke,
Pitt, Burke—were free-traders, and so in the nineteenth
century were Canning, Peel, and Salisbury; the circumstances of the period imperatively demanded the abolition
of mercantilist monopoly and the unification of world
markets.   And even the twentieth-century protectionists
proclaim that, although in a world universally become
protectionist Britain must necessarily defend herself by
means of tariffs, their prime object, vis-à-vis foreign
nations, is to induce them to remove the barriers whereby
British goods are excluded from their markets, so that
trade may flow more freely.   There ought to be no insuperable difficulty as to agreement on this subsidiary
matter, provided only that neither side attempts to make
it a primary concern, a rigid test of orthodoxy.

But before the national government divides into its constituent elements, and so allows the true democratic party
system to resume its sway, there are several tasks before
it which, just because it is a coalition, it can perform more
safely and satisfactorily than could any single-party
administration.   These tasks are necessary but unpopular
tasks which each single party might hesitate to undertake
for fear of alienating and driving into its opponents' arms

large bodies of voters. Not even a national coalition, of course, can wholly ignore the danger of offending the ignorant and unpatriotic portions of the electorate by the effecting of needful but unpleasant reforms; and unquestionably upon the conservative section of the coalition the fury of the disgruntled and the disloyal will be primarily directed. It is to be hoped, nevertheless, that the national government, strong in the overwhelming majority given to it by the electorate in October, 1931, will have sufficient courage and enterprise to perform its duty faithfully. What is this duty? If I may summarise very tentatively the opinions of important people who have recently surveyed the field of politics, it would appear to be as follows.

First, it is the duty of the national government to re-establish British credit by effecting drastic economies in public expenditure, by strictly balancing its budgets, by maintaining the standard of the currency, by resisting all temptations to artificial inflation, by opposing all suggestions to place the banks under political control.

Secondly, it is its duty to do what it can to bring back prosperity to Britain by safeguarding industry, by fostering agriculture, by reducing the present devastating taxation, by removing vexatious restrictions, by encouraging individual enterprise, by resisting socialistic efforts to confiscate profits won by superior energy and skill.

Thirdly, it is its duty to defend and fortify the national character by abolishing the lingering abuses of the dole, by stopping the demoralisation caused by indiscriminate charity, by stirring up the contentedly lazy to useful and elevating self-help, by ending those appeals to anti-social cupidity which have been the main cause of " the corruption of the citizenship of the working man." Well says the prime minister : " It is the poorest of games to make people believe that they can get money endlessly for nothing, and to call it ' socialism.' "*

Fourthly, it is its duty carefully to revise the whole system of unemployment insurance, making the system

* Mr. Ramsay Macdonald, reported in the *News-Chronicle* of September 15, 1932.

actuarially sound and solvent, and possibly substituting payments in kind for those payments in money which have been so generally abused and misapplied.

Fifthly, it is its duty to do what in it lies to terminate the intolerable tyranny of the socialist oligarchies who have captured the trade unions. To this end it is particularly necessary to maintain the liberties conferred on loyal working men by the Trade Union Act of 1927, and further to take away the iniquitous licence to commit wrong conferred by the Trades Disputes Act of 1906.

Finally, it is the duty of the national government to restore the balance of the constitution by means of (1) the reform and rehabilitation of the house of lords; (2) the elimination, through a scheme of "second ballot" or otherwise, of the anomaly whereby, owing to the existence of three parties, minority candidates win seats and misrepresent majorities; (3) the re-establishment of the connection between representation and taxation, so as to remove the crying scandal whereby one-tenth of the electorate—$2\frac{3}{4}$ millions out of 28 millions—provide 65 per cent. of the expenses of government; this tax-paying minority lying, as sheep to be shorn, helpless at the feet of the irresponsible and comparatively untaxed majority.

§ 79. THE FUTURE OUTLOOK

But, beyond the period of the rule of the national government, conservatives must look forward to the day when once more as a party, with a policy and a programme of their own, they will appeal to the electorate. What shall be the nature of their appeal? Shall they attempt to outbid the liberals in the loud assertion of personal rights, in promises to lower franchises, in offers to extend the domain of the dominant democracy? Or shall they attempt to compete with the socialists in holding out to the proletariat, under the seductive title of "social reform," enormous bribes of other people's money—lifelong doles for all who do not want to work, old-age pensions from the moment of birth, and so on? Far be it from them to do so. For one thing they cannot succeed: liberals

can always outbid them in assertions of individual claims;
socialists can always outbribe them in promises of public
assistance. For another thing, in making these essentially anti-social appeals they would display a profound
misunderstanding of the character of the British electorate
as a whole. Although there are ignorant and immature
sections of it that think of little except personal rights,
and although there are depraved and debased sections to
whom cupidity is the prevailing motive, the hearts of the
majority—and especially of those portions of it which have
long possessed the franchise—are sound. The patriot
resents and repudiates the lure of proffered privilege and
the corrupting offer of unearned increments of other
people's property. One of the most impressive features
of the huge vote that placed the national government in
power in the autumn of 1931 was the fact that out of the
14,539,403 who supported the policy of solvency and
honour there must have been several millions of the unemployed and otherwise unfortunate who would have stood
to gain immediately by the success of the socialist policy
of continued doles, slackened administration, extended
borrowings, and increased raids upon capital.

To gain immediately! Yes; and beyond the immediate
present (so urgent are its necessities) it is scarcely possible
for many of the unfortunate to look. But those whose
circumstances and whose abilities enable them calmly to
envisage the more distant future are aware that the facile
promises of the radicals and the seductive lures of the
socialists are all too often heavy with presages of ultimate
disaster. If the radical policy of anarchic individualism
were really good for the people, and if the socialist scheme
of a general confiscation of private property supplemented
by a universal system of outdoor relief were really conducive to national prosperity, there can be little doubt
that the patriotic minority, who are doomed to suffer
under it, would accept it *pro bono publico*. But it is precisely because conservatives are convinced that the programmes of the present-day radicals and socialists, if
carried out, will result in widespread and irremediable
calamity, and even if not carried out, will cause much

baseless and debilitating unrest, that they oppose and
denounce them. And their opposition and denunciation
are not grounded on mere speculation or prejudice. They
have history on their side. For the record of all radical
revolutions is one of disappointment and disgust, while
(as I have elsewhere remarked) the story of socialism, in
all its protean forms, is a long and lamentable chronicle of
unrealised theories, addled experiments, and disillusioned
dupes.*

If, however, conservatism opposes and denounces the
subversive projects of the radicals and the predatory programmes of the socialists, what does it offer in their place ?
Why, it may be asked, should it offer anything except the
negative blessing of protection against the dangerous
activities of the two rival parties ? Is it not enough that
it should safeguard ancient and admirable institutions,
defend venerable traditions, and maintain menaced liberties ? The answer is that at the present time this, although
incalculably important, is not by itself sufficient. The
condition of the world—social, economic, political, cul-
tural—is changing so rapidly before our very eyes that it
is imperatively necessary that conservatives—in the spirit
of their great old leaders, Bolingbroke, Burke, and
Beaconsfield—should be prepared to adapt institutions
however sacred, and ideas however immutable, to the
circumstances of the day.

Conservatives, fortunately, are for the most part awake
to this necessity. Nevertheless, three things must be said.
First, too much power is still possessed within the party
by the mere reactionaries, by the antiquated and obsolescent, by those whose only claim to distinction is title
or wealth; too little influence is allowed to the young,
the energetic, the far-sighted, the men of intellectual
eminence. Secondly, too little use is made of the conservative working man, too little consideration is given
to his peculiar problems, too little opportunity is offered
to him for a great and successful career in conservative
politics. The strength of socialism as a political organisation rests in the fact that it is a proletarian organisation.

* Cf. above, p. 2.

Its highest places are easily accessible to the lowliest rank-and-file member.' Of course, conservatism can never become a merely proletarian party : its very genius affirms, on the one hand, the solidarity of the nation and the unity of all classes in the whole; on the other hand, the gradation of classes and the propriety of leaving predominant political control in the possession of those who are by descent, by character, by education, and by experience best fitted to exercise it. Nevertheless, at the present day the old "governing classes" have an excessive share of influence in the party. Well says Mr. Harold Begbie : "To do its work in the world conservatism must draw its strength from the confidence and affection of the working classes."* Thirdly, the progressive programmes promulgated by conservative leaders in recent years somehow lack effectiveness of appeal. It may not be generally true that, as has recently been asserted, "conservatives are hampered by the lack of inspiration and enthusiasm,"† but it is undoubtedly a fact that the pronouncements of conservative policy made since the break-up of the coalition in 1922 have fallen somewhat flat. I have already remarked that the manifesto of 1924, entitled *Looking Ahead*, was considered by some ardent young imperialists to be deficient in " vim " and " pep." The same criticism might be applied to half a dozen general statements concerning the principles and the programme of conservatism that have been promulgated since the date of that publication.

§ 80. The Problem of a Programme

Space fails me to examine in detail the half-dozen or more formal statements of conservative principles and policy that have been made on public platforms or in the press during the past eight years. Nor is it necessary to do so, for they all display the same characteristics, and say much the same things. They all, accepting the socialist lead, lay almost exclusive emphasis on economic con-

* *The Conservative Mind*, by " A Gentleman with a Duster " (1924), p. 23.
† Goddard and Gibbons, *Civilisation* (1926), p. 41.

cerns. The following is typical. It is, moreover, at once both the most succinct and the most authoritative of the series. Issued in October, 1930, it outlines " the policy which the party will put before the country at the next general election." A lengthy statement concludes with the summary : " Rigorous economy; reduction of taxation; thorough reform of the unemployment system; effective protection for our manufacturing industries against foreign competition by the immediate introduction of an emergency tariff; a guaranteed wheat price for the British farmer, combined with a tax on foreign malting barley, and the prevention of the dumping of foreign oats and other produce; a system to secure a definite market for home-grown and empire wheat; and, finally, concerted action with the dominions in order to promote the economic unity of the empire."* This programme no doubt includes some excellent and most necessary proposals, but how enormous its omissions ! " Man does not live by bread alone," nor even by bread supplemented by porridge and beer.†

Expositors of the nine proposals of this meagre, trivial, and exclusively economic programme will of course defend them by the same sort of argument as modern civilians employ in expounding and defending the scantiness and pettiness of the famous Twelve Tables of the Roman Law. They will say that the general principles of conservatism are assumed; that it is taken for granted that they are universally known and accepted, and that all that is attempted in the nine propositions laid before the electors is a statement of conservative policy in relation to the specific problems of the moment. To this line of argument I would reply, first, that, unhappily, the general principles of conservatism are not known nearly so well as they should be by vast numbers of good conservatives; secondly, that outside the ranks of conservatives, not only are they unknown, but their very existence is unsuspected

* *The Times*, October 16, 1930.

† *Cf.* Maurois, André, *La Vie de Disraëli*, p. 197 : " Un parti doit avoir une foi. Ou ne peut pas exciter l'imagination des hommes avec des lois douanières."

or denied; and, thirdly, that pressing and urgent as the economic problems treated in this manifesto may be, there are others not less insistent that go far deeper below the surface of the national life, reaching to the very foundations of both religion and polity.

One of the factors which in old days made constitutional government possible in this country was that the two great political parties had much in common, that they were agreed on fundamentals, that they differed only respecting secondary principles or details of administration. Both of them recognised Christianity and favoured the maintenance of an established church; both of them accepted the form of government by king, lords, and commons, and were prepared to abide by the verdicts of legalised electorates; both of them respected the monarchy and the social system of which it was the apex and crown; both of them reverenced the law, regarding it as the authoritative utterance of the general will; both of them supported the institution of private property, and the general principles of the so-called capitalist system; both of them were earnestly devoted to the welfare of the mother-country, the unity and prosperity of the empire, the honour and dignity of world-wide British Commonwealth. But this happy unanimity concerning fundamentals can no longer be postulated. Since the advent of Karl Marx and the spread of atheistic communism, and in particular since the growth in the European system of the deadly cancer of Bolshevism, everything is challenged; nothing can be taken for granted. The very foundations of Christian civilisation are menaced, and all that both liberals and conservatives hold dear is threatened with destruction. Well says Mr. Arthur Boutwood in his brilliant and impressive book entitled *National Revival* (p. 10): " It is hardly possible to exaggerate the gravity of the situation. The fundamental facts of the existing order are becoming central topics of debate."

Socialism, and particularly socialism in its logically final form of communism, is what conservatism has now especially to combat. And socialism has become a creed that reaches out far beyond the limits of economics into the innermost sanctuaries of ethics, politics, and religion. It tends to subvert not only the system of industry and commerce which has made England wealthy and powerful, but also the moral order upon which our civilisation is based; the religious principles by means of which that order is sustained, and the political institutions which have been erected upon the foundations of sanctity and faith. It menaces equally the church, the constitution, the crown, the family, the social organism, the economic system, and the liberties of the individual. It is to be combated by conservatism, and indeed by all men of goodwill, not in the interests of any exclusive or privileged classes, but in the interests of the nation as a whole. For in the long run it is the poor, even more than the rich, who suffer from the absurdities and iniquities by means of which socialism seeks to ease the discomforts of its votaries. In the long run the policy of confiscation, repression, collectivisation, regimentation, redistribution, and demoralisation reacts with results the most disastrous of all precisely upon those whose necessities it has momentarily relieved, whose hopes it has falsely raised, whose energies and self-reliance it has sapped, whose vices and weaknesses it has condoned and encouraged. For socialism is a disease to which the wretched and the ignorant are peculiarly liable, and communism is a cancer —generated by Jewish atheism in the morass of German economics—which spreads most rapidly and dangerously in the criminal underworld. The menace of socialism to the well-being of the whole community is largely due to the fact that the socialist party depends for its strength "upon the support of the feckless, the improvident, the loafer, and the half-witted."*

* Hugh Melson in *Nineteenth Century*, March, 1930.

CHAPTER XX

CONCLUSION: THE CONSERVATIVE TASK

" If I have devoted a good many pages to political history, it is because I am firmly convinced that most of the rash judgments and fantastic hopes prevalent to-day are due to ignorance of that subject."—SIR R. MITCHELL-BANKS.

" The conservative believes that the only salvation of the country is to concentrate on the individual, and to continue to cherish in him a spirit of character, the virtues of thrift, hard work, and prudence, that they might spread from the individual into the community."—STANLEY BALDWIN.

" The fundamental weakness of the unionist party to-day lies in its present confusion of thought. It has no clear policy on immediate problems; it has no clear goal towards which it feels itself to be striving; it has too many open questions, and too many closed minds."—HAROLD MACMILLAN.

THE task of the modern conservative is an onerous one, and as noble as it is burdensome. It is nothing less than to save Christian civilisation from its would-be destroyers; to preserve the priceless heritage of the past; to use the institutions of old days, reforming and supplementing them where necessary, in such a way as to further the well-being of the present and realise the hopes of the future. And modern conservatism, fortunately, does not lack leaders who perceive the magnitude and importance of their task, and are prepared to devote themselves to its achievement. In particular, Mr. Baldwin is gifted with prophetic vision, and has shown himself capable of sounding the high authentic note of noble captaincy. He stands in the great succession of Bolingbroke, Burke, and Beaconsfield. When he speaks of England his words burn with the fire of the true patriotism; when he labours for peace in industry he is striving to realise that very ideal of national unity which inspired the author of *Sybil*; when with infinite patience or profound sympathy he conducts international negotiations he displays that large humanity

298

which is the mark of the genuine citizen of the world. He has already, as we have seen, rendered invaluable service to conservatism. It was he who emancipated conservatism from the corrupt and strangling coalition of 1922; it was he who did most to stop that shameless sale of honours which was threatening to reduce our noble peerage to the level of a Bœotian plutocracy; it was he who ended in the councils of conservatism the evil dictatorship of the commercialised press. He will have, if all goes well, still greater services to render both to conservatism and to country in the future. For his is the spirit of confidence and hope peculiarly needed in these dark days of anxiety and doubt. " No one," he finely and bravely says, " who knows our people can be a pessimist; nor should he be an alarmist." He realises that the same firm courage, the same patient endurance of suffering, the same tolerant good humour as carried the nation through the terrors of the war, will carry it through the horrors of the present peace, provided only that a proper appeal is made to these fine and heroic qualities of the British people, and that these qualities are not corrupted and destroyed by the hateful and hate-inspiring falsities of socialism and communism.

It rests, then, with Mr. Baldwin and his colleagues to proclaim the full conservative creed, as it has been developed during the past four centuries of British history, adapting it to the conditions of to-day, modifying it to suit the circumstances of the new age, supplementing it in the same manner, and in the same spirit, as it was built up by the masters of old.

In detail, what does this mean? It means, I think, that conservatives should, in season and out of season, make it clear that they stand for the following principles:

(1) *The Recognition of Religion.* Never before has this fundamental principle of conservatism been challenged as it is challenged to-day by the communist atheocracy. Bolshevik Russia presents the appalling spectacle of a great and instinctively religious people persecuted into a bestial materialism. The would-be Bolsheviks of Britain aim at the same atheistic and sordid tyranny. Conservatism is

committed to undying resistance to this abomination. Its witness for religion may not, and probably will not, take the form which it assumed in early days. The majority of conservatives probably will not stand, as the majority stood four hundred years ago, for Roman Catholicism. None will seek to restore the exclusive Anglicanism of the Test Acts and Acts of Uniformity. All will accept the wide toleration advocated and introduced by such leaders as Halifax, Bolingbroke, Burke, Peel, and Disraeli. Some, indeed, who, like the great Bolingbroke himself, find themselves compelled to dissent from all forms of the Christian creed, will display the religious spirit in a still wider latitude. But in all it will be there; for the religious spirit— the spirit of awe, of reverence, of instinctive worship—is of the very essence of conservatism. This spirit will determine the attitude of modern conservatives toward the difficult problem of disestablishment, which is becoming every year more and more prominent. Their desires will undoubtedly be to maintain that union of church with state which Hooker expounded and Burke eulogised. If they are constrained to follow the Bishop of Durham (Dr. Henson) in denouncing the state as secular, and in demanding for the church emancipation from its control, they will do so with profound reluctance and regret. But probably they will not feel constrained to do so. For the state is not so secular as it appears to be. Its basis, like that of modern society, is the Christian civilisation of the middle ages. And the supreme authority of the law of Christ is still recognised by the majority even of those who no longer accept the anglican formularies.

(2) *The Maintenance of the Constitution.* Parliamentary government has well been described as " the greatest contribution of our race to the political institutions of the world."* And the feature of this parliamentary government which specially commends itself to conservatives is the balance of powers and equilibrium of interests which in its perfect form it displays. That balance and that equilibrium have been destroyed by recent legislation. The *Parliament Act* of 1911 established

* Bryant, A., *The Spirit of Conservatism* (1929), p. 41.

the ascendancy of one house in the legislature; the *Franchise Acts* of 1918 and 1928 established the ascendancy of one class in the electorate. The inequitable results of the *Parliament Act* need to be redressed by the reform and the rehabilitation of the house of lords; those of the *Franchise Acts* by a reduction of the pauper vote, by a raising of the standard of electoral qualifications, and by the increase of the voting power of the educated and thrifty classes. It is particularly imperative for conservatives, whether alone or as partners in a national government, to face and to solve the house of lords problem. They undoubtedly ought to have done so during their years of grace 1924-29. The details of the settlement, perhaps, are difficult. But the general principles seem to be clear. On the one hand, there must be no break with the past: the hereditary principle must be left intact. But in respect of peers of the United Kingdom it should be modified as it has been in the case of Scottish peers; that is to say, it should be supplemented by means of election. No peer should sit in his own right. A fixed number—say 100— should sit as representatives of the whole body. On the other hand, new elements should be added, and in particular representatives of the great interests which are not, as such, recognised at present in either part of the legislature. To each parliament should be called as "lords" the elected leaders of the chief churches, of the great trade unions, of the commercial and financial magnates, of the civil servants, of the press, of the universities and schools. As to the franchise, everything should be done that can aid in restoring the lost balance and equilibrium of classes, and in securing a return to the two-party system. All such seductive but subversive devices as proportional representation—devices designed to multiply fanatical groups and exactly calculated to enable log-rolling minorities to secure control over unsophisticated majorities—should be resolutely shunned. But far more important than any reforms of the parliamentary system is the maintenance of the authority of the parliamentary system itself. Government by discussion must be vindicated against government by violence. The determina-

tion of policy by direct action, by general strikes, by mob
terrorism, by open rebellion, or even by the irrelevant
expedient of abstaining from food, must be steadily and
consistently resisted. The mere fact that an end is sought
by these illegitimate means should be made the ground of
its firm refusal. Naughty children who snatch are properly
punished by deprivation.

(3) *The Defence of the Crown.*   The institution of
monarchy is at present under a cloud. Since the war, and
as a result of the war, many thrones have fallen, and in
the places of emperors and kings, republican presidents and
popular assemblies have been installed. The only persons
who have cause to rejoice at these changes of régime are
the communistic revolutionaries through whose machinations they have mainly been effected. They have brought
perceptibly nearer the day of the universal confiscation.
Weak and unstable administration, constant privy conspiracy and rebellion, frequent persecution, flagrant in-
justice, all the horrors of semi-anarchy, have characterised
the countries that have rashly allowed their ancient royal
houses to be expelled. Some of them, probably, will never
return to even moderate prosperity until the *ancien régime*
is re-established. But if monarchy is essential to the
security of, say, Spain or Germany, much more so is it to
the unity and integrity of Britain and the Empire. The
king in this country and throughout the dominions is the
primary bond of social and political cohesion, the centre
of loyalty, the symbol of kinship, the inspirer of patriotism and devotion. In the actual working, too, of our
complex constitution he plays an incalculably valuable
part, enabling almost revolutionary changes of ministries
to be effected easily, without disorder or bloodshed;
advising transient officials out of his stores of accumulated
experience; aiding the conduct of diplomacy by the majesty
of a dignity raised above the arena of international conflict.   Happily, at the moment the British monarchy is
safe in the loyal affection of all the nations, peoples, and
tongues that constitute the world-wide British empire.
But the day may come in no distant future when conservatives—in the widest sense of the term—will have to

fight to defend it against the assaults of the wild communistic ideologues who are seeking to achieve a world revolution.

(4) *The Preservation of the Unity of the Nation.* Nothing more sharply differentiates the conservative from the communist than the principle of national unity. The key doctrine of communism is the pernicious Marxian dogma of the class war. The Marxian fanatic, obsessed by a false philosophy of history, sees the nation irreconcilably divided into two sections, the proletariat and the bourgeoisie; and he wickedly incites the proletarian masses to wage remorseless war upon their imagined enemies until they have extirpated them and secured their property. A propaganda such as this is, of course, destructive of the nation as a unit; it is the very negation of the conservative conception of society as an organism in which every class serves, and is served by, every other. In fact, in this organic idea you have one of the leading differentia of conservatism. The liberal looks to the individual; the socialist to the class; the conservative to the nation as a whole. Under laissez-faire liberalism the devil takes the hindmost; under confiscatory socialism he gets the foremost; only under conservatism is an effort made to prevent him from securing any at all.

(5) *The Improvement of the Condition of the People.* Since the nation is a unit, and since no class and no individual can suffer without the whole community's being the worse, the true conservative is profoundly concerned for the condition of the people. He is convinced, however, that no permanent improvement of this condition can come by means of indiscriminate charity, or promiscuous doles, or any other device that debilitates, demoralises, and degrades. He sees the way of improvement to lie—however hard its beginning may be to discover— along the line of intelligent self-help, cultivated ability, enhanced skill, increased specialisation, bettered physique, elevated character, enlarged faith. He sees hope in eugenic reform; in the segregation or sterilisation of the unfit; in the purification of the race; in the growth of temperance and self-control. He would gladly see a

smaller population in Britain, provided its standard were higher. His ideal is that not of a pauper proletariat dependent on the state (*i.e.*, on other people's confiscated possessions), but of a property-owning democracy.

(6) *The Protection of Agriculture, Industry, and Commerce.* Since the establishment of a property-owning democracy depends upon the restoration of Britain's temporarily-lost economic prosperity, the conservative is necessarily deeply interested in all that concerns Britain's financial solvency—*e.g.*, the stability of her currency, the security of her credit, the efficiency of her industry, the success of her agriculture, the preservation and extension of her markets. He looks with favour upon all means—whether tariffs, or bounties, or international treaties, or imperial conferences—that seem likely to increase employment, relieve the burden of taxation, or remove hindrances to economic revival. He is a strenuous defender of the "capitalist system" against its socialistic traducers and assailants; for he realises that this unjustly maligned "system" is merely the condition of economic freedom in which every man can use his wealth and his talents in the way that seems to him most likely to bring him the largest legitimate reward in return for the most effective social service that he can render. "Production for service" is the capitalist watchword: profit is the rightful reward of success in such production. To the socialist, "production for service" merely connotes a long series of insatiable strikes for higher wages, shorter hours, increased interference with management, and a persistent reduction of output that culminates in bankruptcy. The conservative ideal is not "down with capitalism," but "every citizen a capitalist." The joint-stock company is the way of hope to the industrious, capable, thrifty conservative working man.

(7) *The Conservation of the Empire.* One of the main elements of hope and confidence for the future is the existence of the vast commonwealth of nations known as the British Empire. Comprising as it does more than one-fifth of the land area of the globe, and including as it does over one-fifth of the human race, it stands as one of the

corner-stones of the modern world system. Communists loathe it as the main obstacle to the triumph of their propaganda; Bolsheviks ceaselessly plot against it as the chief barrier to their advance towards world dominion; socialists of the milder type speak of it with dislike or contempt as something unfavourable to their little schemes; even liberals tend to be lukewarm in their imperial enthusiasm. But to conservatives the Empire's continued existence, its growing solidarity, its closer federation, its progressive development, its increasing prosperity, are matters of vital importance. The Empire stands in the world as a monument of freedom, of justice, of peace, of health, and of general well-being. The primitive peoples who come within its compass are, except through faults of their own, incomparably happier and more prosperous than they were before admission. It is itself an organic league of nations which functions immeasurably better than the laboriously constructed engine of Versailles and Geneva. It may be expected to provide increasingly expanding markets for British manufactures, inexhaustible stores of raw materials for home industries; fields for emigration and enterprise; invaluable aid in days of difficulty and danger. It is the task of conservatism to prevent the disintegration of the Empire, whether it is threatened by a fanatical minority in India or by a handful of republican conspirators in Ireland.

(8) *The Provision of Imperial Defence.* The defence of the Empire cannot safely be trusted to either socialists or liberals. The socialists, filled with illusions concerning the solidarity of the cosmopolitan proletariat, would reduce the navy, deplete the army, starve the air force, until the Empire would lie impotent in a world that is still governed by deeds and not by words. The liberals, leaning with a generous faith upon the League of Nations, would make confiding gestures of disarmament, in the hope that the spectacle of a vast defenceless dominion would set a noble example to the quarrelsome and re-arming races of mankind. The conservative has as profound a love of peace as the most sentimental socialist, and as ardent a desire for the stoppage of the insane race for armaments as the

most large-souled liberal, but he is more disposed than either of them to face the facts of the political situation. He realises that an undefended British Empire would be the most effective of all lures to predatory war, and that a British Empire unable to implement its policy by force would cease to exercise any useful influence among the armed and restless nations of the earth. Above all, he remembers that the British Empire is founded upon sea power, and that the loss of the command of the sea for a single day might mean the permanent destruction of that great commonwealth upon which the hope of the peaceful progress of mankind so largely depends. Hence the conservative will see to it that behind the British Empire, and behind the League of Nations, there is a British navy, a British army, and a British air force adequate to the performance of the heavy and responsible duties that fall to Britain's lot.

(9) *The Safeguarding of English Liberty.* The maintenance of the British Empire and the consequent provision of forces sufficient for its defence are, from the point of view of the outside world, specially desirable because Britain has become the embodiment and model of what is known as " English liberty." This " English liberty "; this freedom limited by legality; this right to do that which the laws permit; this heritage of long prescription; this gift of the Anglo-Saxon peoples to their Celtic fellow-citizens, to their countless imperial allies, and to the world at large—this " English liberty " used to be the peculiar protégé of English liberalism. But modern liberalism, especially since it passed under the disastrous dictatorship of Mr. Lloyd George and suffered the corruption of his pernicious fund, has lost its soul and betrayed its trust. It has declined to bureaucracy; it has run to regulation; it has abandoned economy; it has piled up taxation; it has increased inspection; it has condoned direct action; it has surrendered to trade-union violence; it has played with socialism. And socialism (with communism as its superlative) is of all the products of human perversity the most deadly foe to personal freedom. Its watchword is equality, and equality is essentially and eternally incom-

patible with liberty. If men are free they are bound to become unequal; if they remain equal it can only be because all of them have become slaves. To conservatism, then, falls the task of safeguarding English liberty. It can appropriately undertake the task; for English liberty is not licence unrestrained by law. It is not the enemy but the offspring of that authority which it is the special province of conservatism to emphasise. It is the conservative task to protect all menaced institutions, and no institution in this country is more gravely threatened at this moment—threatened by bureaucrats, by tax collectors, by trade-unionist oligarchs, by socialistic politicians, by communistic conspirators—than is " English liberty."

(10) *The Salving of Civilisation.* " English liberty " is only one, although an incalculably important one, of the factors that go to make up modern civilisation. The whole fabric of that civilisation, slowly constructed by the faithful labours of many generations of noble men and women, is menaced by the subversive activities of misguided revolutionaries. The institutions of religion, the heritage of the prophets and priests of Israel, and of the apostles and martyrs of the early Christian church, are assailed with a diabolical ferocity that recalls the persecutions of pagan Rome. The institutions of marriage and the family, upon which as foundations our whole social structure is erected, are undermined by the seductive propaganda of a semi-scientific sensuality. All the precepts of Christian ethics, consecrated by the lives of an unbroken succession of saints, and confirmed as beneficent by the experience of unnumbered generations of common men, are decried and attacked. To conservatives above all others—although in this cause all good men are conservative—falls the task of defending the menaced citadel of civilisation and maintaining the eternal sanctity of the moral law.

THE END

BOOK LIST

BOOK LIST

ADAMS, W. H. D.: English Party Leaders. 2 vols. 1878.

ALINGTON, C.: Twenty Years (1815-35). 1921.

ALISON, SIR A.: Lives of Lord Castlereagh and Sir Charles Stewart. 3 vols. 1861.

ANON. [Members of the 1924 Club, Liverpool]: The Conservative and Unionist Party, 1832-1929. 1929.

ARNOLD, MATTHEW: The Zenith of Conservatism (*Nineteenth Century*, 1887).

ASPINALL, A.: Lord Brougham and the Whig Party. 1927.

ATTERBURY, F.: English Advice to the Freeholders of England (in Somers Tracts, vol. xiii.). 1715.

BALFOUR, EARL OF: Chapters of Autobiography. 1930.

BANKS, SIR R. M.: The Conservative Outlook. 1929.

BAUMANN, A. A.: Burke, the Founder of Conservatism. 1929.
Persons and Politics of the Transition. 1916.
The Last Victorians. 1927.

BEACONSFIELD, EARL OF: Whigs and Whiggism, etc. Edited by W. Hutchens. 1913.
Lord George Bentinck. Edited by C. Whibley. 1905.
Speeches on Parliamentary Reform. Edited by M. Corry. 1867.
Selected Speeches. 2 vols. 1882.
Novels: the Bradenham Edition. 12 vols. 1927.
Letters. Edited by Lord Zetland. 2 vols. 1929.

BEGBIE, HAROLD ["A Gentleman with a Duster"]: The Conservative Mind. 1924.

BENN, SIR E.: Account Rendered. 1930.
Honest Doubt. 1932.

BENTINCK, LORD HENRY: Tory Democracy. 1918.

BIRKENHEAD, LORD: see Smith.

BLACKSTONE, SIR WILLIAM: Commentaries on the Laws of England. 4 vols. 1765-69.

BOLINGBROKE, VISCOUNT: Collected Works. Edited by David Mallet. 5 vols. 1754.
Letters to Sir William Trumbull (published in the Easthampstead Papers by the Hist. MSS. Commission, 1924).

BOOTHBY, R., AND OTHERS : Industry and the State. 1927.

BOSANQUET, B. : A Philosophic Theory of the State. 1899.

BOUTWOOD, A. [otherwise "Hakluyt Egerton"] : Patriotism. 1905.
    National Toryism. 1911.
    Constructive Toryism. 1912.
    National Revival. 1913.
    National Principles. 1914.

BRANDES, G. : Lord Beaconsfield. 1880.

BROWNING, A. : Life of Thomas Osborne, Earl of Danby. 1913.

BRYANT, A. : The Spirit of Conservatism. 1929.
    King Charles II. 1931.

BURGHCLERE, LADY : Strafford. 2 vols. 1931.

BURKE, EDMUND : Collected Works. 8 vols. 1854-57.
    Speeches. 4 vols. 1816.
    Correspondence. 4 vols. 1844.

BUTLER, SIR GEOFFREY : The Tory Tradition. 1814.

CANNING, G. : Speeches, with a Memoir. 6 vols. 1830.

CECIL, ALGERNON : British Foreign Statesmen. 1927.

CECIL, LADY GWENDOLEN : Life of Robert, Marquess of Salisbury. 4 vols. 1921-32.

CECIL, LORD HUGH : Conservatism. 1912.

CHURCHILL, LORD RANDOLPH : Speeches, 1880-88. 2 vols. 1889.

CHURCHILL, W. S. : Lord Randolph Churchill. 1907.

CLARENDON, LORD : History of the Rebellion and Civil Wars. Edited by Warburton. 7 vols. 1849.

CLARK, G. KITSON : Peel and the Conservative Party. 1929.

CLARKE, SIR EDWARD : Benjamin Disraeli. 1929.

COBBAN, A. : Edmund Burke. 1929.

COLERIDGE, S. T. : Complete Works. 7 vols. 1853.

COLLINS, J. C. : Bolingbroke and Voltaire. 1886.

COOKE, G. W. : Memoirs of Lord Bolingbroke. 2 vols. 1835.
    History of Parties. 3 vols. 1836-37.

COOPER, E. : Life of Thomas Wentworth, Earl of Strafford. 2 vols. 1874.

CRAIK, SIR H. : Life of Clarendon. 2 vols. 1911.

CRISP, DOROTHY : The Rebirth of Conservatism. 1931.

CROKER, J .W. : Correspondence and Diaries (1780-1857). 3 vols. 1884.

Curzon, G. N. (Marquess): The Conservatism of Young Oxford (*National Review*, June, 1884).
   The Conservatism of Tennyson (*Oxford Review*, February 25, 1885).

Delahaye, J. V.: Politics: A Discussion. 1929.

De Quincey, T.: Political Parties of Modern England (in vol. ix. of Collected Works, 1890).

Dibdin, Sir L.: The Establishment in England. 1931.

Dibelius, W.: England. (Translated by M. A. Hamilton.) 1930. [On political parties, pp. 188-207.]

Dicey, A. V.: Law and Public Opinion in England. 1905.

Dickinson, G. L.: A Modern Symposium. (New edition.) 1930.

Disraeli, Benjamin: see Beaconsfield.

Elliot, Walter: Toryism and the Twentieth Century. 1927.

Feiling, Keith: Toryism: Political Dialogues. 1913.
   History of the Tory Party, 1640-1714. 1924.
   What is Conservatism? 1930.
   Sketches of Nineteenth-Century Biography. 1930.

Firth, Sir Charles H.: Edward Hyde, Earl of Clarendon. 1909.

Froude, J. A.: Beaconsfield. 1890.

Gifford, John: Political Life of William Pitt. 6 vols. 1809.

Gordon, Sir A. [Lord Stanmore]: The Earl of Clarendon. 1893.

Gorst, H.: The Earl of Beaconsfield. 1900.

Grigg, Sir E.: Three Parties or Two? 1931.

Guedalla, P.: The Duke. 1931.

Halifax, Marquess of: Complete Works. Edited by Walter Raleigh. 1912.

Harrop, R.: Bolingbroke, a Political Study. 1884.

Hassall, A.: Life of Viscount Bolingbroke. 1889.
   Viscount Castlereagh. 1908.

Henson, H. H., Bishop of Durham: Disestablishment. 1929.

Herries, E.: Memoirs of J. C. Herries. 2 vols. 1880.

Hill, R. L.: Toryism and the People (1832-46). 1929.

Hobbes, Thomas: Leviathan. 1651.

Hume, David: Essays Moral and Political. 1741-42.

Huskisson, William: Speeches with Memoir. 3 vols. 1831.

Inge, W. R.: England. 1926.
   Christian Ethics and Modern Problems. 1930.

" Janitor ": The Feet of the Young Men. 1928.

JEYES, S. H. : The Marquis of Salisbury, etc. 4 vols. 1895-96.

KEBBEL, T. E. : A History of Toryism, 1783-1881. 1886.

KELTON-CREMER, R. W. : Early Life of William Windham. 1930.

KENNEDY, J. M. : Tory Democracy. 1911.

KENT, C. B. R. : Early History of the Tories (1660-1702). 1908.

KNOWLER, W. : Letters and Despatches of Thomas Wentworth, Earl of Strafford. 2 vols. 1740.

LECKY, W. E. H. : History of England in the Eighteenth Century. 8 vols. 1879.

LISTER, T. H. : Life of Clarendon. 3 vols. 1838.

LOFTUS, PIERSE : The Creed of a Tory. 1926.

LONDONDERRY, MARCHIONESS OF: Robert Stewart, Viscount Castlereagh. 1904.

LONDONDERRY, MARQUESS OF: Memoirs and Correspondence of Lord Castlereagh. 8 vols. 1848-51.

LORD, W. F. : The Development of Political Parties under Queen Anne. 1910.

LUDOVICI, A. M. : A Defence of Conservatism. 1927.

LYMINGTON, VISCOUNT : Ich Dien. 1931.

MACAULAY, L. : The Decadence. 1929.

McCARTHY, J. : Sir Robert Peel. 1891.

MacCUNN, J. : The Political Philosophy of Burke. 1913.

MACKNIGHT, T. : Life of Henry St. John, Viscount Bolingbroke. 1863.
Life and Times of Edmund Burke. 3 vols. 1858-60.
Benjamin Disraeli. 1854.

MAHON, LORD, AND CARDWELL, E. : Memoirs of Sir Robert Peel. 2 vols. 1857-58.

MAINE, SIR HENRY : Popular Government. 1885.

MALCOLM, SIR IAN : Lord Balfour : A Memory. 1930.

MALLOCK, W. H. : Memories of Life and Literature. 1920.

MARRIOTT, SIR J. A. R. : Life and Times of Lord Falkland. 1908.

MAUROIS, A. : La Vie de Disraeli. 1927.

MAXWELL, SIR H. : The Creevy Papers [1768-1838]. 2 vols. 1904.
Life of Wellington. 2 vols. 1899.

MEYNELL, W. : Benjamin Disraeli. 2 vols. 1904.

MIDLETON, EARL OF: Ireland—Dupe or Heroine. 1932.

MONYPENNY, W. F., AND BUCKLE, G. E. : The Life of Benjamin Disraeli, Earl of Beaconsfield. 6 vols. 1910-20.

MORGAN, W. T.: English Political Parties, 1702-10. 1920.

MORLEY, J. (LORD): Burke, a Historical Study. 1867.
Burke, a Biography. 1879.

MURRAY, D. L.: Disraeli. 1927.

NEWMAN, B.: Edmund Burke. 1927.

NORTH, ROGER: Examen. 1740.
Lives of Francis North, etc. 2 vols. 1740-42.

OPZOOMER, C. W.: Conservatismus und Reform: eine Abhandlung über Edmund Burke's Politik. 1852.

PARKER, C. S.: Peel from his Private Papers. 3 vols. 1891-99.

PARKER, R., AND OTHERS: A Declaration of Tory Principles. 1929.

PAYNE, E.J.: Select Works of Burke. 3 vols. 1874.

PEEL, G.: Private Letters of Sir Robert Peel. 1920.

PEEL, SIR R.: Speeches in the House of Commons, 1810-50. 4 vols. 1853.

PELLEW, G.: Life and Correspondence of Henry Addington, Viscount Sidmouth. 3 vols. 1847.

PERCY, LORD EUSTACE: Democracy on Trial. 1931.

PETRIE, SIR C.: George Canning. 1930.
The Jacobite Movement. 1932.

PHILLIPS, W.: Life of George Canning. 1905.

PITT, WILLIAM: Speeches in the House of Commons. 3 vols. 1817.

RAMSAY, MISS A. A. W.: Sir Robert Peel. 1928.

RAPIN, PAUL DE: Dissertation sur les Whigs et sur les Tories. 1717.

RAYMOND, E. T.: Disraeli, the Alien Patriot. 1925.

ROBERTSON, J. M.: Bolingbroke and Walpole. 1919.

RONALDSHAY, LORD: Life of Lord Curzon. 3 vols. 1928.

ROSE, J. HOLLAND: William Pitt and the National Revival. 1912.
William Pitt and the Great War. 1911.
Short Life of William Pitt. 1925.

ROSEBERY, EARL OF: Pitt. 1891.
Lord Randolph Churchill. 1906.

RUVILLE, A. VON: The Earl of Chatham. (Translated by Chaytor and Morison.) 3 vols. 1907.

ST. JOHN, HENRY: see Bolingbroke.

SAINTSBURY, G.: Earl of Derby. 1892.

SALISBURY, MARQUESS OF: Essays on Foreign Policy. 1903.

SAMUELS, A. P. I.: Early Life of Burke. 1923.

SCOTT, JAMES: The Whigs and other Essays. 1929.

SELLON, H. G. R.: The River of Conservatism (in *Ashridge Journal*, August, 1931).
Whither England. 1932.

SICHEL, WALTER: Bolingbroke and his Times. 2 vols. 1901-02.
Disraeli. 1904.

SMITH, F. E. (LORD BIRKENHEAD): Toryism. 1903.
Unionist Policy. 1913.

STANHOPE, EARL: Life of Pitt. 4 vols. 1861-62.

STAPLETON, A. G.: George Canning and his Times. 1859.

STEPHEN, SIR J. F.: Liberty, Equality, Fraternity. 1873.

SWIFT, JONATHAN: Complete Works. 13 vols. 1768.

TAYLOR, G. R. S.: Seven English Statesmen. 1929.

TAYLOR, W. C.: Life and Times of Sir Robert Peel. 4 vols. 1846-51.

TEMPERLEY, H. W. V.: Life of Canning. 1905.

TOMLINE, G.: Memoirs of the Life of William Pitt. 3 vols. 1821.

THURSFIELD, J. R.: Peel. 1893.

TRAIL, H. D.: The Marquis of Salisbury. 1891.

TREVELYAN, G. M.: The Two-Party System in English History. 1926.

TWISS, SIR TRAVERS: Public and Private Life of Lord Eldon. 3 vols. 1844.

WALPOLE, SIR SPENCER: Life of Spencer Perceval. 2 vols. 1874.
Studies in Biography. 1907.

WELLINGTON, DUKE OF: Speeches in Parliament. 1854.
Despatches: Civil Series. Vols. vii. and viii. 1930-34.

WHIBLEY, CHARLES: William Pitt. 1906.
Political Portraits. 2 vols. 1917.
Lord John Manners and his Friends. 1925.

WILKINSON, W. J.: Tory Democracy. 1925.

WILLIAMS, BASIL: Life of Chatham. 1913.

WINDHAM, WILLIAM: Speeches in Parliament. 1812.

WINGFIELD-STRATFORD, E.: History of British Civilisation. 2 vols. 1928.

WOLFE, A. B.: Conservatism, Radicalism, and Scientific Method. 1923.

WOODS, MAURICE: A History of the Tory Party. 1924.

WOODWARD, E. L.: Three Studies in European Conservatism. 1929.

YONGE, C. D.: Life and Administration of the Second Earl of Liverpool. 3 vols. 1868.

INDEX